The Worth of the Social Economy

An International Perspective

P.I.E. Peter Lang

Bruxelles · Bern · Berlin · Frankfurt am Main · New York · Oxford · Wien

CIRIEC
(edited by Marie J. BOUCHARD)

The Worth of the Social Economy

An International Perspective

Social Economy & Public Economy
No. 2

Les activités, publications et recherches du CIRIEC sont réalisées avec le soutien du Gouvernement fédéral belge – Politique scientifique et avec celui de la Communauté française de Belgique – Recherche scientifique.

La recherche a bénéficié en outre des Fonds spéciaux pour la recherche – crédits classiques de la Communauté Française (Belgique).

© P.I.E. PETER LANG s.a.
Éditions scientifiques internationales
Bruxelles, 2009
1 avenue Maurice, B-1050 Bruxelles, Belgique
www.peterlang.com ; info@peterlang.com

Printed in Germany

ISSN 2030-3408
ISBN 978-90-5201-580-4
D/2009/5678/78

Library of Congress Cataloging-in-Publication Data
The worth of the social economy : an international perspective /
[compiled by] Marie J. Bouchard.
p. cm. — (Économie sociale & économie publique ; no. 2)
ISBN 978-90-5201-580-4
1. Economics. I. Bouchard, Marie J.
HB171.5.W896 2010   330—dc22   2010001838

CIP also available from the British Library, GB

Bibliographic information published by "Die Deutsche Bibliothek"
"Die Deutsche Bibliothek" lists this publication in the "Deutsche National-bibliografie"; detailed bibliographic data is available on the Internet at <http://dnb.ddb.de>.

Contents

Acknowledgements

The present book is the result of the CIRIEC international Working Group on Methods and Indicators of Evaluation of the Social Economy that met on a regular basis during three years (2005-2008) in order to explore this theme. At the closing of this work, I would like to thank all the members of the Working Group and the contributors to this book for their collaboration and the quality of our conversations. I also want to acknowledge the support of the national sections of CIRIEC that hosted our meetings, namely CIRIEC France, CIRIEC Belgium and CIRIEC Spain. This book could not have been produced in the absence of the support of CIRIEC international staff, in particular Christine Dussart, and of the Canada Research Chair on the Social Economy, namely Monique K. Desève, as well as without the involvement of Nadine Richez-Battesti (CIRIEC France), Rafael Chaves, President of the CIRIEC International Scientific Commission "Social and Cooperative Economy", Benoît Lévesque, President of the CIRIEC International Scientific Council and Bernard Thiry, General Director of CIRIEC international. May they be thanked.

Marie J. Bouchard

INTRODUCTION

The Worth of the Social Economy

Marie J. BOUCHARD

*Professor and Director of the Canada Research Chair on
the Social Economy, Université du Québec à Montréal (Canada)*

The social economy constitutes a form of economy that is distinct from the capitalist and public economy. Co-operative, nonprofit and mutual benefit organizations, as well as foundations, union funds and nongovernmental organizations, etc., are known for their capacity to respond to emerging needs and to new social demands, particularly in periods of crisis marked by important socioeconomic transformations. Many reasons plead to explore and better understand how the social economy is being evaluated in the present context.

Over the past thirty years, the social economy has increasingly come to the forefront of discussions about job creation and work insertion, decentralization of social services, sustainable development, etc. Its size and scope have been growing in the recent decades as it is playing an important role in responding to emerging social and economic needs as well as to new collective aspirations. Social economy organizations are increasingly involved in areas where the market or the public sectors seem to fail. The social economy is no longer a residual phenomenon but a veritable institutional pole of the economy.

In this context, evaluation takes a new importance. Demands have been formulated by the public authorities, the donators and by the social economy players themselves, to measure the sector and evaluate its contribution. However, not much is known about how the social economy should be evaluated and of what is needed to recognize its contribution to development.

Even if there has been a fair number of publications about of how the social economy should be evaluated – namely the nonprofit organizations –, very little is known about how it is actually being evaluated. Especially when considered for their common values and shared institutional characteristics, organizations of the social economy – which include nonprofit, co-operative and mutual organizations – could benefit from an understanding of whether or not their evaluation schemes recognize and enhance their specificities. Under the patronage of CIRIEC international, a Working Group was created to study the methods and indicators for evaluating the social economy in different institutional environments.

Though the questions about *how should we* go about evaluating the social economy are numerous, there had not yet been a comprehensive study or *how it is* being evaluated now. Rather than being upfront prescriptive about this important – but how delicate – question, we chose to start by taking a look at the actual trends in evaluation, trying to typify and analyze them in the light of what evaluation *means* for the present and future development of the social economy. Our aim was to eventually see how the evaluation practices contribute to the very definition of the field of the social economy and to deduce – from these empirical observations – some relevant and hopefully useful suggestions to social economy actors and policy makers. This work came to its ending in 2008 and the results are presented in this volume.

This book fills a gap in the literature about the social economy. It addresses the questions of *how* the social economy is being evaluated, and *what it means* to be evaluated in those fashions. It outlines the actual trends in methodologies and indicators of evaluation applied for the social economy in different national contexts. One of the goals is to give a critical glance at what evaluation practices reveal about the social economy itself. The cases presented here expose a great range of evaluation practices, each needing to be understood in the particular national context in which it takes place. We will have understood that this book does not pretend to give an exhaustive survey of the current practices, but rather to analyze a number of significant experiences. Each has been considered with reference to a common analytical framework as well as in relation to each other in order to allow the comparison.

The different chapters of this volume take stock of the methods and indicators that are being used to measure the specific contribution of the social economy in different parts of the world. The authors propose a critical assessment of today's interests that the social economy must cater to and for which questions of evaluation appear to be the most telling. To conduct this comparative study, the Working Group referred to a common analytical framework.

The first part of this volume offers four conceptual contributions. Chapter one exposes the general framework of the Working Group and is signed by its coordinator, Marie J. Bouchard. She summarizes the focus and orientation as well as the questions that this book addresses. The approach of the Working Group is based on two postulates. The first is that evaluation is never neutral. Consequently, different approaches and different methodologies will reveal contrasted stakes for the social economy. The second postulate is that the evaluation of the social economy reflects the role the social economy is expected to play in the development model and its transformations. The framework proposes analytical categories for discussing the complexity of evaluation practices. It also exposes the intricacy of the social economy not only in its various definitions, which may vary from one country to another, but also in the variety of forms and activities of the organizations.

The next three chapters offer different views on the relation between the nature of the social economy and that of evaluation. In his essay, Bernard Perret highlights the complex rationality that underlies the social economy and which therefore should be taken into account in its evaluation. Because the social economy is not in itself a public policy – pursuing objectives that have been formalized and validated by democratic procedure – its evaluation calls for a shared conception of the common good. He defines evaluation as a cognitive process by which common grounds for interpreting the actions are being constructed. Since there is a never-ending array of legitimate conceptions of social welfare, evaluation should reflect the various perspectives with which an action can be viewed rather than be a rational authoritarian exercise. The issue is at once of a democratic and cognitive order, and calls for the establishment of places and procedures to facilitate confrontation among the heterogeneous logics underlying non-standard social practices, and the development of tools to facilitate the objectification and measurement of the values at stake.

In his text, Bernard Enjolras questions the normative foundations of the social economy, on the one hand, and of public policies on the other. The different paradigms used to qualify the social economy (market and government failures, social economy, solidarity economy and civil society) can be synthesized into three social functions of the social economy organizations: solidarity function, democratic function and productive function. The confrontation between the normative foundations of these organizations (what ideally they should be) and the normative foundations of public policies (what public policies aim at) reveals the paradoxes of the evaluation of the outputs and outcomes of social economy organizations. This leads the author to conclude about the paradoxical character of public policy evaluation of social economy organizations.

On his part, Bernard Eme aims to question the axiological and normative basis of evaluation processes. According to the author, these processes should themselves continuously question the values and norms which, often implicitly, constitute their foundations. An evaluation aiming to take into account the quality of organizations must reveal a plurality of "worlds" or value judgements that underlie the social and solidarity based economy. Therefore, evaluation is a process tool of a deliberative democracy, respecting the controversies that must be talked through according to the forms of argumentation that are legitimated by the actors.

The second part of the book is constituted of seven chapters presenting the situation in different parts of the world: France, Quebec, United Kingdom, United States of America, Brazil, Portugal and Japan. The evaluation practices that were observed concern the organization (micro level) and the sectors (meso level), situated in their national context (macro level). Each of these contributions is organized following a common pattern. A first section describes the major trends that characterize the context of the social economy in recent years. A second section illustrates the major trends in evaluation with the support of relevant data and examples. A third section is dedicated to analyzing the major incidences the evaluation methods have over the practices of the social economy organizations and sectors.

The French contribution is cosigned by Nadine Richez-Battesti, Hélène Trouvé, François Rousseau, Bernard Eme and Laurent Fraisse. The authors identify two important trends in the evaluation of the social and solidarity based economy in France: social utility and societal balance sheet (*bilan sociétal*). These two evaluation modalities have been chosen not so much because of their ample diffusion in France, but because they have been the objects of debates between the different categories of actors in the past fifteen years. What comes out of this analysis is that what's at stake with evaluation is also – and above all – the definition of field of the social and solidarity based economy and of its modes of regulation.

The situation in Quebec is presented by Marie J. Bouchard. Based on the observation of tools utilized in more than fifteen sectors of activities where the social economy is active, three main trends have been identified where evaluation may be based on the objectives, the mission or on the specificity of the social economy. These practices reveal different expectations posed upon the social economy, whether it should make up for development failures, complete the market and the public sphere by responding to emerging needs, or present itself as a distinctive reality that calls for specific performance and risk evaluation criteria. This analysis illustrates the relative influence that the stakeholders, the mission and the very nature of the social economy have over the evaluation procedures.

In his text, Roger Spear reviews the recent evolution of the evaluative frameworks in the United Kingdom and shows their increasingly influential nature, namely on the governance of the social economy organizations. Referring to a resource dependency view, the author examines four evaluation frameworks associated with different subsectors in which the social economy operates: social return on investment, social balance sheets, performance indicator based methods, and social audit. According to the author, there is a necessity to undertake a collective action to create legitimacy for social accounting, beyond the measures already in existence. This leads to a view that sectoral initiatives to develop processes of institutionalization may be more important to develop rather than merely promoting the growth of individual social economy organizations' actions.

To present the situation in the United States, Charles Patrick Rock chooses to concentrate his observations on the evaluation of nonprofit organizations (NPOs). One of the main issues concerns the demands for accountability coming from the federal government as well as from nongovernmental intermediary organizations that support nonprofits. In the recent years, evaluation seems to be spreading everywhere throughout the nonprofit sector. Even if generalizing about evaluation patterns in the US is a risky business, a variety of ways are observed: cost-benefit analysis, evaluation of behavior change of the beneficiaries, evaluation focused on developing the organization itself, and more unusually, evaluation that creates popular citizen activism in social movements. The paper traces the financial flows, seeing how those who control them often determine the evaluation framework.

The Brazilian contribution is coauthored by Mauricio Serva, Carolina Andion, Lucilla Campos and Erika Onozato, and focuses on the evaluation of non-governmental organizations (NGOs). To the extent that those are more and more active in managing and providing public services, their evaluation are mainly oriented towards control, accountability and transparency. According to the authors, this is a proof of the hierarchical subordination of the social economy to the State in Brazil. It also reflects a functionalist conception of the role of the social economy in the execution of public policies. The analysis also reveals the feeble accountability of the social economy actors, which cannot be efficiently reinforced without more involvement of the stakeholders, namely the managers, the members and the users of the social economy organizations. This could also reinforce the institutional domain of the social economy in Brazil.

Isabel Nicolau and Ana Simaens discuss the case of social solidarity organizations (SSOs) in Portugal. Growing competition between for profit and social economy organizations – but as well as between social

15

economy organizations themselves – bring evaluation to play an important role in the governance. Internal voluntary initiated evaluation usually has a strong impact on the organization, namely to improve the transparency that creates legitimacy and reinforces the principles of the social economy. But it can also be limited to a meaningless *pro forma*. External evaluation asked by funders is mainly a tool to control the use of the funds by the organization. Nevertheless, the procedures to apply for European funds and the ongoing evaluation obligations that come with it have contributed to improve internal routines and some management practices in the Portuguese social economy organizations. Still, some limitations may be pointed out, namely the rigidity in the use of such funds.

The situation in Japan is presented by Akira Kurimoto. Three modalities are identified: evaluation of performance and process for improved management, such as the ISO standards; evaluation according to the specific mission, namely health care; and evaluation according to the specific nature, with examples coming from the co-operative sector. The author points out to the difference between evaluating the outputs (direct and short term results) and the outcomes (indirect and long term effects), the later being much more difficult. However, an observable impact is how Japanese co-ops have played a "pacemaker role" or provided a "competitive yardstick" in terms of environmental and food security issues. Secondly, the author discusses the risks of isomorphism coming with the ISO and third party evaluation practices which, according to him, are relatively low as both are, at the present time, voluntary.

The conclusion of the book summarizes the findings of this study and proposes some reflections addressed to policy designers, evaluation specialists and social economy actors.

PART I

CONCEPTUAL FRAMEWORKS

Methods and Indicators
for Evaluating the Social Economy

Marie J. BOUCHARD

*Professor and Director of the Canada Research Chair on
the Social Economy, Université du Québec à Montréal (Canada)*

Introduction

The social economy is a large and growing pole of social utility within a plural economy, positioned between the capitalist sector and the public sector. It includes associations (or nonprofit organizations), cooperatives, mutual societies and foundations, as well as other types of organizations that follow common values and principles[1] and share institutional traits.

As the social economy tends to play a greater role in solving new social problems, the question of how it is evaluated and by who comes to rise. Yet, the social economy is still a relatively under-theorized phenomenon. The evaluation methodologies and indicators specific to the social economy have not yet gained wide recognition, either in political or academic spheres (Bouchard, Bourque and Lévesque, 2001; Rondot and Bouchard, 2003). There is no consensus about what methodologies or indicators can that take into account the specific characters of the social economy. This undermines its position and reduces its capacity to take part in the great debates of society.

One of the reasons for this is that the social economy is a complex and diversified field in terms of the forms of the organizations and their functioning, of the types of activities it develops and how, and of the way it relates to public institutions and to for-profit agents. The social economy is composed of a "large and diverse group of free, voluntary microeconomic entities created by civil society to meet and solve the

---

[1] For example in Europe, see the *Charter of Principles of the Social Economy* promoted by the European Standing Conference of Co-operatives, Mutual Societies, Associations and Foundations (CEP-CMAF).

needs of individuals, households and families rather than remunerate or provide cover to investors or capitalist companies [...], and is involved in a varied spectrum of activities, market and non-market, of mutual interest or of general interest" (Chaves and Monzón Campos, 2006). This complicates the evaluation work that applies to them. Another factor that contributes to the difficult recognition of a methodology for evaluating the social economy is the variety of conceptions that underlie the exercise of evaluation.

The CIRIEC Working Group's common framework for tackling the issue of how the social economy is now being evaluated in different national contexts is presented in this chapter. Rather than propose a theoretical background from which to deduce generalities about the observed phenomena, this framework aims at providing a set of common concepts which can be used to conduct empirical research.

We first expose the rich complexity of the social economy. Next, we develop some comments about the importance of the context in which the questions relating to its evaluation need to be situated. Finally, we present some landmarks for reflecting upon the various types of evaluation practices, and about the approaches and paradigms that underlie their conception.

The Rich Complexity of the Social Economy

Given its distinctive organizational features and institutional rules, as well as its special relationship with the State, and the market, the social economy constitutes a special sector that merits recognition and should be differentiated from other sectors (Defourny and Monzón Campos, 1992). However, it is a polysemic term, since the definitions and practices that claim to adhere to it are highly varied (Lévesque and Mendell, 2004; Chaves and Monzón Campos, 2006). Indeed, the social economy consists of various legal statuses, broad spectrum of economic activities (in the primary, secondary and tertiary sectors) and diverse social missions (either of mutual or of general interest), etc.

While complex and composed of a rich diversity, there is still a great unity inside the social economy "family". The following remarks primarily aim at assisting the formulation of hypotheses towards the differentiation of performance criteria that apply to different types of organizations, different types of activities and in different institutional contexts.

A first comment is that various *definitions* of this field coexist:
- social economy (Chaves and Monzón Campos, 2006; Gide, 1890; Desroche, 1983; Lévesque and Malo, 1992; Quarter, *et al.*, 2003b; Vienney, 1980; etc.);

- solidarity-based economy (Eme, 1997; Eme and Laville, 1994; Laville, 1999; Enjolras, 2002; Evers and Laville, 2004; Gardin, 2006; etc.);
- social enterprises (Borzaga and Defourny, 2004; Kerling, 2006; Nyssens, 2006; etc.);
- cooperatives (Angers, 1975; Vienney, 1980; etc.);
- nonprofit or third sector (Anheir and Ben-Ner, 2000; Ben-Ner and Van Hoomissen, 1993; Hansmann, 1980; James, 1983; Salamon and Anheir, 1998; Weisbrod, 1977; etc.).

The definition adopted in the present book intends to be large and inclusive, but bases itself on the general consensus reflected in previous CIRIEC's works (Defourny and Monzón Campos, 1992; Chaves and Monzón Campos, 2006).

Another remark concerns the *forms of organization* adopted by social economy enterprises, which is sometimes formally recognized by special legal frameworks (laws on cooperatives, associations, nonprofit organizations, mutual societies, foundations, etc.), or corresponds to organizational practices that take place within a general legal framework. For some, the social economy also includes certain informal associations.

The *activities* undertook by these organizations may be primarily economic (as in the case of cooperatives or mutual societies) or primarily social (as in the case of associations providing services to individuals) (Lévesque, 2006). Their mission may include: combating poverty; providing improved services to meet the special needs of a target population (not necessarily economically disadvantaged); providing assistance in the self-organization of workers or producers who seek to create work or a marketing structure for themselves (Weisbrod, 1997). Their production may be meant for a group of members that control the organization (mutualist organization) or be addressed to people or collectivities that are not involved in the governance (altruist organization) (Gui, 1992).

Their *vocation* may derive from a desire to democratize the economy, or as a response to the new or pressing needs of vulnerable groups or territories (Lévesque, 2006).

Their *revenues* may come mainly from market, government or philanthropic sources (Salamon, *et al.*, 1999), or from a mix of them (Eme and Laville, 1994), etc.

In addition, social economy organizations, like all organizations, go through various *stages* in their development: the transition from the informal to the formal stage (Dussuet and Lauzanas, 2007), diversification of activities (typically, the twinning of non-market and market activities), upstream and downstream integrations (Desforges, 1980), development of subsidiaries, generation of spin-offs, etc.

We have to consider that the above-noted distinctions are often, in reality, not so clear-cut. For example, the social impact of these organizations' activities are often more important than their economic weight would indicate. They frequently have multiple objectives, which may derive not only from unmet or poorly met needs but also from a desire to propose alternatives to market or the public sector. The resources that are mobilized are often combined (subsidies, public contracts, sales, voluntarism), helping to prevent from the dependency to any of them (insolvent demand; insufficiency of voluntarism; centralization of public policies) (Salamon, *et al.*, 1999). It also generates hybridization and compromises among the various types of logic with which each type of resource is associated (redistribution, market, reciprocity) (Eme and Laville, 1994).

The Importance of Context

Social economy enterprises generally emerge in clusters, as the result of socio-economic pressures, and usually during a major economic crisis (Lévesque, 2006). Since crises are never identical, different generations of the social economy have different identities, especially since social economy participants and promoters differ from one generation to the next. In particular, social economy organizations occupy niches that may be very different form one another, depending on the sector to which they belong. Within any given sector, the social economy niche also depends on the niches occupied by the public and private sectors (Weisbrod, 1997). Thus, the supply of public services or competitive market services, as well as the State regulation, may limit the space occupied by the social economy. Hence, the place and role of the social economy will vary from country to country, or from region to region – each of which has its distinct institutional environment – and will change according to transformations in their environment.

With the beginning of this new century, growing privatization and merchandization of social services introduce competition in fields of activities so far withdrawn from market influence. Services which were traditionally public services appear as new markets for social and collective entrepreneurs. Relocations and shutdowns of large enterprises bring forth the issue of re-developing regions on the basis of activities that are anchored into the local space while still being linked to the global market. This also leads to wondering about the requirements of a more sustainable development. Those trends converge to give to the social economy an important role to play between the Market and the

State, within a new plural economy where the Civil Society is asking to have a larger say.

The powers and responsibilities of the State, of the business enterprises and of civil society tend to be reorganized in new institutional and organizational arrangements. On the one hand, public authorities are turning to partnerships with the private sector – namely social economy organizations – for the production and provision of social and health services, but also concerning the responsibility for local and regional development. On the other hand, societal concern for ecology and a more "fair" development brings corporate businesses into showing more signs of being socially and environmentally responsible, of having positive impacts on communities, etc. This doesn't go without questioning the specificity of the social economy.

The boundaries between the social economy, the public economy and the capitalist economy are permeable. The social economy develops service contracts with public authorities to provide social and health services of general interest (Enjolras, 2002). The field is evolving: there is a new legal status for cooperatives that develop services of general interest (solidarity or social cooperatives); associations are increasingly availing themselves of market-based revenues and there is a growing demand for external capital; some federations of cooperatives take the form of holdings (Côté, 2000); there are new governance structures without legal status (such as the *Centres financiers aux entreprises* Desjardins) (St-Pierre and Bouchard, 2005); etc. A "competition" also exists on the specificity of the social economy via social balance-sheet and audit activities and by social certification actions of capitalist enterprises (Bouchard and Rondeau, 2003), entraining a risk of bastardization of the social economy to the profit of the discourse and practices of social responsibility of capitalist enterprises (Zadek, Pruzan and Evans, 1997). But only the organizations of the social economy mix together the social and the economic at institutional level (laws, rules, conventions) (Demoustier, 2001; Vienney, 1980), rather than a simple organizational and discretionary (ergo variable and unstable) response (Gendron, 2000).

Evaluation is tied up inside a force field where the State, the Corporate World and Civil Society reciprocally define their area of competences, at the different scales of the society's architecture. The growing complexity of how the general interest is being assured, engaging a variety of socioeconomic actors (public, private, social economy), imply the growing complexity of the criteria for evaluating activities which are susceptible to contribute to its achievement. The multiple stakeholders do not come to a consensus over what should be evaluated or how. In general, the identities of economic and social actors are in the process of redefining themselves: "Strategic State", "Corporate Citizen", "Organized Civil Society". The notion of new governance carries the idea that responsibilities that used to be those of the State are progressively in the hands of social actors and, by way of consequence, decentralized. Governance is there to arbitrate between two contradictory forces, one being the demands for autonomy coming from social actors, the other being the need for a better coordination between policies that cross about the frontiers of ministries and public agencies. At each level concerned, the principle of subsidiarity asks for the subordination of each party to the general will of society. The actors to which responsibilities are being bestowed become accountable. Autonomy of management is challenged by the dependency to public funds, in the case of non-market services, and to public opinion, as it is more often the case of market goods and services.

This explains why evaluation of the social economy cannot come from anything but a complex proposition. It has to refer to the specificity of the social economy and of its contribution. It also raises the question of which paradigm of the development is the social economy expected to contribute to, and how.

A Working Framework

Evaluation is never neutral. Different approaches and different methodologies should reveal the interests shown for the social economy in different ways. As mentioned previously, the reality of the social economy is not independent of the transformations of the market or of the State, the social economy enterprises being a sort of laboratory for social innovations *vis-à-vis* the for-profit and the public sector. The institutional arrangements vary from one country to another. We pose here that evaluation methods and indicators of the social economy refer to the development models and to their transformations, revealing the expected role of the social economy in the process.

The following notes aim at sharing common markers for a comparison of methods and indicators of evaluation in different institutional contexts.

Methods and Indicators

As to methods, evaluation may find expression in national accounts (macro), the sectoral or regional portrait (meso), program analysis (objectives, process, results, impacts) or balance-sheet and organizational functioning (micro). It may consider the standardization of norms (audit, certification, ISO), conformity to program (summative evaluation) or improvement of practices (formative evaluation). It may be based on quantitative or on qualitative information or combine the two. It may be done by an external assessor or produced in participative manner with the players (negotiated evaluation) (Bouchard and Dumais, 2001; Rondot and Bouchard, 2003). In the context of this Working Group, we propose to concentrate our observations on evaluation of enterprises and organizations of the social economy (EOSE) and their sectors of activity. Hence, the evaluation under study will be of *organizational* (micro) or *sector-based* (meso) reach.

As to indicators, the social and economic repercussions are difficult to separate from the methods of functioning of social economy enterprises. We can identify three dimensions, distinct and yet complementary, on which evaluation of the social economy may be based (Bouchard, 2004b; Bouchard, Bourque, Lévesque, 2001; Bouchard and Fontan, 1998):

- the *organizational* dimension, which concerns the particular performance of social economy enterprises in terms of quality, efficiency, productivity etc.;
- the *social utility* dimension, which concerns the impacts such as the reduction of social inequalities or exclusion, the structuring effects on sectors and territories, the mobilization of actors in the environment, the partnerships with other social players, the redistribution effects, etc. (see: Gadrey, 2002 and 2004; the works commissioned by DIES in France);
- the *institutional* dimension, which concerns the social innovations *vis-à-vis* the governance of economic activities at the territorial and sectoral level, the emergence of new rules of the game, the interfaces between the social economy, the public and the commercial economies, etc.

Methods and indicators

The key research questions that the Working Group considers concerning the methods and social indicators of the social economy are the following:

- What *methods* are used to evaluate the SE in terms of scale (macro, meso, micro), of objectives (accountancy, conformity, quality), of approach (national statistics, program evaluation, social balance-sheet, etc.).
- What are the *advantages* and *limits* of those approaches?
- What are the *indicators* of the performance and impacts of the SE as regards:
  a) the organizational dimension of enterprises;
  b) the social utility dimension of their activities;

---

c) the institutional dimension of relations between the SE and the State and between the SE and the market?
- What are the *criteria* for performance and social impact according to type of organization, type of activities, the institutional context in which they are set?
- What are the *links* between the organizational performance, social utility and institutional contribution of the SE?

Evaluative Approaches and Paradigms

Evaluation poses the question of the type of judgement of perform-ance and the forms of justification used in analysis. No judgement of social utility or otherwise can escape the social relations in which the activities take place (Zarifian, 2002). In this sense, each evaluative action implies an epistemological position that is rarely explicit among evaluate subjects and the parties requiring evaluation (where they are not the subjects themselves). Demands for evaluation of the social economy are subtended by "visions" of the role that the social economy plays in the economy and in society, themselves informed by contrast-ing theories or paradigms.

The relevant conceptual categories for evaluating the specific contri-bution of the social economy are varied and reflect the various concep-tions of the social economy, and indeed the social utility of its evalua-tion. Different *notions* are used, such as social cost-effectiveness, social wealth, social return on investment (Aeron-Thomas, *et al.*, 2004), social accountancy (Quarter, *et al.*, 2003a), social utility (see Gadrey, 2004, and the works in France commissioned by DIES), social innovation (see Bouchard, 2004a and the works of CRISES), added value (Mengin and Pascal, 2002), outcomes or externalities (Fraisse, Gardin and Laville, 2000), collective benefits (Gadrey, 2002), etc.

The interests of evaluation of the social economy will be perceived in different ways according to the different *underlying approaches*.

- By way of examples, in a *managerial and strategic* perspective largely inspired by a rational choice approach, evaluation refers above all to internal and external accountancy, social balance sheet, social and environmental reporting, social audits, etc. Giv-en their nature, the enterprises of the social economy must have a good social organizational performance in the dimensions meas-ured by the social balance sheet (Mugarra Elorriaga, 2001). To the extent that the practice of the social balance sheet in social economy enterprises might even reverse the burden of proof to-wards private enterprises (Fraisse, 2001). However, the tools sprung from theories of management and standard economy are unwieldy as regards the organizational dimension of the social economy, particularly for taking account of just what makes these enterprises good performers, among other things the "social" factor.

- The *neo-institutionalist economy* inspires evaluative studies of the social economy in terms of capacity to fill in gaps in the market and public action (Weisbrod, 1977) and to assess the specific performance of the nonprofit organizations (Ben Ner, 2006). This perspective helps governments identifying those organizations that can introduce competitiveness in providing some social services, in respect of the principle of subsidiarity. Now, history shows, for one thing, that the social economy precedes the creation of public services (Salamon and Anheier, 1998) and, for another thing, that it succeeds in becoming profitable without thereby being absorbed by the commercial economy, as witness the example of Mondragon. Nevertheless, a "competitive regime of governance" also brings new challenges to the social economy as more for-profit enterprises are also penetrating the field of social and health services, as the previous CIRIEC Working Group has demonstrated (Enjolras, 2008).

- Looking at it from a *cognitive approach*, evaluation of public policies is seen as a social construction or as a collective action (Perret, 2001). In this sense, public policies are not the result of rational decisions made by a centralized and sovereign actor. Rather, it is the result of social interactions within a system of actors. Those interactions give way to the production of ideas, representations and common values that enable the collective actions. Taken from such a constructivist perspective, evaluation can be seen as a tool helping to optimize the interaction and knowledge processes that "produce" collective actions.

- In the perspective of *institutionalist sociology*, the demands for evaluation exceed the only sector of the social economy but concern every organizational body within plural or mixed economies. Evaluation takes a greater importance as concern and weariness about the economy needs are growing within the civil society. Evaluation reviews the social or societal contribution of the social economy to the democratization of the development model (Lévesque, 2006), to the renewal of public action (Salamon *et al.*, 1999), to the creation of middle paths between the economic and the social (Piore, 2001), of public spaces for debate (Eme and Laville, 1994), to the creation of mixes of instruments and public intervention in other instruments of the private sector and the social economy (Monnier, 1999; Bernier,

27

Bouchard and Lévesque, 2003). However, evaluation of this type of contribution poses the problem of isolating the effects proper to the intervention of the changes that will have occurred independent of the action of the latter (Perret, 2001).

To evaluate means to measure, to compare, to judge. These different meaning have evolved with time. Since the end of the 19th century, at least four *generations of evaluation* have been observed (Guba and Lincoln, 1989). They respectively consist in:

1. Measuring the gaps between objectives and results;
2. Describing what is being evaluated to explain the gaps;
3. Appreciating the relative efficiency accordingly to the values and merits of the evaluated object;
4. Inviting the concerned actors to participate and negotiate the meaning of their action in a pluralist perspective of evaluation.

These forms have not evolved in a linear fashion since different generations of evaluation can coexist and that elements from one generation may be present in the next. Some call upon a fifth generation, more political, that consists in:

5. Creating a space for deliberation about the values and the social relevancy of the object being evaluated (Bouchard and Fontan, 1998).

Any indicator thus conveys an implicit message. Not exposing the motives that govern the choice of indicators cannot give the evaluation report more than a veneer of neutrality. On the other hand an evaluation based solely on the subjectivity of the players concerned, if it serves the purposes of self-evaluation, does not allow account to be taken of the collective choices that direct the action of the group or organization. Evaluation must therefore necessarily arbitrate between a (false) posture of scientific neutrality and radical constructivism (Zúñiga, 2001).

We note different *types of indicators* associated with different postures of evaluation in relation to different modalities of the democratic decision-making:

– *Deterministic* indicators, that are deduced from a program's objectives and may be connected to representative democracy that speaks in the name of the general will;

– *Experimental* indicators, that come from the co-production of the demand and of the offer by the users and the producers, and may be associated with direct democracy;

– *Alternative* indicators, that may be produced in a context of co-production of public policy by a plurality of social actors – being representatives of the civil society, of the business interests, of the workers or of government – that may take place in deliberative democracy and eventually rise to collective players participating to in social democracy.

The objective of the CIRIEC international Working Group is to analyze the various contributions expected of the social economy according to the different *theoretical and methodological fields or approaches*. This aims at a critical assessment and fuelling the debate on what is expected from the social economy.

Approaches and paradigms

The main research questions that we now address concerning the approaches and paradigms underlying the evaluation of the SE are the following:

- What are the relevant *conceptual categories* for evaluation of the SE?
- What are the different *approaches* to the SE that underlie evaluative actions? What are the advantages and limits of those approaches?
- What are the different relevant *paradigms* of evaluation for the SE in its organizational, social utility and institutional dimensions?
- In what way do the evaluation practices participate in the actual *construction of the field* of the SE?

Some Relevant Data for Describing and Analyzing Evaluation Practices of the Social Economy

The studies are conducted on the basis of review of empirical research (evaluative sectoral research, evaluation tools in force in the social economy, surveys of evaluation needs, etc.). They may contain elements such as:

- *Querents and methods of evaluation*. Evaluations may be requested by different types of querents and for different reasons. It is a matter of identifying the principal clients (public administrations, sectors of the social economy, social movements, other) and the main interests connected with these evaluations (taxation, public contracts, financing of activities, external recognition, compliance with values, internal functioning, etc.). Evaluation may proceed in various ways, including or disregarding social and economic dimensions, qualitative and quantitative dimensions and short-term or long-term effects. The evaluation framework may be imposed by an outside authority, developed by the players themselves, or negotiated. What are the main trends in evaluation method? What interests are involved? Might these evaluations have a standardizing effect on the sectors (certification, labelling, etc.) or on organizations (adaptation of mission in order to comply)? Or, on the contrary, might they have structuring effects (recognition, reinforcement of autonomy, awareness-raising and mobilization of the movement, legislative adaptations)?

– *Evaluation objectives.* This is a matter of identifying the primary objectives of evaluation that depend on the position of the social economy in varied national situations. The integration of continental Europe raises questions in terms of competition and general interest. The French speak of social utility. In Quebec and in Canada, solidarist financiers raise the question in terms of co-dependence between the viability of the enterprise and that of the association. The international cooperative movement seeks to prove its contribution to an equitable, more even-handed globalization (fair globalization). In Central America and in Quebec they are developing audits of conformity with cooperative values. What sense are we to assign to these choices? What development dynamic do they reveal? What are the links between the organizational performance, social utility and institutional contribution of the social economy?

– *Evaluation indicators.* This concerns identifying the indicators of performance and impacts of the social economy as regards: a) the organizational dimension of enterprises; b) the dimension of social utility of their activities; c) the institutional dimension of relations between the social economy and the State and between the social economy and the market.

References

Aeron-Thomas, D., Nicholls, D. J., Forster, S., Westall, A., *Social Return on Investment. Valuing what Matters. Findings and Recommendation from a Pilot Study*, London, New Economics Foundation.

Angers, F.-A., *La coopération, de la réalité à la théorie économique*, Montréal, Fides, 1975.

Anheir H. K., Ben-Ner, A., *Advances in Theories of the Nonprofit Sector*, 2000.

Ben-Ner, A., "For-profit, State and Non-profit: How to Cut the Pie", in J.-P. Touffut (ed.), *Advancing Public Goods*, The Cournot Centre for Economic Studies, Cheltenham, UK/Northampton, MA. USA, Edward Elgar, 2006, pp. 40-67.

Ben-Ner, A., Van Hoomissen, T., "Nonprofit Organizations in the Mixed Economy", in A. Ben-Ner and T. Van Hoomissen (eds.), *The Nonprofit Sector in the Mixed Economy*, Ann Arbor, The University of Michigan Press, 1993.

Bernier, L., Bouchard, M. J., Lévesque, B., "La prise en compte de l'intérêt général au Québec. Nouvelle articulation entre l'intérêt individuel, collectif et général", in M.L. Von Bergman, B. Enjolras and O. Saint-Martin (dir.), *Économie plurielle et régulation socio-économique*, Bruxelles, CIRIEC-International, 2002.

Borzaga, C., Defourny, J. (eds.), *The Emergence of Social Enterprise*, London, Routledge, 2004.

Bouchard, M. J., "De l'expérimentation à l'institutionnalisation positive, l'innovation sociale dans le logement communautaire au Québec", *Annales de l'économie publique, sociale et coopérative*, 77-2, 2004a, pp. 139-165.

Bouchard, M. J., "Vers une évaluation multidimensionnelle et négociée de l'économie sociale", *RECMA Revue internationale d'économie sociale*, 292, May 2004, 2004b, pp. 59-74.

Bouchard, M. J., Bourque, G., L., Lévesque, B., "L'évaluation de l'économie sociale dans la perspective des nouvelles formes de régulation socio-économique de l'intérêt général", *Cahiers de recherche sociologique*, March 2001, pp. 31-53.

Bouchard, M. J., Dumais, L., *Rapport sur les enjeux méthodologiques de l'évaluation de l'économie sociale et solidaire*, Site du projet de coopération France-Québec sur l'économie sociale et solidaire, 2001: http://www.unites. uqam.ca/econos/index.htm.

Bouchard, M. J., Fontan, J.-M., *L'économie sociale à la loupe. Problématique de l'évaluation des entreprises de l'économie sociale*. Présenté au 66e congrès de l'ACFAS, 1998. http://www.omd.uqam.ca/publications/ telechargements/evaluation.pdf.

Bouchard, M. J., Rondeau, J., "Le financement de l'économie sociale, à la croisée des intérêts privés et publics. Le cas du Réseau d'investissement du Québec", *Économie et solidarités*, 34, 1, 2003, pp. 123-135.

Chaves, R., Monzón Campos, J. L., *L'économie sociale dans l'Union européenne*, Liège et Bruxelles, CIRIEC international et Comité économique et social européen, 2006.

Côté, D. (dir.), *Les holdings coopératifs: Évolution ou transformation définitive?*, Bruxelles, De Boeck Université, 2000.

Defourny, J., Monzón Campos, J. L. (eds.), *Économie sociale: entre économie capitaliste et économie publique/ The Third Sector: Cooperative, Mutual and Nonprofit Organizations*, Brussels, CIRIEC and De Boeck-Wesmael, Inc., 1992.

Demoustier, D., *L'économie sociale et solidaire. S'associer pour entreprendre autrement*, Paris, Syros, 2001.

Desforges, J.-G., "Stratégie et structure des organisations coopératives", in J.-G. Desforges et C. Vienne (dir.), *Stratégie et organisation de l'entreprise coopérative*, Montréal/Paris, Éd. du jour/CIEM, 1980, pp. 287-311.

Desroche, H., *Pour un traité d'économie sociale*, Coopérative d'information et d'édition mutualiste (CIEM), 1983.

Dussuet, A., Lauzanas, J.-M., *L'économie sociale entre informel et formel*, Rennes, PUR, 2007.

Eme, B., "Aux frontières de l'économie, politiques et pratiques d'insertion", *Cahiers internationaux de sociologie*, Paris, PUF, CII, juillet-décembre 1997.

Eme, B., Laville, J.-L. (dir.), *Cohésion sociale et emploi*, Paris, Desclée de Brouwer, 1994.

Enjolras, B., *L'économie solidaire et le marché*, Paris, L'Harmattan, 2002.

Enjolras, B. (ed.), *Gouvernance et intérêt général dans les services sociaux et de santé*, Brussels, P.I.E. Peter Lang, 2008.

Evers, A., Laville, J.-L., *The third sector in Europe*, Cheltenham, Elgar, 2004.

Fraisse, L., *Les enjeux politiques de l'évaluation*, Site du Projet de coopération France-Québec sur l'économie sociale et solidaire, 2001. http://www.unites.uqam.ca/econos/index.htm.

Fraisse, L., Gardin, L., Laville, J.-L., *Les externalités dans l'aide à domicile: une approche européenne*. Rencontre des délégations française et québécoise, Projet de coopération franco-québécois en économie sociale et solidaire. Montréal, Centre Saint-Pierre et UQAM, 5-9 February, 2000, Montréal, 2000.

Gadrey, J., *Bénéfices collectifs, externalités collectives, et économie solidaire: commentaires sur le rapport européen du CRIDA*, Lille, Université de Lille 1, Laboratoire CLERSE, 2002.

Gadrey, J., *L'utilité sociale des organisations de l'économie sociale et solidaire. Une mise en perspective sur la base de travaux récents*, Rapport synthèse pour la DIES et la MIRE, Lille, Université de Lille 1, CLERSE-IFRESI, February 2004, Lille 2004.

Gadrey, J., Zarifian, P., *L'émergence d'un modèle de service: enjeux et réalités*, Rueil-Malmaison, Éditions Liaisons, 2002.

Gendron, C., *Le questionnement éthique et social de l'entreprise dans la littérature managériale*, Montréal, CRISES, No. 0004, 2000.

Gide, C., *Économie sociale, Rapports du Jury international, Exposition universelle de 1900*, 1900.

Guba, E.G., Lincoln, Y., "Competing Paradigms in Qualitative Research", in: N.K. Denzin and Y. Lincoln (eds.), *Handbook of Qualitative Research*, Thousand Oaks, Sage Publications, 1994, pp. 105-107.

Gui, B., "Fondement économique du Tiers Secteur", *RECMA Revue des études coopératives, mutualistes et associative*, 72, 247, 1992, pp. 160-173.

Hansmann, H., "The Role of the Nonprofit Enterprise", *Yale Law Journal*, 89, 2, 1980, pp. 835-898.

James, E., "How nonprofits grow: a model", *Journal of Policy Analysis and Management*, 2, 3, 1983, pp. 350-66.

Kerling, J. A., "Social Enterprise in the United States and Europe: Understanding and Learning from the Differences", *Voluntas*, 17, 2006, pp. 247-263.

Laville, J.-L., *Une troisième voie pour l'emploi*, Paris, Desclée de Brouwer, 1999.

Lévesque. B., "Le potentiel d'innovation sociale de l'économie sociale: quelques éléments de problématique", *Économie et solidarités*, Vol. 37, No. 1, 2006, pp. 13-48.

Lévesque, B., Malo, M.-C., "L'économie sociale au Québec", in J. Defourny et J. L. Monzón Campos (eds.), *Économie sociale, entre économie capitaliste et économie publique*, Bruxelles, CIRIEC and De Boek, 1992, pp. 384-446.

Lévesque, B., Mendell, M., *L'économie sociale au Québec: éléments théoriques et empiriques pour le débat et la recherche*, Montréal, CRISES, Working Papers No. 9908, 1999.

Mengin, J., Pascal, F. (dir.), "Les plus-values de l'économie sociale", *La tribune fonda*, 154, May 2002.

Monnier, L., *Fondements et dynamique de l'économie plurielle*, Congrès annuel de l'Association canadienne-française pour l'avancement des sciences, Colloque du CIRIEC-Canada, Ottawa, May 10-11-12 1999.

Mugarra Elorriaga, A.M., "Responsabilidad y balance social hoy en día: un reto para las cooperativas", *CIRIEC España: Balance social en la Economía social*, 39, 2001, pp. 25-50.

Nyssens, M. (eds.), *Social Enterprise*, London, Routledge, 2006.

Perret, B., *L'évaluation des politiques publiques*, Paris, La Découverte, 2001.

Piore, M., "The Emergent Role of Social Intermediaries in the New Economy", *Annals of Public, and Cooperative Economy/Annales de l'économie publique, sociale et coopérative*, 72, 3, September 2001, pp. 339-350.

Quarter, J., Mook, L., Richmond, B. J., *What Counts. Social Accounting for Nonprofits and Cooperatives*, Toronto, Prentice Hall, 2003a.

Quarter, J., Mook, L., Richmond, B. J., *What is the Social Economy?* Centre for Urban and Community Studies, Research Bulletin, 13, 2003b.

Rondot, S., Bouchard, M. J., *L'évaluation de l'économie sociale. Petit aide-mémoire*. Montréal, ARUC-ÉS, Collection recherche, Cahier R-03-2003, 2003.

Salamon, L. M., Anheier, H. K., "Social Origins of the Civil Society: Explaining the Non-Profit Sector Cross-Nationally", *Voluntas*, Vol. 9, No. 3, 1998, pp. 213-248.

Salamon, L. M., Anheier, H. K., List, R., Toepler, S., Sokolowski, S. W. and ass., *Global Civil Society: Dimensions of the Nonprofit Sector*, Baltimore, The Johns Hopkins University, Centre for Civil Society Studies, 1999.

St-Pierre, J., Bouchard, M. J., "De l'alliance à la gouvernance, logiques d'action et logiques d'acteurs dans un centre financier aux entreprises Desjardins", *Annales de l'économie publique, sociale et coopérative*, 76, 4, décembre 2005, pp. 585-620.

Vienney, C., *Socio-économie des organisations coopératives*, Paris, Coopérative d'information et d'édition mutualiste (CIEM), 1980.

Weisbrod, B. A., *The Voluntary Nonprofit Sector*, Lexington, MA: D. C. Heath, 1977.

Zadek, S., Pruzan, P., Evans, R., *Building Corporate Accountability*, London, Earthscan Publications Limited, 1997.

Zarifian, P., "Service et efficience: le rôle essentiel de la compétence professionnelle", in J. Gadrey et P. Zarifian, *L'émergence d'un modèle de service: enjeux et réalités*, Rueil-Malmaison, Éditions Liaisons, 2002, pp. 121-155.

Zúñiga, R., "L'évaluation sur la place publique: science, éthique et politique", *Cahiers de recherche sociologique*, No. 35, pp. 15-30, 2001.

Evaluating the Social Economy
Clarifying Complex Rationality

Bernard PERRET

*Head of the Mission "Evaluation of the Public Policies"
at the General Council for Environment and
Sustainable Development – CGEDD (France)*

For the social economy to grow, it must be evaluated. While this assertion might seem self-evident, we need to understand its underpinnings and implications. First, evaluation continues to establish its value as a tool for reporting on, guiding and legitimising collective action; this is essential if democratic societies are to function properly. The legitimising function is especially useful in the case of the social economy, which has a low profile and precarious social status. However, that is not all. On a more fundamental level, the realm of evaluation and the social economy both have the same outlook, the same rebelliousness against market logic and bureaucratic standardization. Thus, evaluation may be defined as the social construction of a belief concerning the value of an action or activity. It therefore breaks away from the economic presupposition whereby it is possible to "naturalize" value by determining its monetary equivalent. Likewise, the social economy is defined by the fact that it includes, amongst its aims, non-monetary impacts on society. For it, too, the social value of an activity cannot be reduced to its market value.

The subject matter developed below concerns mainly the evaluation of public policy and public programme. That said, the social economy is not a policy but, rather, a set of structures. Nonetheless, the policy-evaluation model can be easily adapted to the evaluation of structures (enterprises, organizations, etc.) inasmuch as these are collective action mechanisms targeting a set of goals tied to the common good. Interrelated with the question of evaluation is that of societal indicators, which we treat here as mechanisms for shaping and "producing" (or presenting) information.

I. Evaluating Public Policy

A. *Epistemological Preliminaries: Information and Assessment*

Before presenting avenues of research for evaluating the social economy, we should set out a few epistemological preliminaries. Evaluation aims to establish a *value judgment* with a view to *action* (*policy*), and is based on information. How should we clarify the links among information, evaluation and action?

First, we should acknowledge that our assessments are largely determined by the nature of the information on which they are based. In this connection, Amartya Sen employs the idea of 'information base': "Every evaluation of a situation is determined by the "information base" supporting it. Every evaluative approach is characterised by an information base: the information needed to make assessments within the framework of this approach and – no less important – the information excluded from the evaluation process. The information excluded is an important element in the evaluative approach" (Sen, 2000: 56).[1]

We might be tempted to deduce from this that an assessment will be particularly thorough when it is supported by a very large information base. However, experience shows that this is far from always being the case. In reality, too much information is almost as harmful as a total lack of it. We are continuously overloaded with so much irrelevant information (the spam phenomenon is a good example) that we are obliged to devote much time and energy to it – often at considerable cost. We are obliged to acknowledge that not all information is useful. Someone who has drawn our attention to this phenomenon in a very clear way is the Nobel Prize winner in economics, Herbert Simon: "In a world where attention is one of the scarcest major resources, information may be a luxury we can ill afford since it can divert our attention from what is important towards what is not. We cannot allow ourselves to process information simply because it is there" (Leca, 1993).[2]

This has an important consequence: information must be assembled and arranged with specific needs in mind. In this light, evaluation and indicators may be viewed as processes for selecting, combining and interpreting information. Their objective is to draw attention to important information, and "produce" or present it in an appropriate way. This constructivist view of evaluation can be linked to the view of human intelligence that emerges from progress made in biology and the cognitive sciences. In this view, the human brain does not function like a

---

[1] Translator's translation.

[2] *Id.*

computer but, rather, like a self-sufficient system. Its operation and 'routines' are determined by the history of its relations with its environment. We do not absorb all of the information that reaches us, but select what interests us based on our practical concerns, beliefs and ideological interests.

B. What is Evaluation?

Authoritative sources on the topic define evaluation as an activity measuring the impact of an action. This 'positivist' view does not reflect the realities of actual practice. I prefer the following definition, which is more complex yet more precise: 'an analytical and research activity dealing with the implementation and outcomes of a public action (policy), conducted within a (more or less) formal methodological and institutional framework to provide accountability and/or improve this action (policy)'.

To be more precise, an evaluation has four principal objectives:

- to put public funds to good use' (accountability);
- to establish a more rational foundation (as part of a strategic perspective or with the more immediate goal of optimising the allocation of public resources);
- to mobilise for and give meaning to action; and
- to share information, and find common ground for different interpretations.

The first two objectives are those that come to mind most naturally, and that are advanced by authoritative sources. In my own experience, the second two (learning, forming common interpretations) are in practice more important.

The cognitive approach to public policy (Muller and Surel, 2000) provides a relevant framework for understanding the role of assessment. In this approach, public policies are not decided in a rational and centralised way by a sovereign political actor, but result from social interaction among a system of actors. This interaction fosters shared ideas, representations and values facilitating the emergence of collective action that sometimes takes the form of public policy. Stated in this way, evaluation may be viewed as a mechanism for optimising the interactional and knowledge processes that 'produce' public policy.

C. Evaluation as an Institutionalised Process

To ensure that the function of producing a collective assessment is efficient, evaluation must be institutionalised. Beyond the diversity of political contexts and participant interaction, institutionalization of evaluation essentially means that:

- the evaluation refers to explicit aims (a legitimate actor in the system of action must indicate why she/he wishes an evaluation);
- the actions taken form part of a plan;
- there is mediation between the 'scientific' aspect of the evaluation and the decision-making aspect. This is the role assigned to the "evaluation authorities", who are responsible, among other things, for collectively questioning and setting in motion a debate on the conclusions;
- the evaluation report meets the requirements of transparency and traceability.

Working out which questions to ask is a crucial step. To evaluate a policy one must first question it. The formulation of evaluative questions finalises an agreement made by the evaluation's protagonists. It aims to establish a common language and a compromise between, on the one hand, the operational expectations of the decision makers, managers and/or actors and, on the other hand, the requirements of objective and detached knowledge. The choice of questions is preceded by broad collective consideration of the evaluation issues, and makes reference to the operational concerns and *a priori* assessments of the system or action to be evaluated. Stated differently, it involves making a diagnosis and formulating hypotheses that must be tested against reality. In any event, the execution stage of the evaluation (gathering information, initiating new surveys or research, recruiting implementers, etc.) should not be broached before taking the time to formulate good questions and, if necessary, identifying rudimentary answers already available in existing information and research.

The term "evaluating board" refers to a place or a function rather than a model mechanism. Whatever the scope of the evaluation and the desired degree of objectivity, there must be a clear emphasis on the collective aspect of the assessment. This is primarily what distinguishes evaluation from inspection or expertise. All complex social practices must be examined from a variety of viewpoints. While evaluating authorities cannot present every possible viewpoint, they must reflect its diversity. It is important to clarify that the evaluating authority does not provide a sphere for negotiation among vested interest groups; instead, based on scholarly research that must preserve its specificity and autonomy, it provides an opportunity to cross-fertilise views and enrich interpretive grids.

Aside from its role in formulating questions and organising debate on the research, the evaluating board can conduct investigations and hold field trips, etc. In addition, once the authority has completed the evaluation, it has an important role to play in disseminating and explaining its conclusions.

D. Methodological Problems

The principal task in evaluation is usually considered to be that of measuring the social and economic impact of an action or activity. In practice, the issues associated with evaluation are broader than this. They deal, amongst other things, with:

- implementation (conformity with certain texts, resources and actors, etc.),
- the attainment of objectives (how the problem that justified the policy evaluation is evolving),
- the effects themselves (their effectiveness *vis-à-vis* the targets established),
- systemic effects,
- action mechanisms (why and how the policy functions),
- contextual influences (what aspects of the context have an impact on implementing and attaining the objectives satisfactorily).

Indicators play an important but not exclusive role in evaluation. An indicator is a figure that provides information on a phenomenon or its evolution. It may also be viewed as a 'system for the optimal aggregation of information'. Its function is to draw attention to a fact or important trend. By itself, it generally cannot be used to evaluate the success of an action.

Every evaluation relies on figures, though the role played by indicators as a mainstay of conclusions is highly variable. They sometimes resolve evaluation issues by themselves but, as a rule, they need to be interpreted and completed by qualitative information. In any case, what should or should not be considered relevant to measure can never be taken for granted.

II. The Question of a Reference System: How Does One Objectify the Common Good?

The social economy is not a policy. Developing it does not involve pursuing objectives that have been formalised and validated by democratic procedure. What benchmark should be used in devising a reference system for social economy enterprises? There does not seem to be any way round approaching the problem indirectly, namely, by formulating a shared conception of the common good. This was what was intended, amongst other objectives, by consideration in France of views on 'social utility'. However, we should keep in mind that there is a never-ending array of legitimate conceptions of social welfare, as demonstrated for example by the burgeoning projects on social indicators.

A. Social Indicators

The question of social indicators has a close and explicit link with that of evaluation. According to a UN definition, social indicators are "statistics that reflect important aspects of social conditions in a useful way and facilitate the evaluation and evolution of these conditions". However, as Heinz Herbert Noll observes: 'The principal function of indicators is not to directly monitor or test the efficiency of programmes and policies but, rather, to broaden our perspectives on society and provide basic information to improve the policy development process in a less direct way (Noll, 2002: 172). The development of social indicators is often motivated by a desire to complement and correct the measurement of social wealth carried out by the system of national accounts. The limits to this system are well known: ignorance of the non-monetary and non-utilitarian aspects of welfare, arbitrary measurement of non-material production, ignorance of the negative externalities of growth, etc.

Over the last few years, there have been several attempts to introduce other ways of measuring social welfare. These attempts are of two types: composite indexes (obtained through the arbitrary weighting of heterogeneous indicators), the best know example of which is the human development index of the United Nations Development Program (UNDP), and extended economic indicators (obtained by combining the monetary wealth indicator with non-monetary aspects of welfare that have been "monetised").

The diversity of the global indicators advanced and the heterogeneousness of the concepts that underpin them (Economic Welfare, Quality of Life, Human Development, Social Health, Sustainable Development, Social Capital, etc.) clearly demonstrate the difficulty of the task. In contrast to economic indicators, which are univocal and coherent, social indicators have no sure conceptual basis on which to rely. There is no rational argument to help select and give weight to the basic indicators of community life (demography, the state of people's health, employment, poverty, inequality, social cohesion, education, innovation and research, the environment and natural resources, the quality of life, the quality of public services, social involvement and institutional development).

III. Improving the Clarity of Social Issues to Facilitate Recognition of Non-Standard Forms of Analysis

We must admit that there is no theoretical argument that would allow us to favour such an approach to social indicators to the detriment of others. The relevance of the indicator systems can only be measured in terms of their ability to explain the social changes that are most important from the standpoint of society's expectations and needs. Ultimately, and as in the case of public policy evaluation, the only way to establish their legitimacy is to prompt a debate on analytical frameworks and assessment criteria within appropriate institutional frameworks. Thus, it is necessary to link the indicator issue to that of public debate and, more generally, the deepening of democracy. Viewed in this way, consideration given to the methods and approaches of evaluation has the merit of being explicitly structured around epistemological and political themes. It suggests an opportunity for and indicates the importance of applying the requirements of rigour and objectivity, which have made science successful, to a wider class of socio-cognitive processes. In this way, we can look forward to the possibility of developing methods and practices designed to make human society's introspective effort more structured, systematic and carefully thought out.

Now, the development of tools and practices likely to make society more understandable to itself also constitutes one of the pre-conditions for greater recognition of the social economy. What does the social economy produce? How can we objectify and measure this production? Of course, social economy enterprises participate in the monetary economy. Within this framework, they are required to balance their accounts and thus cannot avoid being tested through financial assessment of their activities. Nevertheless, they also generate non-monetary resources and claim to function in the spirit of non-economic values. They therefore must be able to demonstrate that they have increased social value, whether the latter is formulated in terms of social utility, social capital or any other concept. The identification and social acknowledgement of this increased social value constitutes a fundamental issue. The issue is at once of a democratic and cognitive order, and calls for the establishment of places and procedures to facilitate confrontation among the heterogeneous logics underlying non-standard social practices, and the development of tools to facilitate the objectification and measurement of the values at stake.

References

Leca, J., "Sur le rôle de la connaissance dans la modernisation de l'État", *Revue Française d'administration publique*, 66, April-June 1993.

Mullet, P., Surel, Y., *L'analyse des politiques publiques*, Paris, Montcherestien, 2000.

Noll, H.-H., "Social Indicators and Quality of Life Research; Background, Achievements and Current Trends", in N. Genov (ed.), *Advances in Sociological Knowledge over Half a century*, Paris, ISSC, 2002.

Sen, A., *Development As Freedom*, Anchor Books, 2000.

The Public Policy Paradox
Normative Foundations of Social
Economy and Public Policies

Which Consequences for Evaluation Strategies?

Bernard ENJOLRAS

Director of Research, Institute for Social Research, Oslo (Norway)

Organizations from the social economy are often involved in implementing public policies in various policy fields (social services, health,
education, environment, employment, etc.). If evaluation conducted or
ordered by public authorities is not the only perspective from which
social economy organizations can be assessed, it constitutes a decisive
type of evaluation since it conditions their access to critical resources
and influences their legitimacy. This chapter sets in relations two normative perspectives that are at play when social economy organizations
are evaluated from the viewpoint of a public policy, on the one hand,
the public policy normative perspective and, on the other hand, the
normative discourse on the social economy. The often paradoxical
character of public policy evaluation of social economy organizations
will appear as a result of this confrontation.

To evaluate consists in determining the value of things. But in matters of values as well as when it comes to distance, to measure supposes
having a measure instrument, an etalon allowing to determine the value
or the distance one seeks to measure. In order to evaluate it is therefore
necessary to define a reference making it possible to construct a value
scale. When it comes to social economy organizations, one possible
reference is given by the "normative foundations" of these organizations
i.e. by the specificities that ideally differentiate those organizations from
other organizational types such as governmental or for-profit. This
chapter will therefore in the first place identify theses normative foundations starting with a discussion of the main paradigms that are used to
define those organizations. These paradigms are constructs resulting
from interactions between actors' self-conceptions and the theoretical
efforts of the academic world, and are articulated in normative dis-

courses on and by these organizations. In other words, these paradigms contribute to building a normative and ideal understanding of those organizations. The synthesis of these paradigms allows defining a normative reference for the evaluation of social economy organizations along three functions: solidary, democratic and productive.

Another normative reference is given by the perspectives embedded in public policies. Historically, evaluation inscribes itself in a tradition – since Aristotle advising Philip of Macedonia – where knowledge and rationality have been used to serve the Prince. Evaluation conducted from a public policy perspective is also characterized by normative foundations, embedded in policy-making and policy-evaluation processes that are not necessarily congruent with the normative foundations of the social economy.

I. The Normative Foundations of Social Economy Organizations

The characterization of the specific features of social economy organizations differs according to the nature of the analytical paradigms mobilized: market failures, social economy, solidary economy, civil society. These paradigms have different origins and do not fit well all types of social economy organizations (associations, mutual organizations and cooperatives). However, all are concerned with association (in the broad sense of the term), whatever the properties form taken by the association. To the extent that voluntary associations, mutual organizations and cooperatives are associations of members, all paradigms have some relevance for all types of social economy organizations. These analytical paradigms influence the modalities by which these organizations justify their "utility" and the way the actors of the field conceive themselves. The synthesis of these paradigms points towards three main social functions that are specific to these organizations: solidary function, democratic function and productive function.

A. Analytical Paradigms

1. Market Failure and Government Failures

For the tenets of market and government failure approaches, the main characteristic of nonprofit organizations consists in the fact that they cannot distribute their profit. This characteristic of nonprofit organizations is referred to as the non-distribution constraint. It is worth noting that such a focus excludes mutual organizations and cooperatives from the field of interest.

The government failure approach (Weisbrod, 1977) considers the provision of public goods by nonprofit organizations. Purely public goods possess two distinctive features: it is virtually possible to exclude or ration their use, neither is it desirable to do so. In order to illustrate the role of nonprofit organizations in the provision of public goods, Weisbrod (1977) describes an economy where two types of goods exist: private and public goods. The question raised by Weisbrod is what will be the level of consumption of public goods that will be satisfied by the Government. The level of public goods supplied by the Government is determined by the electorate, i.e. by the median voter. This leads to a situation where many consumers are unsatisfied, some being over-satisfied, some being under-satisfied. The more heterogeneous the population in terms of preferences, income, wealth etc., the higher is the degree of dissatisfaction. The under-satisfied consumers have the option of setting up nonprofit organizations in order to increase the supply of public goods. The production of public goods by nonprofit organizations appears as a second best solution, but by comparison with public organizations, possesses the characteristic of being able to satisfying heterogeneous and/or minority demands.

The market failure approach focuses on the informational characteristics of the goods offered by nonprofit organizations, especially the existence of informational asymmetries. It is possible to distinguish two types of informational asymmetry. The first refers to situations of moral hazard where one party must carry out an action, while the other party cannot perfectly control nor constrain the action carried out. The second refers to situations of adverse selection, where the knowledge relevant to the transaction that one party possesses but which is lacked by the other. The existence of information asymmetry opens up the possibility of contractual failure (Hansmann, 1980) and leads for-profit organizations to be less effective in their relations to consumers. In this case, the constraint of non-distribution (of profits) characterizing nonprofit organizations reduces the incentive to exploit informational asymmetries. In the presence of informational asymmetry, nonprofit organizations appear to be more trustworthy than for-profit organizations and in consequence are to be preferred by consumers.

The paradigm of market and government failures justifies tax privileges given to nonprofit organizations due to their "social utility" since they offer goods and services in quantity and quality that neither the market nor the government are able to provide.

2. Social Economy

The social economy paradigm stresses the specific rules that characterize the functioning of social economy organizations (Vienney, 1994; Demoustier, 2001). The economy is conceived as a sphere of activity regulated by social rules relative to the distribution of property rights, the mechanisms of distribution of surpluses, and the distributive and allocative mechanisms by which resources are allocated. From this viewpoint the economy is divided in three sub-sectors, capitalist economy, public economy and social economy, each of these sub-sectors being characterized by specific rules. The social economy is, from this perspective, characterized by (i) the equality of the associated members independently of their participation in the funding and in the activities of the organization; (ii) the collective property of the reinvested surplus; when admitted, the sharing of the surpluses among the associated members is effectuated on the basis of their participation to the activities of the organization. Based on ideological origins of different nature (Socialism, Christianism, Solidarism, Republicanism) the social economy justifies social economy organizations in terms of an alternative to Capitalism (Gueslin, 1998). The social economy justifies itself also from the viewpoint of its contribution to a more equal distribution of social wealth (as a complement of the welfare state) following in this the approach initiated by Léon Walras.

3. Solidary Economy

The paradigm of solidary economy (Eme and Laville, 1994; Laville, 1994) considers organizations that hybridize three of Polanyi's economic principles, market, redistribution and reciprocity. Three features of these organizations are identified: they constitute public spaces of proximity when solidarity bonds can be weaved, they provide services which modalities result from a joint construction of both supply and demand, and they hybridize three types of economy, market economy (the sale of services), redistributive economy (public funding) and reciprocal economy (volunteering). The reciprocal dimension that includes voluntary action and active participation of the users to the production of the services confer the solidary feature of these organizations. The justification of solidary economy organizations is based on their social utility and on their contribution to the solution of macro-social problems. By putting solidarity at the heart of their functioning, these organizations are said to contribute to the regeneration of social bonds, to social cohesion and to job creation. Furthermore, they are said to contribute developing an intermediate sphere between state and market that re-balance, by promoting a plural economy, the disequilibrium due to Fordist regulation.

4. Civil Society

The paradigm of civil society emphasizes the political role of civil associations that do not belong to the state's sphere or the market's one. The concept of civil society is a polysemic concept which has been given different contents by authors like Ferguson (1995), Kant (1991), Hegel (1967), Tocqueville (1955), Arendt (1958) or Habermas (1996). It is however possible to identify three dimensions of civil society more or less emphasized by these authors. Civil society is conceived as sphere of morality, as constitutive element of the public sphere, and as basis for the civic community.

As a matter of fact, for Ferguson, following the tradition opened by Hobbes and Locke, civil society is the society without the state. The question is to determine how conflicting interests between individuals as well as the exercise of arbitrary power can be limited and regulated. Ferguson's answer is morality, the moral sentiments. Kant and Hegel affirm against Hobbes, Locke and Hume, the preeminent place of morality in opposition to interest as a foundation of the common life and of civil society.

The dimension of public sphere put forward by Kant, Arendt and Habermas is based on the distinction made by the ancient Greeks between the private sphere (family, household) which is also the sphere of necessity, and the public sphere (the *polis*) which is the sphere of freedom and where the public opinion is made.

The last dimension, that of civic community, emphasized by Tocqueville and Putnam (1993, 1995a, 1995b, 2000), considers civil society as a sphere of mediation between the individual and the state allowing the union between individual interests and the common good. Civic associations are the locus where public spirit, civility, trust, cooperation and social capital are constituted, making possible the emergence of a common good, a civic community beyond particular interests.

The civil society paradigm justifies consequently civil society organizations on the basis of the role they play in democracy's functioning (public spaces, intermediation, and school of democracy) as well as their role as agent and spaces of morality allowing the transcendence of particular interests and the constitution of a common good.

Analytical paradigms of social economy organizations

Analytical paradigms	Instituted identities	Contribution to public policies	Justification
Market and government failures	Third sector Philanthropy	Private provision of collective and trust goods	Social utility justifying tax privileges and public funding
Social economy: organizations a systems of rules	Social economy	Complement to the welfare state/ democratization of the economy	Alternative to capitalism, democratic organizations
Plural and solidary economy	Solidary economy	Jobs creation, social cohesion, new services, local development, environment	Social innovation, social utility, social integration, democracy
Civil society, social movements	Voluntary sector, New social movements	Democracy, social integration, public spaces	Social capital, community, democracy, advocacy, interest representation, social transforma-tion

B. The Functions of Social Economy Organizations

It is now possible to synthesize these different paradigms in order to identify the main specific features of these organizations, and by so doing to establish a normative referent for their evaluation around three functions, solidary, democratic and productive.

1. Solidary Function

Both the solidary economy and civil society paradigms emphasize the community dimension of social economy organizations. The notion of solidarity has a judicial and economic origin: in commercial law the solidary debtors are considered as one by the creditors. In other words, solidary individuals are unified by a bound and constitute a whole. Social economy organizations fulfill a solidary function as far as they constitute a social space where, contrarily to what characterizes social institutions like the family, the market or the state, individuals, by being members to these organizations, are able to belong to a community which is both immediate and voluntary. Indeed, solidarity among family members is non-voluntary, ascribed, whereas solidarity among market actors (Durkheim's division of labor) is a mediated solidarity as it is the case with solidarity resulting from citizenship rights or social rights. Solidarity within social economy organizations is based on – even if other mediated modalities are also at play – face-to-face relationships and reciprocal exchanges. This kind of solidarity is build upon common interests but also in most of the cases upon common values which guarantee the cohesion of the associated individuals. Contrarily to the solidarity among shareholders characterizing the capitalist corporation, the associative solidarity that unifies the members of a social economy organization guarantees vote equality (one man = one vote) independently of the participation to the capital (when it comes to cooperatives) or to the amount of the fees (when it comes to associations and mutual organizations). Beside the internal solidarity among members, social economy organizations are also likely to generate external solidarity when their activities are partially or totally oriented towards non-members.

2. Democratic Function

Social economy, solidary economy and civil society approaches stress the democratic role of social economy organizations. Modern democratic governments, contrarily to what characterized the antic democracy, are not direct or participatory democracies but representative democracies where the people participate in politics through its representatives. This characteristic of modern democracies makes civil society organizations – of which social economy organizations are a significant sub-set – privileged actors of democratic processes. A first reason is that, due to the representative character of democratic institutions, social economy organizations constitute social spaces where participative democracy can be exercised and where the members have the possibility to organize themselves according to democratic principles. Participation potentialities provided by social economy organizations allow them to be "schools of democracy" where the members are able to develop political skills and civic virtues.

In addition, democratic processes can be conceived along a continuum, with on the one side democracy understood as a process allowing to deal with conflict between interests and democratic institutions as preferences aggregation methods (through vote and election); and on the other side, democracy understood as a process allowing to reach a common good and democratic institutions as deliberative mechanisms oriented towards preferences transformation and consensus seeking. In practice, democratic institutions implement these two dimensions of politics. Social economy organizations play an important role along those two dimensions. They allow, on the one hand, interests expression and representation, and on the other hand, they constitute public spaces and deliberative spaces where different conceptions of the common good can be expressed and elaborated.

3. Productive Function

All four paradigms (market and government failures, social economy, solidary economy and civil society) emphasize different dimensions in which social economy organizations are different from other organizational types in the way they conduct economic activities. Social economy organizations have a specific productive function that differs from that of governmental and for-profit organizations. The service function of these organizations may be analyzed along five dimensions characterizing the production of services: *inputs, pooling-resources processes, outputs, allocation mechanisms, surplus affectation mechanisms*. All organizations do not possess all the dimensions discussed here, but all present some specific features concerning one or several of those dimensions.

a. Inputs: Voluntary and Mixed Resources

Social economy organizations are characterized by specific inputs or resources. Whereas the funding sources of for-profit are constituted by the markets where they operate, social economy organizations may find their funding sources by selling goods and services on different markets, by attracting voluntary labor, by collecting donations, through the contribution of membership-fees, by receiving grants from or by contracting with different public agencies. In other words, the service function of social economy organizations will involve a mix of several types of resources, including public funding.

b. Pooling Resources and Co-Production

Collective goods are often "pooled" within social economy organizations, according to some principles of solidarity and reciprocity (Horch, 1994). People with shared interests associate and put in common resources in order to further these interests. Organizations that produce collective goods will typically not charge prices in order to finance its activity but will rely on voluntary inputs (voluntary work and donations) as well as on membership fees which are decoupled from the individual value of the service consumed. Self-help and advocacy organizations will display such a service function based on pooled resources and the production of collective goods. Even when social economy organizations operate on markets or receive public funding, they distinguish themselves from for-profit and governmental organizations due to the fact that they associate members and pool resources according to a non-capitalist principle i.e. not based on individual property of organization's capital. In addition, some organizations will be characterized by the fact that the beneficiaries of the services are associated to the service production as co-producer of the services.

Community centers for the elderly may be partly run by the elderly, music and cultural activities may be carried out by the participants etc.

c. Outputs: Collective Goods and Trust Goods

Following Sugden (1984) one may argue that the social economy's provision of goods and services differs from the profit-making sector in that exclusion by the price mechanism is not a main mechanism. Goods and services produced by those providers may wholly or partly be collective goods implying that a person who has contributed towards the costs does not have any entitlement or priority. Thus, one person's contribution typically confers benefits on a group of people. Collective goods may be produced within members-based organizations where the members are also the beneficiaries and most of the time the producers of the organization's service. Collective goods may also be produced by social economy organizations without implying resources-pooling but by the play of public funding within a system of third-party government (Salamon, 1995). Information asymmetry may occur between those who produce and receive welfare services, opening for what has been labeled *contractual failure* (Hansmann, 1980). In such cases, these organizations have a reduced incentive to exploit informational asymmetry (Ben-Ner & Van Hoomissen, 1993). Consequently, they appear to be more trustworthy than for-profit ones, particularly when it is difficult to obtain a precise measure of the product's quality.

d. Allocation Mechanisms: Externalities

Goods that are non-rival but partly excludable (it is possible to exclude individuals from their benefit) generate external effects.[1] The concept of *externality* refers to the fact that the production and/or consumption of goods or services affect other producers or consumers. For example, health services affect not only the users of the services but have an impact on the general health of a population. Better education or better health has a positive effect on the entire community. The externality requires in general some form for institutional mechanism other than the market for the externality to be internalized.[2] In the absence of such a mechanism the allocation of the good is likely to be inefficient, the external effect not being taken into account by individual

---

[1] The notion of externality refers to the fact that an action (production or consumption) affects positively or negatively other actors than those involved in the action. Educational services affect for example not only the "consumers" of those services but also the population's human capital generating external effects on political behaviors, productivity, economic growth etc.

[2] In the presence of transaction costs or when property rights are not well defined, a Coase solution i.e. a decentralized market-like solution, to the externality problem is not available.

actors the good may be undersupplied. One internalizing mechanism providing an alternative to market mechanism is collective action mobilized within an association.

Some externalities linked to social economy organizations' activities are due to the nature of the services they produce. Most of the services within the fields of education, health and social services are characterized by the existence of external effects. That characteristic justifies among others reasons governmental intervention within these fields. Other external effects may be due to the social economy organizational form and to the specificities attached to those organizations' functions. The production of collective and trust goods may lead to lower prices charged for the services and to redistributive effects that benefit to the community. Social economy organizations may also generate territorial effects taking the form of community development as well as integration effects due to their contribution to the maintenance of social capital and solidarity. Some organizations may also produce environmental effects by enhancing sustainable techniques of production whereas others generate poverty reduction, social insertion and equal opportunities effects because of their activity or because of their human resources policies.

e. Surplus Affectation Mechanisms

Social economy organizations, as it is the case with for-profit organizations, are able to realize profits, but contrarily to for-profit organizations they do not distribute their profits on a capitalist basis. Dependent on their statuses, they affect profits totally or partially to the reserves of the organization, and in some cases they distribute the profits to their members not in relation to the members' share of the capital but proportionally to the members' activity.

The organizational modalities (associated members, one man = one vote) as well as the socio-economic principles (resources pooling; volunteerism, surplus affectation mechanisms) defining social economy organizations differentiate them from for-profit and governmental organizations. These organizational modalities allow them, at least potentially, to make a social contribution in terms of solidarity, democracy and provision of goods and services. However, when these organizations are involved in the implementation of public policies, their organizational modalities and their socio-economic principles are in most of the cases taken into account neither by public policies objectives nor by evaluation procedures.

II. Public Policy Evaluation and Social Economy Organizations

Public policies that involve social economy organizations in order to attain their objectives are often top-down policies which are based on a rational model of public policy. These policies implement incentive-based or coercive policy tools which are not neutral in the ways they affect social economy organizations' behaviors and characteristics. The confrontation between the normative foundations of these organizations (what ideally they should be) and the normative foundations of public policies (what public policies aim at) reveals the paradoxes of the evaluation from a public policy perspective of the outputs and outcomes of social economy organizations.

A. Top-down and Rational Models of Public Policy Implementation

1. Top-down Policy Implementation

Public policies take in most of the cases a top-down form, as exemplified by figure 1, where public authorities define standards, objectives and resources. Social economy organizations may have been involved in the definition of these standards and objectives through participation in policy networks (Rodhes, 1997) or Advocacy Coalitions (Sabatier, 1998). However, once adopted, public authorities implement the policy with a focus on the attainment of the objectives.

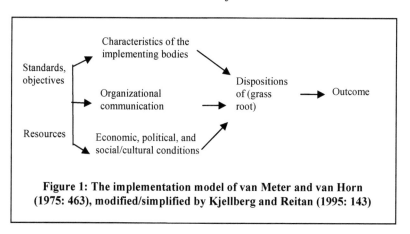

Figure 1: The implementation model of van Meter and van Horn (1975: 463), modified/simplified by Kjellberg and Reitan (1995: 143)

In this process, as illustrated by figure 1, the effects and outcomes are conditioned by the dispositions and behaviors of the implementers, for our purpose the social economy organizations. If social economy organizations may dispose a relative autonomy in implementing public policies, as we will see, the nature of policy tools used may affect their behavior and consequently their functioning.

2. *Tools of Government*

The term 'tool of government' is used here to cover those instruments that public authorities bring into use to realize public goals. Such tools usually consist of some kind of financial, regulatory or informative instruments and conditions that are attached to their use. The use of a particular tool is intended to realize a public goal, and it has an impact on the practice of an implementing agency. Following Salamon (2002), *incentives, coercion and information* form the main types of governmental tools. On a mid-level, tools relevant for our purpose can be specified as follows.

Tool	Product/activity	Vehicle	Delivery System
Social regulation	prohibition	rule	public agency
contracting	good or service	contract and cash payment	business, civic actor
grant	good or service	grant/cash payment	public agency, civic actor
loan/ loan guarantee	cash	loan/loan guarantee	bank, civic actor
tax expenditure	cash, incentives	tax	tax system
government corporations	good or service	direct provision/ loan	quasi-public agency

The scheme above illustrate that different tools are transformed into different products or activities, they are brought into action by certain 'vehicles' which work through particular delivery systems. An important point is that these delivery systems have logics of their own, which affects the distribution welfare goods or services. The study of interactions between public goals and non-public delivery systems is an important part of this project.

Following Salamon (2002) we assume that when social economy organizations are used as delivery systems, different tools will produce effects in three directions. From the perspective of public agencies they will be more or less *manageable* (they may demand managing skills, effects may be more or less visible and measurable), they may be more or less *effective* and they may demand higher or lower degree of *political support*. For social economy actors, different tools may have intended and/or unintended consequences for their structure and goal attainment.

3. Tools-effects Linkage

The relations between tools, their use and their produced effects on social economy organizations may be schematized as follow (Figure 2).

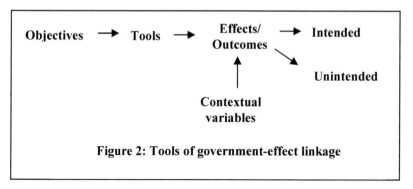

Figure 2: Tools of government-effect linkage

The tools of government produce both intended and unintended effects trough a linkage system. The impact analysis aims at (i) assessing the effects but also (ii) identifying the linkages through which the tools work. The linkage in this schema designs the social mechanisms that link tools of government and their effects on social economy organizations. These social mechanisms, i.e. the ways the tools of government influence actors' behaviors, have to be made explicit for each tool. Following Salamon (2002) we consider any tool as a package that contains a number of different elements, including a type of good or activity; a delivery system, that is a set of organizations that are engaged in providing the good or activity; and a set of rules, whether formal or informal, defining the relationships among the entities that comprise the delivery system. Some elements of the mechanisms that make the linkage between tools and effects are build into the tools of government, such as the incentives and constrains that are associated to a given tool and the institutional context (delivery system) in which the tool operates. Other elements such as actors' behavior in response to incentives and constrains as well as the institutional processes characterizing the relationships between actors and their institutional environment, including the delivery system, have to be made explicit in order to describe the linkage.

4. Means of Action

One possible way to classify the tools of government consists in identifying the elements of the service provision function they act upon as well their means of action. A usual classification of the means of action differentiates coercive and incentive mechanisms. The tools may act upon different dimensions of the service provision function: inputs, outputs, production processes, and allocation mechanisms. Combining means of action and action target one obtain the following typology of tools of government:

Tools classified by means of action and action target

	Coercive	Incentive
Outputs	Contract Regulation	Contract
Inputs	Contract Regulation	Grant Tax subsidy Vouchers
Production processes	Contract Regulation	
Allocation mechanisms	Regulation	Tendering

B. Public Policy Instruments and Effects on Social Economy Organizations

The way the organizations part of the delivery system will respond to constraints and incentives incorporated into the tools of government will depend on the determinants of their behavior. Considering the main conceptions of the relationships between organizational behavior and environmental pressures developed by organization-theorists allows us to make some conjectures about possible behavioral responses.

1. Goal Displacement vs. Goal Achievement

A well known dilemma in organization theory is that of "rational model versus natural system model" Panebianco (1982). According to the rational model, organizations are instruments for the realization of specific goals whereas the natural model sees the organization as a structure which responds to, and adjusts itself to, a multitude of demands from various stakeholders, and which tries to maintain balance by reconciling these demands. According to the natural model, the real aim of an organization is a facade behind which the real aim, the survival of the organization and the perpetuation of the leaders, is concealed. Official aims cannot be however reduced to a mere facade as far as they are part of an ideology necessary to maintain the identity of the organization in the eyes of its supporters (members, funders, donators). But at the same time, organizations develop a tendency toward self-preservation and growing diversification of aims under the pressure of its environment. One of the environmental pressures is the one exercised by public authorities implementing different tools of government. One possible impact of this governmental activity on social economy organizations is the displacement of organizational goals, the official aims being replaced by aims imposed by the environmental pressures.

2. Resources Dependency and Crowding out Effects

No organization is self-sufficient and must engage in exchanges with the environment as a condition of their survival (Pfeffer and Salancik, 1978). The need to acquire resources creates dependencies between organizations and external units. How important and how scarce these resources are will determine the nature and the extent of organizational dependency. Since social economy organizations have different sources of income (monetary donations and time from private individuals, government funding, membership fees, sale of ancillary goods and services), the relationship between each type of resource and their eventual crowding-out effect (Steinberg 1991; Kingma 1995) may be affected by governmental activity.

3. Isomorphism

Another possible effect of governmental activity is that of isomorphism (DiMaggio and Powel, 1983). Organizations may be seen as competing not only for resources and customers but for political power and institutional legitimacy. The organizational environment may be thought in terms of *institutional field* i.e. a recognized area of institutional life constituted by key suppliers, resources and product consumers, regulatory agencies, and other organizations that produce similar services and products. Governmental activity upon social economy organizations may lead to an inexorable push towards homogenization of institutional fields (*institutional isomorphism*). Three types of institutional isomorphic change have been identified by DiMaggio and Powel (1983): *coercive isomorphism* that stems from political influence and the problem of legitimacy (government regulation, legal environment, fiscal regulations); *mimetic isomorphism* resulting from standard response to uncertainty (innovation processes, management techniques); *normative isomorphism* associated with professionalization (formal education and legitimating by universities, development of professional networks).

4. Oligarchy vs. Democracy

According to Michels (1949) almost all democratic organizations are characterized by the "iron law of oligarchy" i.e. the control of the organization by those at the top and a restriction of members' influence. Large organizations tend to develop bureaucratic structures, that is, a system which is both rationally and hierarchically organized. But the price of bureaucracy is the concentration of power at the top and the limitation of members' influence. By controlling resources (knowledge, means of communication, and skills in the art of politic) the leaders may gain advantage over members who have neither the time nor resources to allow them to compete with the leaders for positions of power. Governmental activity may influence the internal democratic processes and favor the development of oligarchic leadership.

5. Likely Organizational Impact of Tools on Social Economy Organizations

Given each tools' means of action and action target it is possible to anticipate the following likely impacts of the tools of government on social economy organizations:

Likely Impacts of Tools

	Goal displacement	Crowding out	Isomorphism	Oligarchy
Regulation	moderate	low	high	low
Contract	high	high	high	moderate
Grant	low	moderate	low	low
Tax subsidy	high	high	high	high
Vouchers	high	high	high	high
Tendering	high	high	high	high

Regulative tools impose a coercive constrain on the organization. They may generate a goal displacement if the constrain contradict the organizational goals. The likelihood that this kind of tools induces crowding-out effects is low at least so long regulative tools do not influence the availability of the resources. Regulative tools, because they are coercive, have a high propensity of generating isomorphic tendencies within a given field. Finally, they are likely to have a low impact on democratic functioning since they have no direct influence on the internal balance of power.

Contracts present a coercive element as well as they incorporate incentives. Indeed a contract may be described as a conditional payment. The recipient of a contractual payment has to meet conditions listed in the contract in order to fulfill the contract and to get the payment. The conditional part of the contract exercises coercion on the recipient whereas the monetary part of the contract, and particularly the device according to which the payment is made, generates an incentive for the recipient to fulfill his contractual obligations. Coercion and incentives attached to a contract are likely to induce a change in organizational behavior. The likelihood for goal displacement, crowding out effects and isomorphism are therefore high. In addition the management of contractual relations supposes competences what in turn may enhance oligarchic tendencies within the organization.

Grants contrarily to contracts do not generate coercive pressure on the recipient. They however generate incentives that can easily lead to crowding out effects.

Tax subsidies and *vouchers* have the effect of transforming the activity of the organization into market-based service provision. They are highly likely to generate goal displacement, crowding out effect and isomorphism. They also transform the members and users of the organization into customers favoring in turn members' disengagement and oligarchic tendencies.

Tendering, in addition to the contractual relations it supposes, implies competition between potential providers. The mix of competitive and contractual elements is likely to induce high degrees of goal displacement, crowding out effects, isomorphism and oligarchic tendencies.

III. Conclusion: Consequences in Terms of Implementation and Evaluation of Public Policies

There exist different models of evaluation (Vedung, 2000) in terms of goal-attainment evaluation, of side-effects evaluation, of goal-free evaluation, comprehensive evaluation, stakeholders evaluation, and so on. However, in most cases, public policy evaluation is based on the goal-attainment model. From such a perspective, evaluation focuses on the question to know in which extent a public intervention has attained the objectives initially assigned to it. Such an evaluation model is susceptible to be criticized on two grounds: (i) it ignores the discretionary power of the actors of the implementation, and (ii) it does not consider the unintended or side effects of the intervention. In spite of its shortcomings, this evaluation model is currently used in public policy evaluation for one reason: politicians and policy-makers are accountable for the results of their action and are keen to evaluations that allow them to show the results of their policies. However, the policy tools mobilized by public policies, as pointed by our analysis above, are likely to affect the behaviors and organizational characteristics of the implementing agents, and in our case of the social economy organizations engaged in the implementation of a public policy. It is clear that the effect of policy tools on social economy organizations is not mechanical. First, implementing agents dispose of a margin of autonomy (depending of the nature of their resources and power) in implementing policies. Second, implementing agents have often the latitude of reinterpreting and accommodating locally the objectives and goals of public policies.

Finally, implementing agents are able to use strategically, for example in order to increase their legitimacy, public policy tools. However, in spite of these margins of autonomy, public policies and government tools have a structuring effect on the organizational fields and on the organizational practices as a result of resources dependency effects and coercive, mimetic and normative isomorphic processes.

Putting into relation, on the one hand, the potential effects of policy instruments on social economy organizations, and on the other hand, the normative foundation of these organizations, leads to identifying what could be labeled a public policy paradox. Indeed, the social and societal contribution of social economy organizations (solidarity, democracy, specific productive organization) are linked to their organizational specificities, whereas public policy implementation and evaluation is mostly devoted to goal-attainment and not to assessing the functioning modalities of these organizations. In other words, by maximizing goal-attainment, public policies that have recourse to social economy organizations for their implementation do not generally take into account the specificities of these organizations, and non-intently, through the policy instruments they mobilize, risk undermining the social and societal contribution of these organizations.

The normative foundations of social economy organizations are more ideals in direction to which they tend towards, than realities. If in practice, social economy organizations greatly vary according to the degree to which they conform to these ideals, they all display some features of these normative foundations and therefore have some form of social and societal contribution. Given this fact and given the analysis above it is possible to draw some conclusions concerning the ways the evaluation of the action of social economy organizations engaged in the implementation of public policies is conducted. As already pointed, even if several evaluation models are available, the most widespread one is that of goal-attainment as a result of political pressures. Evaluation conducted from a public policy perspective should not only focus on goal-attainment, but also on the side effects of the policy and the policy tools mobilized on social economy organizations. Evaluation strategies should assess not only how the policy-goals are realized, but also to what extent the policy affects the social and societal contributions of social economy organizations. Such evaluation strategy would require a shared understanding of the social and societal contribution of social economy organizations. Unfortunately, such a shared understanding is still far to be reached and the concepts of social economy as well as those of nonprofit and voluntary organizations, associations, third sector, civil society, solidary economy organizations, are contested concepts leading to contested normative understandings and to contested evaluation strategies.

References

Almond, Gabriel og Sidney Verba, *The Civic Culture. Political Attitudes and Democracy in Five Nations*, Boston, Little, Brown and Company, 1963.

Arendt, H., *The human condition*, Chicago, Chicago University Press, 1958.

Ben-Ner, A., Van Hoomissen, T., "Nonprofit organizations in the mixed economy", in A. Ben-Ner and T. Van Hoomissen (eds.), *The nonprofit sector in the mixed economy*, Ann Arbor, The University of Michigan Press, 1993.

Demoustier, D., *L'Économie sociale et solidaire*, Paris, Syros, 2001.

Di Maggio, P. J., Powel, W. W., "The Iron Cage Revisited, Institutional Isomorphism and Collective Rationality in Organisational Fields", *American Sociological Review*, 48, 4, 1983, pp. 147-160.

Dockès, P., *La société n'est pas un pique-nique*, Léon Walras et l'Économie sociale, Paris, Economica, 1996.

Eme, B., Laville, J. L. (dir.), *Cohésion sociale et emploi*, Paris, Desclée de Brouwer.

Enjolras, B., *Le marché providence*, Paris, Desclée de Brouwer, 1995.

Etzioni, A., *The Spirit of Community. Rights, Responsibilities and the Communitarian Agenda*, New York, Crown Publishers Inc., 1993.

Etzioni, Amitai, *Society The New Golden Rule. Community and Morality in a Democratic Society*, New York, Basic Books, 1996.

Ferguson, A., *An Essay on the history of civil society*, New Brunswick, Transaction Publishers, 1995.

Giddens, A., *The Third Way and its Critics*, London, Polity Press, 2000.

Gueslin, A., *L'invention de l'Économie sociale*, Paris, Économica, 1998.

Gui, B., "Beyond transactions, on the interpersonal dimension of economic reality", *Annals of Public and Cooperative Economics*, 71, 2, 2000, pp. 139-169.

Habermas, J., *Between facts and norms*, Cambridge, MIT Press, 1996.

Hansmann, H., "The Role of Non Profit Enterprise", *Yale Law Journal*, 89, 2, 1980, pp. 835-898.

Hegel, G.W.F., *The philosophy of rights*, Oxford, Oxford University Press, 1967.

Hood, C. C., *The Tools of Government*, London, The Macmillan Press, 1983.

Horch, H.D., "On the socio-economics of voluntary associations", *Voluntas*, 5-2, 1994, pp. 219-230.

Kant, I., *Political writings*, Ed. H. Reiss. Cambridge, Cambridge University Press, 1991.

Miseries and Worth of the Evaluation of the Social and Solidarity-based Economy

For a Paradigm of Communicational Evaluation

Bernard EME

Professor of Sociology, Faculty of Economic and Social Sciences, Université de Lille 1 and CLERSE (France)

Introduction

One need hardly underline the fact that "evaluation" refers to "value", i.e. the worth or the price of a person or a thing (14th century) according to a specific quantitative scale based on a benchmark, which is always arbitrary. But evaluation also aims to assess the *qualities* of a person (late 18th century), i.e. it is a social or institutional process of *social qualification*. This process assigns – or does not assign – qualities, and it establishes a mode of recognition of beings and actions by legitimate bodies of society.[1] However, not emphasizing this fact does not amount to ignoring the *primary ambivalence* of evaluation, which is divided between quantitative and qualitative approaches: on the one hand, calculation, which disenchants the world, as Max Weber diagnosed – what are the quantitative measures and the benchmarking of things and beings? –, and on the other hand, the quality of beings, actions, organizations and, ultimately, their identity and way of life, the latter referring to multiple spatially and temporally determined ontologies of the world. It is thus not necessary to dwell on the fact that there is a permanent tension between this evaluative quantification and this kind of qualification: the first refers to a *universal axiological horizon* (techniques of calculation and their general equivalent), whereas the second is more respectful of *the plurality of the worlds wherein things and beings exist, and of their socio-cultural recognition.* From this point

---

[1] In the wake of Axel Honneth's work, one can see scientific and political battles on evaluation as *fights for the recognition of beings and things* (Honneth, 2000).

of view, the evaluation of practices and organizations of a social and solidarity-based economy (henceforth referred to as SSE) in reference to their normative basis and goals (their contributions to society and the measure of the gap between their goals and those contributions, *i.e.* efficiency), one understands that an evaluation aiming to take into account the quality of organizations must reveal a plurality of SSE worlds.

But a further analysis of the origin of the word "evaluate" cautions us to be vigilant. This origin reveals a *dogmatic* – religious and legal – *basis* inherent in the word. "Evaluating" did indeed initially refer to a "religious expression having *force de loi*" (the *religious oath*); and, later, it assumed a legal meaning (the "law"). The origin of the word indicates that the act of evaluating implies *dogmatic institutions* which constitute the basis for a creed and its rituals, on the one hand, or a "fiction" with its legal devices and its codified behaviours, on the other.[2] The value judgment made on a thing or a being was thus based on a truth guaranteed by a dogmatic institution that aimed at universality.

In fact, this position of universality may still prevail. It could have evolved, in an underground process, into an *instrumental and technical positivism* – mainly "the measure of an action's effects"[3] – which is increasingly pronounced and is generated by the requirements of public authorities (the European Union, the state, regional authorities) that demand that a "managerial spirit" (Ogien, 1995) be combined with a "culture of results", imported from the bourgeois city, and which nowadays is encapsulated in a "neo-liberal political rationality" (Brown, 2007: 50ff[4]). Indeed, the whole life of citizens is supposed to conform to this rationality, of which the State becomes both the prescriber and the actor by implementing a new form of *government* of beings (Foucault, 2004). This form of rationality requires, simultaneously, that the value of beings be measured (evaluation) according to its more or less hidden normative presuppositions – being an "entrepreneur of oneself … on the basis of a calculation of utility, interest and satisfaction" and identifying "moral responsibility with rational action … by reducing the moral sense to an issue of rational deliberation on costs, benefits and consequences" (Brown, 2007: 51, 54). It further postulates a utilitarian and rational objectivization of all aspects of social and economic life. In its

---

[2] We refer to the works that discuss the law as a paternal fiction which "institutes life" and is short-circuited by technicalities of all kinds, and in particular to the books by Pierre Legendre (1999) and to Alain Supiot's (2005) approach.

[3] See the contribution by Bernard Perret in the present book.

[4] Michel Foucault's course in 1978-1979 tackled this question of liberal government-ability and the analysis of neo-liberalism as a mode of governance (Foucault, 2004).

growing extension, evaluation becomes one of the new tools of this governance of people.[5]

The following hypothesis can now be stated: if evaluation tends to become, to an ever-growing extent, this tool of "governmentability", it establishes itself, even more than before, not only as an issue of *knowledge*, but also of *power*. The possible plurality of worlds and ways of life, of which the SSE (itself multiple) is one of the aspects, thus becomes a political issue. Hence, the legitimacy of this plurality is questioned. From this perspective, the present text aims to suggest that an analysis of evaluation cannot settle for or make do with apprehending evaluation from the technical or instrumental points of view, or by producing a typology of its methods. This text aims to question the axiological and normative basis of evaluation processes, in particular with regards to the practices and organizations of the social and solidarity-based economy (SSE). To this extent, it indicates that the processes themselves should continuously question the values and norms which, often implicitly, constitute their foundations. Indeed, evaluation becomes a scientific act only *at a second stage*, once the prerequisites have been defined. The latter are defined by a society that aims at *common goods* through democratic choices among a multiplicity of possibilities. Defined values and norms are linked to these common goods (specific to a group or community), and the former can be used as a basis for evaluation to produce fully objective judgments, based on a good knowledge of the aims and goals. The present text thus suggests that evaluation is an *argumentative battlefield*, where scientific processes are based on preliminary social choices and continuously feed, in total neutrality, a society on these political aims by providing resources and arguments to build democratic controversies on the legitimacy of the aims.

If there is a choice, we have (1) to isolate the principle of a *plurality of possible worlds*, for which theorization is a condition for carrying out relevant evaluations of the SSE. This principle probably implies the pragmatic elaboration of *smaller worlds* than those that are usually employed (Boltanski and Thévenot, 1991; Boltanski and Chiapello, 1999). However, (2) any evaluation must also heed the *tension* inherent in SSE organizations between the instrumental and managerial aspects on the one hand, and the civic and democratic aspects on the other. The

---

[5]   Through successive displacements of meaning, the sector of integration through subsidized work ended up conforming with this governmentability through the imputation of personal responsibility, a summons to become the entrepreneur of one's own project under the constraint of a contract with a company, an individualized production of one's own integration path that puts an abrupt end to older, collective or community-based modes of integration (Eme, 2006b).

production of new values, such as social utility, also demonstrates an inventiveness which goes beyond falling back on the manager. Consequently, it is (3) the proximity relations with the State that call for a questioning of the *principle of autonomy* of these organizations. In the evaluation processes, their own goals must give way to the goals of public authorities, whereas their inventiveness is not, to a significant extent, evaluated as such, but is above all measured in terms of deviation from the norm. Finally, (4) evaluation in its relations to the life of the polity (*polis*) aims to produce *controversies*, to throw them into the limelight, and to facilitate these controversies in public deliberative spaces, which implies not isolating the objects to be evaluated, but apprehending them in their *tensions* with all the concerned actors and objects.

1. A Plurality of Worlds and Value Judgments

When times come to distinguish the specific field of the social and solidarity-based economy (SSE), the question raised is indeed that of *the possible plurality of worlds* as well as the relevance of value judgments adapted to these worlds. Indeed, without falling into post-modern relativism, we should be attentive to a plurality of socio-economic worlds which all possess their own grammars and ways of "specifying the [legitimate] common good" (Boltanski and Thévenot, 1991: 28). If *controversies* among these worlds are possible and desirable in so-called "democratic deliberation" societies,[6] we should also be attentive to the situations where judgments go beyond their sphere of relevance and apply to actions, beings, and organizations belonging to another world whose principles of justice (Walzer, 1997) or scales of value are different. A *principle of non-relevance* emerges from this, which invalidates the judgments made. It is this plurality of worlds which must be isolated in order to escape from the dominant neo-liberal mould, and from the evaluative rationality that constitutes one of its tools.

1.1. The Proper Coherence of Multiple "Large Worlds"

Over and above their different perspectives, many books (Boltanski and Thévenot, 1991; Salais and Storper, 1997; Walzer, 1997; Boltanski and Chiapello, 1999) suggest the existence of a plurality of worlds (or spheres of existence) of individuals' lives that is not part of and does not refer to a *universal Weltanschauung*. Boltanski and Thevenot's (and

---

6   This is a crucial issue, which belongs to the area of political sociology; however, we cannot, in the restricted framework of the present text, dwell upon the limits of the use or exercise of democratic practices when the latter are rooted in and concern different civic worlds (representative, deliberative, participative, etc.).

later Boltanski and Chiapello's) "economies of worth" clearly demonstrate that each polity – be it industrial, market, inspired, domestic, fame, civic, or project-oriented, and whatever the debates regarding the number of polities and their relevance – refers to specific principles and values which, through evaluation and justification, create beings and things great or small in a way that differs from one polity to another (Boltanski and Thévenot, 1991; Boltanski and Chiapello, 1999). The worth of employers' paternalism in the domestic polity is only smallness when submitted to the market trial, or when judged in terms of industrial efficiency. The latter, with its stable hierarchized work positions, is disqualified or made insignificant – thus undergoing the trial of a reversal of values – in the project-oriented polity, which requires mobility, reactivity, nomadism, and non-hierarchical leadership. The state of worth (of legitimate values) or of smallness or unworthiness (of invalidations) is specific to each polity or world and supposes differentiated and compared evaluative axiologies. Similarly, in another perspective, Michael Walzer's (1997) analysis suggests that inequity is generated (the evaluative act is also an act of equity or inequity) when one sphere's values are applied in a non-considered manner to another sphere (money and merchandise to kinship or love, community membership to politics, etc.) and when one of these areas is judged in reference to the axiological basis of the other areas, rather than according to a distribution based on "distinct and 'internal' reasons" (Walzer, 1997: 19), or according to some "appropriate … criteria and devices/plans" (Walzer, 1997: 32). Each sphere has its own axiological horizon, and it aims at "legitimate forms of the common good" (the states of worth), which distinguish themselves from illegitimate values (Boltanski and Thévenot, 1991); but each sphere can also hybridize with one or two other spheres to form a *composite/mixed world* that appears to be legitimate (industrial-civic, market-civic, domestic-civic, etc.).

1.2. Pragmatic Economic Sociology and the Plurality of "Small Worlds"

Are not this plurality of possible worlds and the question of the choice of a unique or composite/mixed world as the horizon of axiological reference for the analysis of a given organization necessary conditions to apprehend and analyze the social and solidarity-based economy and to evaluate it? And can the worlds to which SSE organizations belong – and the values of these worlds – be identified with certainty? This is far from certain.

This question is an object of investigation in itself and would require a research agenda of its own. We cannot dwell on this issue, but the social and solidarity-based economy in France, as in many other countries, is similar to a *nebula* – an "interstellar object, with a cloudy and indistinct aspect", or, in the figurative sense, a "blurry, diffuse cluster", whose spangled and scattered theorized analyses are only a reflection. This is even truer at the international level, in the multiple ideological foundations of the SSEs and the construction of their specific relations with regulating welfare states, which are themselves specific. The world of the SSE is a trail of archipelagos whose main axiological references or benchmarks can differ, both in ordinary practice and in theorizations.[7] The fact that no typology of organizations, associations or concerned sectors of activity has been unanimously accepted, and that none has been able to impose itself indisputably, testifies to this.

Is it not essential to pursue research on the plurality of SSE worlds as a prerequisite to any evaluation (Eme and Laville, 1994; Thévenot, 1994; Enjolras, 1998; Evers, 2000; Haeringer and Traversaz, 2002)? This question needs to be tackled, given the *empirical plurality* of meanings, values, and ways of functioning of economies as social and solidarity-based organizations, but also, more fundamentally, given their axiological and normative foundations (solidarity, democracy, the value of the collective aspect, and other polysemic notions) – a plurality which, in the last instance, still remains to be organized in a reasoned manner.[8]

If, to a first approximation, the SSE refers to composite/mixed worlds combining several worlds, in particular – and in a fundamental way the civic world and the familiar and localized domestic world – one

---

[7] Despite a long-standing theoretical positioning (Eme, 1991) that would require deep-reaching rectifications, given the evolution of the contexts (in particular the marked institutionalization from the late 1990s on of the SSE, which, through the loss of its critical sense, became a regional or municipal public policy), the multiple and controversial terms used to refer to this field in the French context are not taken into account in the present text; however, these terms refer to competing theoretical approaches: the social economy and/or the solidarity-based economy, the third sector (Delors, Gaudin, 1979; Lipietz, 1990), the third sector of the social and solidarity-based economy (Lipietz, 2001; Maréchal, 1995), but also to the quaternary sector (Ferry, 1995; Sue, 1997) or "sphere of unconditionality" (Gorz, 1988). It is obvious – and it does not call for any additional explanation – that power relations in the scientific and practical fields are not absent from this sector. We simply note that the SSE refers to multiple practical and theoretical benchmarks, which make it a controversial field, open to an evaluation of their names and a clarification of their meaning.

[8] The "Social and solidarity-based economy in the regions" programme, carried out under the aegis of the Interdepartmental Delegation for Innovation, Social Experimentation and Social Economy and of the MiRe, enabled producing more than 35 research reports; it generated advances, sometimes of a decisive nature, in terms of the scientific visibility of the SSE; but as far as the formalization of this plurality of SSE worlds is concerned, its contribution has remained incomplete (Chopart, Neyret, Rault, 2006).

can at the same time question the rise in generality of these worlds. We can indeed question the relevancy of these worlds to account more accurately for the SSE practices and organizations. Probably only a *pragmatic sociology* could account for "smaller" worlds and their tensions, which are the only ones likely to open the way for a more accurate understanding of SSE worlds. This can be illustrated by the world of civic commitment, which in Boltanski and Thévenot's works refers to the effacement of individualities to the benefit of commitment to collective entities that represent the common will and the general interest. Individuality thus represents a "state of smallness and degradation of the civic polity." Do we not here witness a remodelling of an ancient civic consciousness? One cannot but observe the emergence within the SSE of new commitments that are "more distantiated" (Ion, 1997), highlight the "I" at the expense of the "we", and are part of an immediate and localized action, without any strong reference to a general interest and a collective narrative. They distrust the old forms of delegation, which represented the benchmark of worth of the civic polity (Ion *et al.*, 2005); rather, they promote a deliberative civic organization, without hierarchy, or a civic organization based on *ad hoc*, problem-linked network coordination (another polity).

2. Tension between the Instrumental and the Political Aspects

2.1. The Productive and the Civic Aspects

The economic, social and cultural effects of the tension inherent in the social and solidarity-based economy should not be underestimated. SSE organizations are torn on a daily basis between an instrumental pole of production (highly diverse in its organizational expressions) of very dissimilar goods and services, and a pole of civic solidarity that is itself multiple in its practices and based on forms of democracy that attempt, as best as they can, to direct its governance and to give it meaning (Vienney, 1980, 1982; Eme, 2001). There is a permanent tension between, on the one hand, an instrumental rationality that governs the productive side – which takes different forms – and, on the other hand, a tugging of the SSE between *policy*, defined as "the construction of desirable institutions" and *politics*, the "instituted guarantor of the monopoly of legitimate meanings in the considered society" (Castoriadis, 1996: 224). One can mention the always uncertain *tension* between the *organization* as a sphere of rules linked to multiple worlds of coordination among actors and the *institution*, which itself constitutes a tension between a democratic aim in political practices and the strategic maintenance of an order of coexistence.

Table 1. Social and solidarity-based organizations' polarity			
Socio-political relations		Socio-economic relations	
Ambivalence:		Ambivalence:	
Democratic relations of solidarity Rationality in values	Social and strategic relations of power Instrumental rationality	Managerial logics Instrumental rationality	Reciprocity logics Rationality of the social link
Solidarity and worlds of the civic society	Strategic power in the organization	Tool of economic utility	Tool of social economy
Institutional processes of policy and politics		Processes of the organization	

On the basis of this – unquestionably simplistic – diagram, evaluation can unfold first at one or the other pole according to reductions that distort the analysis of the operation of SSE organizations. Which pole is privileged? As we have stressed, the pole highlighted in evaluations is, with increasing frequency, that of managerial requirements, of a simplistic "cost-benefit" rationality without taking into account the political common good, which always remains to be questioned and in which multiple values compete. For example, this common good can be examined from the point of view of increasing *inequalities*. In this perspective, one can ask whether the SSE does not, involuntarily, contribute to the latter by generating a *wage precariousness* in multiple areas of activity (Castel, 1995; Eme, 1996[9]). This issue of casualization provides a good example of norms and values being obscured by evaluations of the SSE which, bottom line, are concerned only with the quantitative issue of employment and do not seek to take into account citizens' desires and the kind of world they want.

Some works have attempted to demonstrate that organizations providing integration through publicly subsidized work, contrary to their declared aims, have only reproduced the social question through an increased reproduction of the wage precariousness/casualization that, without leading to stable jobs, is continuously gaining ground in all sectors of the economy. But this process occurs more deeply through the generalization of *precarious ways of life*, whereby individuals are kept dangling and without having the possibility to project themselves into the future since they are stuck in the immediacy of the present (Eme, 1996[10]). Is the increased number of fixed-term contracts or integration

---

[9] For a more economic perspective, see for example Friot, 1998.

[10] Despite an idealization of the general interest represented by the State (an idealization that weakens the point), one can refer for a severe, but relevant from the point of view of the sociology of work, criticism of the SSE to Hély, 2008.

contracts (whose proliferation increases employment rates) in itself a good evaluation indicator? Is the axiological question of *desirable ways of life* overlooked in quantitative evaluations of this sort?

The sphere of socio-economic relations of production can also become the object of an evaluative rationality committed to a neo-liberal "good management" of the economy, imposed by the State or by other public authorities. The evaluation is carried out in an intra-economic way; it measures efficacy (means-goals) or efficiency (means-results) ratios according to a narrow questioning, or it evaluates impact on the basis of purely organizational and economic criteria that meet the implicit or explicit expectations of public sponsors. However, in some cases, this rationality is privileged to such an extent that it obscures the axiological aims of *solidarity*: the economy evolves from being a tool of solidarity to being the aim of the organization (efficiency, input/output ratio/productivity, work optimization). In the area of some integration practices, this major shift from means to goals has been observed. Indeed, the organizational efficiency required to meet increased financial constraints or reinforced administrative requirements has made it necessary to recruit more qualified workers so that the latter can be more competitive...while forgetting that these organizations were intended precisely for those persons experiencing difficulties and with a low performance level.

In the same perspective, evaluative processes very often obscure the issue of the democratic operation of SSE organizations and of the tension between this democratic operation and the strategic forms of power within these organizations. Since the political pole of SSE organizations sometimes becomes a theatre of shadows rather than a scene of actors playing out the daily practice of democracy,[11] it is thrust only to a limited extent under the evaluative limelight. Without this fact being questioned by evaluation, managerial governance takes over from democratic governance, producing a "professional bureaucracy" that combines the legitimacy of rule with that of occupation (Haeringer and Traversaz, 2002). Without this generating many debates, the production of goods and services is no longer conceived in reference to the values of a desirable way of life demonstrated by SSE organizations. Rather, it is thought of in terms of the latter's smooth professional running, which constitutes the new instituting values of these organizations from which their socio-political aims are ultimately derived in a secondary way.

---

[11] This question of the ordinary and daily democracy of SSE organizations remains one of the "black holes" of evaluations, as though the question should not be studied in too much detail or where the normative display of democracy ought to be sufficient.

2.2. The Invention of New Values

No doubt, our words have to be qualified. The evaluative act is constantly being based on new societal values. Those suggest the invention of new composite worlds in which some norms of the SSE are taken into account. Thus, for example, the instrumental level of evaluations refers to a societal horizon of values (the *relations between SSE organizations and society*) promoted by institutions. It also concerns the political and administrative systems whose so-called "social" indicators are used, wholly or in part, by SSE organizations (Sainsaulieu, 1990). The judgments made on the productive structure of SSE organizations are benchmarked against aims that are called *social utility* of activities (Richez-Battesti et al, 2006; Gadrey, 2003, 2005). They are also made in relation to *social responsibility* of organizations and *sustainable development*, questioning the instrumental logics – constituent of Western modernity – of mastering and possessing nature (Descartes); or *social capital* (Perret, 2006; Bevort and Lallement, 2005). These conceptions bring into play solidarity or democracy.

In these evaluative dynamics, the SSE organization and institution rearrange, and the production and the civic solidarity recombine in multiple variants of the latter. But it should be noted that the meaning and conditions of the achievement of solidarity cannot be reduced to normative discourses. Moreover, the daily exercise of democracy in SSE organizations is not simply programmatic. Democracy can be a consensual routine, manipulative on the one hand and agreed upon on the other. It can be absent insofar as the governance instances become obliterated to the eye of the organizational management. It can be directly self-managing or participative. All these gradations and others point to an unrelenting evaluative gaze. The notions of solidarity and democracy are not simple rags, but neither are they SSE organizations' priestly vestments. Evaluation must explore the kitchens, the backstage, the basement and the alleyways in order to know what is really going on. We are pleading here for an evaluation that must become *anthropology of depths*, of roadsides, of closets, of backgrounds, in order to describe SSE houses, their democratic and economic "good governance", and the debates which engender possible new aims and desirable institutions.

3. Public Authorities and Civil Society or the Confusion of Registers

There is no point in deluding ourselves: we are still far from having achieved our goal. Is it not necessary to analyze trenchantly the relations between public authorities – which, in most cases, finance SSE actions and require their evaluation? Given the power relations that any evaluation entails, a fundamental question is that of the social and solidarity-based economy's *autonomy* from public authorities in legal terms. This autonomy remains one of its normative principles,[12] but it can be seriously questioned (Eme, 2006a).

3.1. The Evaluative Heteronomization of the Social and Solidarity-Based Economy

An essential point is the fact that evaluations refer to the aims of the public programmes implemented by SSE organizations rather than to the internal values of the latter, and thus to their specific combination of instrumentality and values. For example, the public values to be achieved, which are often multiple, and the equally multiple values of SSE organizations are not taken simultaneously into account, nor is the evaluation of their degree of compatibility and combination. The public worlds – the civic-industrial world, the civic-market world, or the domestic "socio-local" world (Thévenot, 1994: 252ff) – and the SSE worlds, which are also highly diversified, are constantly being *mixed up* by those asking for evaluations. This constitutes a central issue for reflection on the evaluation of SSE organizations. Evaluations mix, for example, SSE organizations as tools of public policies with SSE organizations as civil society actors, despite the fact that this distinction is essential to the construction and reinforcement of a democratic society (Lefort, 1983). Can SSE organizations not only be seen as micro-social cogs of the latter, but also, despite their imperfections, as spaces of learning or experimentation for economic democracy?

Secondly, evaluation processes do not really question the *autonomy* claimed by SSE organizations. This autonomy is an integral part of and consubstantial with the exercise of a democracy in which the State is not society, and public authority is not the private sector or civil society (unlike the case in totalitarian regimes). From the start, these processes implicitly see the SSE only as a *heteronomous world*, deeply dependent on the values promulgated by public authorities. In this sense, they *de facto* reinforce its heteronomy. The SSE, far from being questioned as an *autonomous supplement*, is considered by evaluations as a *heteronomous complement*. This generates deep biases in terms of SSE organizations' evaluation: technical biases, but also political biases, in that the real contributions of these organizations to society – exercise of democracy, social utility, social capital, and acquisition in terms of individua-

---

[12] The European Social Economy Charter cites "autonomous management and independence from public authorities" as one of the main characteristics of the social economy.

tion by individuals on the intertwined collective and personal levels – is obscured (Simondon, 2005).

3.2. Deviation from the Norm, or Transgressive Inventiveness

The confusion between the two evaluation scales can be understood if one hypothetically admits that "evaluation is a complex form of questioning about, in some cases, coherence, compatibility, conformity, identity between a norm, a matrix, a model and an object, a phenomenon or an event compared heretofore, or, in the absence thereof, the measure of the scaled deviations...; in other cases, the sense and meanings as well as the value that this object, this phenomenon, this event can take on for us, according to a project which is itself explicitly recognized as temporal...." (Ardoino, 1990). As far as the deviation from the norm – the primary aspect of evaluation – is concerned, it can be measured either from the point of view of conformity to public norms or on the basis of SSE organizations' own norms, which does not exactly amount to the same thing. But in usual evaluative practices, are not SSEs' own norms most frequently considered as being derived from (and serving) public norms, which are the only fully legitimate ones? And is not their specificity overlooked? Taking this specificity into account in relation to the coherence of their world and evaluating the tension with the values of public authorities are absolutely necessary steps if a relevant judgment is to be made by the evaluator.

According to the second aspect, evaluation follows a completely different direction: that of evaluation of the social and economic inventiveness of SSE organizations. This inventiveness, which oversteps the latter's own norms or public norms, becomes the object of evaluation, which attempts to measure the contributions of this inventiveness to society in terms of meaning and values (social utility, social capital, human or sustainable development, exercise of a practical democracy, experienced solidarities, etc.). But instead of taking into account the often helter-skelter, inventive, and transgressive swarm of practices, evaluation practices frequently focus mainly on the measure of deviation from a norm embodied in management plans and strategies.[13] Instead of producing fertile controversies on the basis of these practices,

---

[13] Norms exist to be eschewed/misused/sidestepped through the action of individuals who constantly produce deviations from the norm in their life. We can refer here to Canguilhem, that most rigorous philosopher/physician of the "normal and the pathological" (Canguilhem, 1975), who stated that "...a norm is only valid through the deviations that it institutes. The deviation, far from opposing the norm, thus regulates its course. Doesn't this capacity to deviate – normative capacity – presuppose a conception of life qua normativity, i.e. qua power to overthrow/subvert existing norms and to institute new ones?" (Blan le, 2007a: 39-40, 2007b).

which always represent a deviation from the norm, evaluations erase them from social reality.

The measure of deviation from the norm (qualification benchmarked against a matrix/model) and the measure of "ordinary innovation" (Alter, 2000), which is always a transgression of a normative model, seem to be antagonistic approaches, with the latter often having to give way to the former. Instead of being a tool that feeds fertile *controversies* – and, in some cases, controversies that may seem infertile, but are they really so? (Latour, 2006; Richez-Battesti, *et al.*, 2006) – instead of resolving these controversies by democratic deliberation and decision-making processes, evaluations could be nothing more than the tool whereby a measure based on a normative conformity is made.

4. Evaluation and the Actor-Network

An evaluation specific to the SSE in its plurality of dimensions could be based on the tool of *controversy* (whether scientific, ideological, cultural, social, etc.) that nourishes the production and visibility of values and the norms whereby conflicts may be resolved through debate in the public arena. Such could well be the foundation proper to an SSE in the plurality of its dimensions. This kind of evaluation would contribute to an *institutionalization of controversies between the sciences and society.*

Given the importance of the issue, legitimate evaluative institutions, built jointly by the State and civil society, should be set up, and scientific arenas, based on the development of rational argumentation, should be legitimated. The relation between general public goods (the political sphere) and specific common goods, such as those targeted by the SSE, could then be debated. How do specific common goods contribute to the former? To the extent to which they are specific, how do they differ from general public goods while remaining legitimate? And to what extent do they become competitors of public goods, which would call into question their political validity? To what extent do evaluation processes question this relation? From this perspective, evaluation is the tool of a democratic debate that constantly poses the legitimacy of desirable and undesirable goods in reference to multiple spheres of values.

4.1. Renouncing any Organizational Border

What is at stake here is the elaboration of new relations between the societal – political and scientific – sphere, the "socio-local" sphere as a legitimate space of implementation of actions (proximity of detachment, familiarity to be rebuilt in a world of detachment), and SSE organizations. Evaluation must no longer be restricted to a *circumscribed object* (an action, an organization, a strategy). Instead, it must aim at a *local system of actors' interactions*, which is itself affected by many tensions with other territorial levels of regulation.

This is not actually the case, though. In a nutshell, most evaluations aim to assess a *self-enclosed object*. This narrow definition of the object to be evaluated is sometimes imposed by the funding agency; and this constraint itself can also be, in some cases, as convenient justification used by the evaluator and the evaluated object. This object can be an action, an organization, a programme. Obviously, the context or the environment can be taken into account (systemic evaluation), but what is measured primarily are the effects in a positivist perspective enclosed on its object. Most frequently, this is what happens as far as SSE organizations are concerned; and it can be accounted for by the implementation of standardized evaluative processes that, based on the model of the industrial world (Boltanski and Thévenot, 1991), aim at efficiency.[14] But does this mean that we should content ourselves with these measures? One can ask whether the world of evaluative industrial standardization can adequately take into account the composite/mixed worlds of the SSE. Therein lies the paradox of a local delineation of objects that is nonetheless submitted to the generality of evaluation standards whose relevance and legitimacy must be henceforth questioned. This is what can be called the symptom of the *object as bubble*. It refers to a non-scientific neutralization of political and administrative constraints or of the market sphere.

Ex hypothesi, we hold that no delineation of an object is valid as far as evaluation is concerned: any object (actor, organization or institution) exists only through the other objects to which it is linked thanks to *mediators* (discourses, rules, enunciations, values, norms, technical devices, natural objects, etc.) that transform it and constitute an introduction to a constellation of network objects that can go as far as becoming a societal generality (Latour, 2006). The task that has to be performed is not easy: what must be evaluated are the connections between entities, the transformations of these connections in reference to the values of solidarity and democracy, and their location in terms of economic organization. Is not evaluation a *processual approach* extended to a *local* or (even larger in some dimensions) *socio-institutional system* that requires democratic means of action? One can probably infer from this reflection the operative hypothesis that indicators and methodologies of SSE evaluation must be rooted in a local space and

---

[14]   We refer here to the evaluations asked for by the European Social Fund, but also to those required by the French State or local authorities.

must take into account the SSE's multiple connected actors. The evaluation that ensues from this approach is a *democratic and process-based evaluation* of the common goods that the SSE creates in a particular space, quite aside from an instrumental rationality reduced to a process of measure of efficacy, efficiency, or impact.

4.2. The Plurality of Public Spaces

In local spaces, what is at stake in evaluation practices is the exercise of democratic plurality. Is not evaluation therefore a processual tool of democracy? It could be an instrument that, beyond its necessary methodological and epistemological bases, allows us to "ensure that the decisions made by individual or collective actors be taken following processes that respect, in a given context, constraints which are deemed indispensable to a rational justification" (Lenoble, 1994: 18). This occurs in the light of respecting the collective definition of the process; respecting the opinion of all the actors who are local stakeholders; respecting the controversies that must be talked through according to forms of argumentation legitimated by the actors; respecting the process for moving beyond controversies through rational argumentative forms, etc. In this perspective, evaluation would be a tool of democracy, which is itself a tool of solidarity whose productive organization is only a means with its own tools, which are of limited validity (control, reporting, expression groups).

Evaluating local spaces requires an understanding of the redistribution of global forces (the local sphere is never only local: it is always different in the hands of supra-local actors able to effect local actions) as well as catching a glimpse of the fact that the local sphere can be global (a redistribution of actors broadcasting knowledge, know-how, capacities in the societal space). This tension of reciprocal transformation – to be evaluated – between the local and global levels probably requires a multiplicity of *deliberative public spaces* that enunciate the terms of evaluation, follow the process of the latter, and discuss its cognitive and practical acquired skills in reference to a policy of common goods. But such a perspective requires a transformation of the normative modes of regulation of the public sphere and of politics, that are not particularly prone to entering deliberative arenas, through granting all actors an equal and legitimate right and opportunity to express themselves (Eme, 2005b).

Conclusion

Final hypothesis: Should not SSE evaluative practices be based on a *communications action* that itself refers to the principle of deliberative democracy? Far from measuring "misconduct" in reference to established benchmarks, are not these practices a *series of experiments* in the framework of which *controversies* unfold about the values, meaning, and principles of justification of the SSE? But these values, meaning, and principles are most often established *on the basis of missing elements, in a subtractive way*, in reference to other dominant spheres of society – the administrative public authority and the market economy – whose evaluative principles are imported as they are in the SSE, thus entailing a risk of non-relevant judgments.

From this perspective, evaluation would be one of the concrete practices wherein Habermas' vision of society could unfold. This vision is understood as a tension between the instrumental rationality aiming at technical or strategic efficiency and the communicational rationality that "defines the criteria of rationality in reference to the argumentative processes aiming to honour, directly or indirectly, the claims to propositional truth, normative accuracy, subjective sincerity and finally aesthetical coherence" (Habermas, 1988: 372, approximate translation). Whatever the opinion of Jürgen Habermas (Habermas, 1987), this communications rationality could differ from that of the *ordinary city*. It would be instead that of the scientific city where scientific actors and experts/scholars debate, argue, and deliberate. Evaluation would be, by principle and in essence, wholly communicational, from the elaboration of its methods and indicators to its public feedback.

Several characteristics can be inferred from this. First, ought not evaluation processes to belong to *instituted scientific arenas* where they would be questioned in reference to SSE multiple worlds? Though scientific associations exist, the debate taking place in these associations often remains academic and does not really take into account the specificity of evaluation methods according to the *plurality of worlds* upon which they focus. Moreover, these arenas need to open up to an encounter with society, its actors and its associations in "public spaces of proximity" (Eme, 1993a)[15] or "hybrid forums" (Callon, Lascoumes and Barthe, 2001). These democratic deliberations would combine the benchmarks of culture (meaning of actions), society (solidarity among individuals as the fundamental social link), and personality (aiming at the subjectivization of each individual according to an ideal of autonomy). They would focus on the goals, methods, processes, and bases for evaluation between the scientific and expertise spheres, on the one hand, and associations and citizens, on the other. These evaluative processes, which oppose the increasingly pervasive instrumental logics of evaluation, would constitute possible meeting points between scien-

---

[15] This notion comes from a personal work on Jürgen Habermas that has been taken over in many theoretical texts on the solidarity-based economy (Eme, 1993a, 1993b).

tific communication acts and the discussion acts of civil society and public authorities.

Back to the primary question of the source of value judgments, the best pluralistic basis for the latter would probably be constituted by evaluative courts with the legitimacy to judge the value of beings, things or actions in reference to a plurality of spheres of values (but also of justice). These public arenas of deliberation, argumentation, and judgment would, through the implementation of new rules of equality among the participants, bring together citizens, SSE organizations, political and administrative actors, and scientists. In these local public spaces where the tensions are evaluated in reference to the common good (solidarity through activities with social, environmental, and cultural utilities, and not merely instrumental ones), evaluative processes would – or would not – grant common goods the status of collective goods, re-appropriated by society as a whole, or would – or would not – confer legitimacy onto the latter's existence.

The inherited identity of evaluation – its fundamentally instrumental character – is not an idea on which we should remain silent. It underlines the still topical submission of SSE actors to this identity and the fact that their emancipation from public control and guidance is necessary for the unfolding of a world of *controversies* on citizens' life in common.

References

Aballea, F., "Méthodologie de l'évaluation qualitative", *Dossiers pour notre temps*, 46, juillet-septembre, 1988.

Alter, N., *L'innovation ordinaire*, Paris, PUF ("Sociologies"), 2000.

Alternatives Économiques, *L'utilité sociale*, Coll. Pratique, Alternatives Économiques, 2003.

Ardoino, J., *Encyclopédie philosophique universelle, Les notions philosophiques*, Tome 1, Paris, PUF, 1990.

Barbier, J.-M., *L'évaluation en formation*, Paris, PUF, 1985.

Bévort, A., Lallement, M. (dir.), *Le capital social. Performance, équité et réciprocité*, Paris, La Découverte/Mauss, 2006.

Blaie, J.-P., Kurc, A. (dir.), *L'évaluation en travail social*, Nancy, Presses Universitaires de Nancy, 1988.

Blanc le, G., *Vies ordinaires, vies précaires*, Paris, Seuil ("La couleur des idées"), 2007a.

Blanc le, G., *Les maladies de l'homme normal*, Paris, Vrin ("Matière étrangère"), 2007b.

Boltanski, L., Thévenot, L., *De la justification*, Paris, Gallimard, 1991.

Boltanski, L., Chiapello, E., *Le nouvel esprit du capitalisme*, Paris, Gallimard, 1991.

Brown, W., *Les habits neufs de la politique mondiale. Néolibéralisme et néo-conservatisme*, Paris, Les prairies ordinaires ("Penser/croiser"), 2007.

Callon, M., Lascoumes, P., Barthe, Y., *Agir dans un monde incertain. Essai sur la démocratie technique*, Paris, Seuil ("La couleur des idées"), 2001.

Canguilhem, G., *Le normal et le pathologique*, Paris, PUF ("Galien"), 1975.

Castel, R., *Les métamorphoses de la question sociale. Une chronique du salariat*, Paris, Fayard, 1995.

Castoriadis, C., *La montée de l'insignifiance. Les carrefours du labyrinthe IV*, Paris, Seuil, 1996.

Chopart, J.-N., Neyret, G., Rault, D., *Les dynamiques de l'économie sociale et solidaire*, Paris, La Découverte ("Recherches"), 2006.

Commissariat Général du Plan, *Évaluer les politiques publiques*, Paris, La Documentation Française, 1986.

Conan, M., Allen, B., *Recherche sur la mise en place de méthodologies d'évaluation des expérimentations du plan urbain*, Paris, CSTB, 1985.

Deleau, M., *et al.*, *Évaluer les politiques publiques: méthode, déontologie, organisation, Rapport pour le Commissariat général au plan*, Paris, La Documentation française, 1985.

Delors, J., Gaudin, J., *Pour la création d'un troisième secteur, comment créer des emplois*, Paris, Centre de recherche Travail et société, université de Paris IX Dauphine, mars 1979.

DIES, *Guide de l'évaluation, Ministère des Affaires Sociales, du Travail et de la Solidarité*, Paris, 2002.

Eme, B., "Les services de proximité", *Informations sociales*, 13, août-septembre 1991.

Eme, B., "Economie Solidaire et changement social, Jalons pour une problématique", *Travail*, octobre 1993a.

Eme, B., *Lecture d'Habermas et éléments provisoires d'une problématique du social solidariste d'intervention*, LSCI-IRESCO-CNRS, ronéo IRESCO-CNRS, 1993b.

Eme, B., "Gouvernance territoriale et mouvements d'économie sociale et solidaire", *RECMA*, 2005, pp. 42-55.

Eme, B., "La question de l'autonomie de l'économie sociale et solidaire par rapport à la sphère publique", in J.-N. Chopart, G. Neyret and D. Rault, *Les dynamiques de l'économie sociale et solidaire*, Paris, La Découverte ("Recherches"), 2006a.

Eme, B., *Généalogie de l'appartenance déliée. Insertions et société*, Mémoire d'habilitation à diriger des recherches, Université Paris Dauphine, 2006b.

Eme, B., Haddab, K., Regnault, B., *L'évaluation des organisations économiques d'insertion. Méthodes, dimensions, variables et indicateurs retenus*, LSCI-IRESCO-CNRS, 1991, 40 p.

Enjolras, B., *Le marché providence: aide à domicile, politique sociale et création d'emploi*, Paris, Desclée de Brouwer, 1995.

Enjolras, B., "Economie sociale et transformation de l'État-providence: le cas des services aux personnes âgées", *RECMA*, 269, 1998.

Evers, A., "Les dimensions sociopolitiques du tiers secteur. Les contributions théoriques européennes sur la protection sociale et l'économie plurielles", *Sociologie du travail*, 42, 4, octobre-décembre 2000, pp. 567-585.

Ferry, J.-M., *L'allocation universelle. Pour un revenu de citoyenneté*, Paris, Cerf, 1995.

Foucault, M., *Naissance de la biopolitique*, Paris, Seuil/Gallimard ("Hautes Études"), 2004.

Fraisse, J., Bonetti M., de Gaulejac V., *L'évaluation dynamique des organisations publiques*, Paris, Les Éditions d'organisation, 1987.

Friot, B., *Puissance du salariat. Emploi et protection sociale à la française*, Paris, La dispute, 1998.

Gadrey, J., "L'utilité sociale", in J.-L. Laville and A. D. Catani, *Dictionnaire de l'autre économie*, Paris, Desclée de Brouwer, 2005.

Gadrey, J., "L'utilité sociale en question: à la recherche de conventions, de critères et de méthodes d'évaluation", in J.-N. Chopart, G. Neyret and D. Rault, *Les dynamiques de l'économie sociale et solidaire*, Paris, La Découverte ("Recherches"), 2006.

Gorz, A., *Métamorphoses du travail. Quête du sens. Critique de la raison économique*, Paris, Galilée, 1988.

Greffe, X., "L'évaluation des activités publiques", *Recherches économiques et sociales*, 13-14, 1985.

Habermas, J., *Théorie de l'agir communicationnel*, Paris, Fayard, 1987.

Habermas, J., *Le discours philosophique de la modernité*, Paris, Gallimard, 1998.

Haeringer, J., Traversaz, F., *Conduire le changement dans les associations d'action sociale et médico-sociale*, Paris, Dunod, 2002.

Hély, M., "L'économie sociale et solidaire n'existe pas", *Laviedesidées.fr*, 11 février, 2008.

Honneth, A., *La lutte pour la reconnaissance*, Paris, Cerf ("Passages"), 2000.

Ion, J., *La fin des militants?*, Paris, Les Éditions de l'Atelier ("Enjeux de société"), 1997.

Ion, J., Franguiadakis, S., Viot, P., *Militer aujourd'hui*, Paris, Autrement ("Cevipof Autrement"), 2005.

Langer, F., "Économie", in B. Cassin, *Vocabulaire européen des philosophies*, Paris, Seuil, Le Robert, 2004.

Latour, B., *Changer de société. Refaire de la sociologie*, La Découverte, Paris, 2006.

Lefort, C., *L'invention démocratique*, Paris, Fayard ("Le livre de poche, biblio essais"), 1983.

Legendre, P., *Sur la question dogmatique en Occident*, Paris, Fayard, 1999.

Lièvre, P., *Évaluer une action sociale*, Rennes, Éditions de L'ENSP, 2002.

Lipietz A., "Après-fordisme et démocratie", *Les temps modernes*, 524, mars 1990.

Lipietz, A., *Pour le tiers secteur: l'économie sociale et solidaire*, La Découverte, Paris, 2001.

Loquet, P., "L'utilité sociale dans la loi", in N. Richez-Battesti, *Module Utilité Sociale, Campus numérique en Economie sociale et solidaire*, Chap. 2, Réseau 21, Université de Valenciennes, 2003.

Maréchal, J.-P., "Secteur tertiaire ou secteur quaternaire?", *Transversales*, 35, septembre-octobre 1995.

Monnier, E., *Évaluations de l'action des pouvoirs publics*, Paris, Économica, 1987.

Moulinier, P., *L'évaluation au service des politiques culturelles locales*, Paris, La Documentation française, 1994.

Nioche, J.-P., Poinsard, R., *L'évaluation des politiques publiques*, Paris, Economica, 1984.

Ogien, A., *L'esprit gestionnaire. Une analyse de l'air du temps*, Paris, Éditions de l'École des hautes études en sciences sociales, 1995.

Perret, B., *L'évaluation de l'économie sociale. Éléments de problématique*, Conférence au Groupe de travail Méthodes et indicateurs d'évaluation de l'économie sociale, Paris, CIRIEC, réunion tenue à l'Hôtel de ville, 10 février 2006.

Perret, B., "Réflexions sur les différents modèles d'évaluation", *Revue française d'administration publique*, 66, avril-juin 1993.

Renault, E., *L'expérience de l'injustice. Reconnaissance et clinique de l'injustice*, Paris, La Découverte ("Armillaires"), 2004.

Richez-Battesti, N. *et al.*, "ESS, territoires et proximité", *RECMA*, 296, 2005.

Richez-Battesti, N., "Évaluer la production associative par les pouvoirs publics: du contrôle à la coproduction des critères?", in X. Engels, H., Peyrin, and H. Trouvé (dir.), *De l'intérêt général à l'utilité sociale: la reconfiguration de l'action publique entre État, associations et participation citoyenne*, Paris, l'Harmattan (Coll. Logiques sociales), 2006.

Sainsaulieu, R. (dir.), *L'entreprise une affaire de société*, PFNSP, 1990.

Salais, R., Storper, M., *Les mondes de production. Enquête sur l'identité économique de la France*, Paris, Éditions de l'École des Hautes Études en Sciences Sociales, 1997.

Simondon, G., *L'individuation à la lumière des notions de formes et d'information*, Grenoble, Éditions Jérome Million (collection Krisis), 2005.

Sue, R., *La richesse des hommes. Vers l'économie quaternaire*, Paris, Éditions Odile Jacob, 1997.

Supiot, A., *Homo juridicus. Essai sur la fonction anthropologique du Droit*, Paris, Seuil ("La couleur des idées"), 2005.

Thévenot, L., "Nouvelles figures du compromis", in B. Eme and J.-L. Laville (dir.), *Cohésion sociale et emploi*, Paris, Desclée de Brouwer ("Sociologie économique"), 1994.

Thévenot, L., *L'action au pluriel. Sociologie des régimes d'engagement*, Paris, La Découverte, 2006.

Vienney, C., *Socio-économie des organisations coopératives*, 2 tomes, Paris, CIEM, 1980, 1982.

Viveret, P., *L'évaluation des politiques et des actions publiques, Rapport au Premier ministre*, Paris, La Documentation française, 1989.

Walzer, M., *Sphères de justice. Une défense du pluralisme et de l'égalité*, Paris, Seuil ("La couleur des idées"), 1997.

Weber, M., *Économie et société. I, les catégories de la sociologie*, Paris, Pocket (Plon, 1971), 1995.

PART II

NATIONAL CONTRIBUTIONS

Evaluating the Social and Solidarity-Based Economy in France

Societal Balance Sheet-Social Utility and Identity Trial

Nadine RICHEZ-BATTESTI, Hélène TROUVÉ,
François ROUSSEAU, Bernard EME & Laurent FRAISSE

Professor, LEST-CNRS and Université de la Méditerranée (France)
Engineer Council, Associate Researcher, Centre d'économie
de la Sorbonne, Université Paris 1 Panthéon-Sorbonne (France)
Associate Researcher, Centre de recherche en gestion,
École polytechnique (UMR-CNRS) (France)
Professor of Sociology, Faculty of Economic and Social Sciences,
Université de Lille 1 and CLERSE (France)
Socio-economist, Laboratoire interdisciplinaire
pour la Sociologie Économique (LISE-CNAM/CNRS) (France)

Introduction

In reference to the works of Perret (2001; 2005), we consider evaluation as a process of formation of value judgments on an organization, a programme or an activity in an operational perspective: accountability, mobilization, collective learning, and support to decision-making, etc. In France, the interest for evaluation develops in a context which is characterized by a progressive change of the mode of regulation and the mode of governance of public policies and enterprises, according to configurations which appear as not stabilized yet. After the rationalization of budgetary choices (*rationalisation des choix budgétaires*, or RCB) – which had been introduced in 1970 as a form of ex ante evaluation of public policies – was suddenly abandoned in 1984, evaluation practices re-emerged in the early 1990s, thus contributing to the generalization of ex post evaluation, and are currently developing.

The acceleration of the decentralization process, transformations of public policies and extension of market procedures in a narrow conception of competition, and the fact that elements of corporate social responsibility (CSR) were enacted as law[1] all concur to raise the question of the evaluation of the social and solidarity-based economy (*économie sociale et solidaire*, or ESS).[2] Although these transformations (which have been implemented for more than two decades) are still immature and remain to be fully developed, they must not be undervalued in a country whose centralist and statist history guaranteed the old forms of evaluation (Eme, 2005a).

In the field of the social and solidarity-based economy (SSE[3]), we have focused on analysis of the evaluation processes such as they emerge from the debates which have taken place among the different actors of the field in the last 15 years, and which reflect the dynamics currently at work in the renewal of evaluation forms; this leads us to ignore the compulsory social balance sheet in companies employing more than 50 workers or the so-called "co-operative revision", which is a compulsory procedure for co-operatives.

In this perspective, two devices – though still experimental – are particularly prominent. For co-operatives and mutual societies, whose activities are embedded in the market, we analyze the "societal balance sheet" (*bilan sociétal*). This participative tool, which aims to improve practices, has been created, maintained and promoted by the Centre for Young Leaders of the Social Economy (*Centre des Jeunes Dirigeants de l'Économie Sociale*, or CJDES) since the mid-1990s. As far as non-profit organizations are concerned, debates are developing around the notion of social utility, most often in relation with the development of non-market activities. These debates were originally supported by the National Council for Associative Life (*Conseil National de la Vie Associative*, or CNVA) in response to the positions adopted by public authorities; nowadays, they also include local actors, associations and elected officials.

Our goal is thus to shed an analytical light on the operationalization of the notions of social utility and societal balance sheet and on their semantic and strategic use. The issue of the goal of the evaluation of the SSE is called upon in this perspective, because it seems to lie at the very heart of the debates. Is the goal of such evaluations to design a "signalization tool" aiming at the legitimization of SSE practices, or a tool of

---

[1] Article 116 of The Law on New Economic Regulations (*Nouvelles régulations économiques*, or NRE), 2001, makes it compulsory for French enterprises listed on the stock exchange to provide a social and environmental report on their activities.

[2] Without entering the French controversies on the subject, we define the social and solidarity-based economy (SSE) on the basis of the legal forms of the organizations which compose it: co-operatives, mutual societies, non-profit organizations (associations) and foundations.

[3] The acronym SSE will be used hereafter.

public regulation of activities, foreboding the normalization of practices? The data collection methodology is primarily documentary and multimodal. It is based on reports and studies regarding the evaluation of the SSE as well as on data from studies on the subjects of evaluation and social utility carried out in recent years by each of the writers of the present work.[4] In particular, we lean on the "Solidarity-Based Dynamics" (*Dynamiques solidaires*) programme, initiated by the "Inter-Ministerial Delegation to the Solidarity-Based Economy" (*Délégation interministérielle à l'économie sociale*, or DIES) in 2002. This programme contributed to the funding of 36 research reports, with a part dedicated to the issue of social utility carried out by a working group led by Gadrey (2003). The action of new entities, embedded in the field of public policies, such as the "Agency for the Valorization of Socio-economic Initiatives" (*Agence pour la valorisation des initiatives socio-économiques* – see AVISE, 2003; Rousseau, 2007; Duclos, 2007) or books addressing the general public (*Alternatives économiques*, 2003) were also analyzed.

We first describe the French context, which is characterized by a double movement: enlargement of the evaluation indicators and intensification of competition in the production of goods and services traditionally "sheltered". Then, we identify the main trends of evaluation and underline the issues at stake in this regard. Finally, we try to tackle the complex and sometimes contradictory consequences of evaluation practices on the evolution of the SSE; this is all the more important that what is at stake through evaluation is first and foremost the definition and the field of the SSE as well as its modes of regulation. Is evaluation not, in this context, at the very heart of the identity trial?

I. A Context Characterized by the Transformation of the Modes of Regulation and the Assertion of Societal Concerns

The question of the evaluation of SSE organizations cannot be analyzed independently from the transformations of public action, which generate both reconfigurations of public regulations (Trouvé *et al.*, 2006; Trouvé, 2005; Fraisse, 2006) and the emergence of new modes of governance (Enjolras, 2008) whose territorial scales are diversified: municipalities and their new forms of groupings, territorial development contracts etc. (Eme, 2005; Richez-Battesti, *et al.*, 2005; Trouvé, 2004a). It is finally directly linked to the transformations of the welfare-state, in

---

[4] See References.

relation with the "new social question" and the justifications for public funding (Richez-Battesti, 2006).

This renewal of public action was paralleled by the creation and extension, at the end of the 1980s, of the systems of evaluation of public policies.[5] The inclusion of compulsory evaluation in legal and regulatory texts developed rapidly[6] and led, by extension, to the evaluation of the action of the partners of public policies, and in particular of associations. In a way which was complementary to the already existing public rules in matters of control of the use of public funds, the evaluation of associative activities was enacted in generic texts of legal or regulatory origin, thus confirming a slow evolution which tends to associate the legal regime of subsidies with ever more accurate counterparts (Rousseau, 2007).

As if trying to counter this trend, negotiations between representatives of the associative world and two successive governments (namely the Juppé and Jospin governments) led to the "Charter of reciprocal commitments", which was signed by associations and the government in 2001, on the occasion of the 100th anniversary of the law on associations. This charter indicates that the role of evaluation consists in "distinguishing clearly, within the relations between the state and associations, what concerns the evaluation of the partnership action from what concerns the control of the implementation of laws and regulations". In this perspective, the administrative memorandum of December 1, 2000, relating to the pluri-annual goal conventions between the state and associations, made it compulsory for associations to implement an evaluation process of state-funded actions. The evaluation guide whose use is recommended does not define a standard evaluation method; on the contrary, it insists on the necessity to implement partnership-based evaluations, tailor-made and contextualized, i.e. embedded in the legal, administrative, socio-economic, territorial, sector-based, etc., specificities which condition the implementation and the carrying out of the funded associative activities. But in practice, these mainly qualitative evaluation practices are not being used; pluri-annual goal conventions are easily questioned; and the extension of a partnership logic to other territorial levels is limited. The context is thus characterized by the persistence of a strong tension between the tutelary practices of public

---

[5] Decree of January 22, 1990 establishing the Scientific Council for Evaluation (*Conseil scientifique de l'évaluation*), which became the National Council for Evaluation (*Conseil national de l'évaluation*) in 1998.

[6] Administrative Memorandum of December 9, 1993 which associates, to the "State-regions Planning Contracts" (*Contrats de plan État-régions*) and the Town Contracts (*Contrats de ville*), an obligation of evaluation.

authorities, on the one hand, and the renewed partnership practices asked for by associative actors, on the other hand.

Associative leaders are aware of the growing place taken by evaluation as a judgment criterion which is gaining ever more importance for obtaining public resources (including recognition and economic means) which are nowadays more difficult to obtain than in the past – hence the necessity to acquire, in this area, arguments and tools which constitute competences allowing them to adapt to this new environment. But simultaneously, the expectations of the state and territorial organizations, on the one hand, and associations, on the other hand, regarding the contents of evaluation often appear as hardly compatible and, consequently, evaluation is perceived as a threat by associations. This concern is reinforced as a result of the inequality of the various categories of actors in terms of means and maturity as far as evaluation is concerned (Rousseau, 2007).

Debates around the notion of CSR represent another contextual element likely to constitute a new normative framework, still unstable, upon which evaluation procedures depend. CSR is defined as an advanced way, for the enterprise, to take responsibility for social, societal and environmental concerns linked to its activity (Capron and Quairel-Lanoizelée, 2004). Presented as a voluntary process, CSR is in fact largely encouraged by regulatory decisions (Gendron, 2002), in particular those imposed by the states, on the one hand, and by competitive pressures linked to the strategies of large international investors, on the other hand.

Three links can be established between CSR and SSE organizations:

- a first one has been established by the European Commission, which invited SSE organizations to better highlight their CSR practices and to better valorize the latter in their communication policy (CCE, 2001; Charte européenne de l'Économie sociale, 2001);
- a second link results from the "intersection" between CSR criteria and the founding principles and statutory rules of the SSE.[7] In this perspective, the SSE appears as a pioneer, as through its foundations, values and principles, it strives to include the various stakeholders and aims at the adoption of virtuous behaviours towards society;
- a third link concerns the societal balance sheet. The six types of criteria (see below) of CSR can also be found in the societal bal-

---

[7] It has to be noted, though, that these SSE general principles do not include any mention of the environmental dimension.

ance sheet. They allow to define the "societal profile" of the organization in relation to its stakeholders.

Beyond the reconfiguration of French public policies, it appears that the reflection on the evaluation of the SSE is part of a larger, international movement which tries to apply the concept of sustainable development to enterprises (*Rapport Bruntland*, 1987) and aims to redesign wealth indicators from a macroeconomic point of view (Viveret, 2001).

In such circumstances, it seems logical to link the SSE to the whole set of socioeconomic movements which, through the combination of the production of goods and services, political questioning and economic expertise, aim to reintroduce public debate on and democratic regulations of the dominant norms of production, consumption and saving (Fraisse, 2007).

In this sense, the question of evaluation refers to the double function – namely the socioeconomic function and the socio-political one – of SSE organizations which, at least in France, often have an ambition to produce goods and services while simultaneously participating to the construction of the public good, through the revelation of demands and social innovation. The search for an enlarged conception of evaluation is not only carried out by forms of collective entrepreneurship that, through their social goal and their modes of organization – which mobilize co-operative, participation and solidarity principles – produce goods and services in ways that differ from for-profit enterprises and public administrations. It does not result either from the sole search for efficiency in a context of increased market regulation and intensification of competition for the access to public funding. It is also concomitant with the emergence of ethical, solidarity and environmental concerns in daily consumption acts (consuming "fair" products; choosing ethical savings; eating organic food; adopting more sustainable ways of transportation, lighting and heating, etc.) which question the social and environmental effects of large-scale retailing and concurred to the elaboration of labels, certifications and norms to qualify the fair or organic character of goods and services.

The question of evaluation appears as particularly crucial when it comes to the permeability of the boundaries of the institutional field of the SSE. Finally, it is difficult to separate it from the progressive emergence, on the global scene, of an organized civil society which, through large-scale international campaigns (debt relief), the criticism of multilateral institutions' (WTO, IMF, World Bank) policies, which are deemed too liberal, and alter-globalization groupings (social forums), challenges universities, governments and enterprises' monopoly on legitimate economic expertise. Even though their significance in economic terms is limited, non-governmental organizations (NGOs), foundations and protest movements nevertheless claim to be bearers of analyses and economic realities which are increasingly being taken into account in the international agenda.

II. Current Trends: a Renewed Interest for an Enlarged Conception of Evaluation

CSR, societal balance sheet and social utility are part of a double perspective of enlargement of evaluation criteria of organizations and schemes, as they integrate a social, societal, and even environmental dimension, on the one hand, and a dimension of structuration of empirical evaluation tools, on the other hand. We are witnessing both an effort of legitimization of the specific modes of organization and action of the SSE, and an attempt to contribute to the constitution of a vision of the general interest – or at least of the common good in the sense of the theory of conventions – combining a plurality of logics (market, industrial, civic, etc.) and various types of compromise among these logics.

A gap can be observed between the vision of those who ask for evaluation and the actors who are submitted to this evaluation; this gap can probably be accounted for by the fact that, historically, in France, evaluation has often been assimilated to control. Partly because dialogue and exchange on the goals of evaluation are insufficient and an instrumental perspective of the rationalization of organization or intensification of the service relation prevails, evaluation has difficulty in establishing itself as a democratic practice and leads to tensions.

We approach successively the societal balance sheet rather dedicated to mutual societies and cooperatives and the social utility appropriate for the associative sector. We underline then the heterogeneousness of the practices and the stake in the emergence of an actor of interface allowing the evaluation to spread.

A. Co-operatives, Mutual Societies and Societal Balance Sheet: Combining Entrepreneurial and Societal Dimensions?

Far from being fully-fleshed and stabilized, the theoretical corpus, the contents, the methods of analysis and the societal and organizational implications of CSR practices raise debates and controversies (Wood, 1991; Gendron, 2002);[8] as for the societal balance sheet, it still remains relatively little-known.

At the level of the enterprise, the implementation process of CSR is progressive. First, a social and environmental diagnosis must be estab-

---

[8] "Conceptual developments have not been systematically integrated with one another, but usually have been treated as free-standing, implicitly competing ideas."

lished; then orientations have to be defined and goals set; and finally, an action programme must be implemented with a view to achieving an evolution of practices and elaborating specific tools of reporting, i.e. an extra-financial information system that can lead to a social and environmental rating. Six main "families" of criteria are defined: environment, human resources, corporate governance, business practices, local impact and citizenship. But most enterprises simply carry out a social and environmental diagnosis, without this leading to an evolution of their practices or strategies (Alberola and Richez-Battesti, 2005).

In a distinct way, the societal balance sheet was elaborated[9] in cooperation with its subscribers. It was originally intended for market organizations within the SSE, but it is nevertheless applicable to all enterprises as well as to associations.[10] This tool of self-evaluation, self-diagnosis and support to decision-making and mutual consultation among the organization's partners allows to assess the responsibility of an organization on its territory and the adequacy between the declared values and the actual practices, and to conduct a strategic reflection. It is based on 450 questions, grouped in nine areas.

Box: The societal balance sheet	
3 pillars of sustainable development	9 areas of the societal balance sheet
Economic activity	– goods-services and relations with customers, – economic management, – anticipation, innovation, prospective.
Work and social relations	– organization of work and production, – human resources management, – internal actors of the enterprise.
Environment	– human, social and institutional environment of the enterprise, – biophysical environment, – goals-values-ethics.

---

[9] See the CJDES website: www.cjdes.org.

[10] An "associative societal balance sheet" (*bilan sociétal associatif*, or BSA) is indeed being developed; it is slightly simplified in order to make its implementation easier. The first experiments with this tool were carried out in employer associations in Brittany (France) in 2005.

Three stages:
- collection, by the organization, of information about the nine areas,
- realization of the analysis and diagnosis by an external auditor (societal analyst) appointed by the CJDES,
- definition of evolution goals by the organization in co-operation with all the stakeholders within the framework of a joint representation process, with a subsequent evaluation (new societal balance sheet).

Source: CJDES.

Unlike CSR, which gives rise, in most cases, to a positive discourse on the part of leaders (Attarça and Jacquot, 2005)[11] – omitting, for example, to mention the negative aspects revealed by the implementation of the diagnosis –, the societal balance sheet explicitly aims to influence the enterprise's decision-making system, to modify stakeholders' behaviours and to evaluate the results or the progress achieved.

Most organizations having voluntarily chosen to implement the societal balance sheet are mutual societies and co-operatives. The French Confederation of Agricultural Co-operatives (*Confédération Française des Coopératives Agricoles*), for example, has proposed, since 2004, its own model to its members, whereas the MAIF and the MACIF, two French insurance mutual societies, engaged in a reflection, at the internal level, on the adaptation of this tool. Some of these organizations, such as the MACIF, also had a social responsibility audit carried out by a specialized agency, better able to facilitate comparisons with for-profit companies in the same field of activity. All these steps stimulate a complementary questioning on the management of membership, its institutional place and its role in the production of goods or services. However, since the steps taken are still rather recent and the re-evaluation of goals provided for by the societal balance sheet has not yet been carried out, the evolutions that they made possible are still difficult to grasp.

B. Public Action and Evaluation of the Social Utility

Social utility is the other aspect of an enlarged conception of evaluation criteria, correlated with public action and associations. Representatives from the associative world have taken over this concept in relation with the issue of the recognition of associations which contribute to the development of the general interest, and to oppose the fiscal doctrine which has prevailed since the 1970s, and which is considered as ill-adapted to the economic activities of associations. Recent history of the

---

[11] Analysis of 85 annual reports produced by managers of large French, English and German enterprises.

social utility tells in fact of the tension between a dimension which is mainly organizational and market-oriented, on the one hand, and the conception of identity conveyed by associative actors, on the other hand.

Originally, the first reflections on social utility were linked to taxation and limitation of competition. Social utility is defines by non-profit character, altruistic management and a price inferior to the market price or a lack of competition on the market. The notion was subsequently taken over in a notice of the National Council for Associative Life (*Conseil National de la Vie Associative*, or CNVA) of July 9, 1995 aiming at the public recognition of associations through the establishment of a distinction between criteria linked to the not-for-profit character and criteria linked to social utility. Ten criteria thus allow the recognition of the social utility of associations; they are generally synthesized in five points: the primacy of the project over the activity; the not-for-profit character and the altruistic management; the social contribution of associations; the democratic operation; and the existence of an official approval.

At the end of the 1990s, public authorities again used the social utility concept to justify the granting of fiscal advantages or advantages linked to the limitation of competition. Thus, the fiscal instruction of September 15, 1998 establishes an examination procedure on the basis of four criteria which are taken into account in a sequential way. The first relates to the altruistic management of the organization. If this condition is met, the second step consists in analyzing potential situations of competition with the provision by for-profit enterprises. In case of potential competition, the third step evaluates whether the activity is carried out in conditions which are similar to those of a for-profit enterprise. The examination is carried out on the basis of four components: the product, the targeted public, the price fixed and the advertisements; this is the so-called "Four-P rule" (*produit, public, prix* and *publicité* in French). It is used to assess, in a fourth stage, the reasons why, on the one hand, the activity meets a need which is not being met (or at least not satisfactorily met) by the market and, on the other hand, the economic and social situation of the targeted public justifies socially adapted prices.

The definition which can be used is that of the fiscal administration: "An activity of social utility is one which tends to satisfy a need which is not – or not adequately – met by the market. Other official texts mentioning the social utility[12] leave it to the administration to determine

---

[12] For example, in the field of supported employment programmes in the non-market sector, it is considered that there is a social utility component when the jobs are cre-

what is of social utility and what is not. Approaches to the social utility thus waver between the general interest and social action, through the specification of the concerned sectors of activity (*sport, culture, environment*, etc.), the nature of the activity (response to emerging needs) and the targeted public, in relation to public policies of employment and integration.

Current debates about the evaluation of social utility, such as they emerge from the experiments led by AVISE, underline the fact that the issue at stake, for SSE actors, is to achieve the recognition of a conception of social utility appropriate to their vision, which would become a reference and would possibly lead to a better established social convention, around which a balanced partnership between associations and public authorities could be built (Rousseau, 2007). These debates, together with the approaches developed as soon as the early 2000s by the study and advice association, Culture et Promotion, and by the research works funded by the DIES, lead to hybrid forums and to the production of methods of analysis (Duclos, 2007) which can be appropriated by associations on a voluntary basis. They are also accompanied, in some regions, by the joint construction of methods of analysis of the social utility then mobilized by the funding bodies in their support policies for the associative sector. Finally, they are fed by the reflections on positive voluntary externalities produced by SSE organizations; the latter consider that taking into account the degree of intentionality of the output would constitute an effective means of differentiation (Fraisse, 2006).

C. Heterogeneity of Practices and Participation

The results of studies and field observations (cf. Appendix 1) highlight the diversity of procedures and methods of evaluation. This diversity is not limited to the tools and the way in which they are implemented; it also affects the representations that those requesting the evaluation, when they are external to the organization, have about the latter, the activity or the action implemented. The fact that these evaluation processes appear as being only to a limited extent imposed from outside does not mean that their implementation does not generate any tension, *inter alia* because they make it necessary to re-question the project and the stakeholders' mode of association. As a matter of fact, all SSE organizations, whether they integrate evaluation within a societal balance sheet perspective or within a social utility perspective, seize

---

ated in the framework of new activities meeting needs which are not – or not adequately – met and when the workers belong to groups targeted by work-integration devices (young workers, social aid recipients, etc.).

this opportunity to reshape their founding project and use it as a mobilization tool at the internal level.

These evaluation practices lead to (re)consider the initial project and invite leaders to ensure a better internal organization by permanently searching an acceptable compromise between the rationalization of resources and the pre-eminence of the social project. The mainly qualitative tools which accompany any evaluation process enrich the traditional management tools (the majority of which are of a quantitative nature), which are considered as ill-fitted to describe the project. The evaluation thus refers to a complex engineering which implies the acquisition of new knowledge or skills; it will then be possible to diffuse these within the organization, thus making a useful contribution to the reinforcement of the latter's identity, while allowing to better explain the project's utility to the stakeholders (Rousseau, 2007).

However, the SSE organization is all the more deeply rooted in the project that the participative process constituted a key element of the evaluation device. This participative process most often develops in relation with the emergence or the presence of a third party, external to the organization. This third party can be a consultant and/or a body whose credibility is based on its expertise in matters of participative evaluation. It appears both as a facilitator and risk reducer, increasing safety throughout the evaluation process, allowing the expression of tensions without this blocking the evaluation process. The third party facilitates the introduction of an evaluation method, the mobilization and enrolment of stakeholders and the production of criteria. By so doing, it favours co-operative collective learning and the acquisition of know-how. Through the relations which are created or reinforced on the occasion of the evaluation, a shared culture, with a strong identity contents, emerges or capitalizes; this culture is likely to lead to the constitution of a common good, rooted in proximity and little perceivable at first sight, but whose long-term territorial effects are significant.

This interface actor is characterized by its capacity to raise awareness of evaluation and to provide a frame for the conflicts produced by the confrontation between heterogeneous stakeholders' logics of action as well as by the feeling of insecurity generated by the evaluation process. From the point of view of providers and demanders of evaluation, the role of this third party seems substantial.

However, in the French context, this translator could not be a direct emanation of the funding body, in particular in the case of associations whose funding comes, partly or totally, from public authorities, as this would entail a risk of evaluation taking over again its dimension of control. Public authorities can sometimes contribute to the elaboration of guidelines aiming to facilitate the implementation of evaluation, be it directly (as the DIES did, for example), or indirectly, through the action implemented by agencies such as AVISE. But the asymmetry of relations results in the demands for evaluation on the part of public authorities appearing as generally disconnected from the activity carried out by these organizations. Public authorities have specific expectations for each funding body, often limited to quantitative indicators linked to the targeted public; these indicators are supposedly easier to provide, but they are ill-suited to reflect the commitment of the organization and its modes of action. Because of this disconnection, evaluation is perceived as an unavoidable step to which one must submit oneself rather than a tool of dialogue, as a tool enabling public authorities to impose their domination and frame onto associations.

III. Analysis: From the Combination of Registers to the Emergence of a Common Good?

In this context, how can the influence of evaluation practices on the development and on the definition and recognition of the SSE be characterized? Are identity roots being reinforced or is there, conversely, a trend towards a reinforcement of isomorphism? Although the strategic perspective adopted and the semantic registers chosen can apply both to the societal balance sheet and to social utility, we have chosen to tackle these two cases separately. We highlight the importance of the identity register in the societal balance sheet and the predominance of the embeddedness in terms of governance in a strategic perspective. We then analyze the combination of semantic registers made possible by the notion of social utility and the contribution of the latter to the emergence of a common good. Finally, we identify the tension forces which are at the heart of the identity trial.

A. The Societal Balance Sheet as a Tool of Co-operative Governance

The societal balance sheet remains mainly oriented towards the search for adequacy between values and organization and, through this search, towards an identity quest, and it appears as a dialogue opportunity among the stakeholders in the framework of an *embedded* self-evaluation. It aims to influence the governance model by allowing the organization to better combine its values and practices, through more participative dynamics. What is at stake here are indeed changes of behaviours. In this sense, this voluntary process is conceived to affect management and governance rather than for signalling quality or increasing credibility in the eyes of external partners. It goes beyond the legal and contractual obligations imposed by public authorities and the regulation and control bodies and it does not, at any point, rely on a preconceived norm of behaviour in relation to a set of good practices, nor does it lead to a rating grid. Finally, the societal balance sheet is an element of integration of the organization within the territory through the mobilization and reinforcement of interactions among stakeholders. It thus combines an internal and an external dimension of governance. By so doing, it leads to the acquisition of new organizational skills, which reinforce the questioning of the project and its implementation and generate an intensification of proximity relations with stakeholders.

B. Registers of Social Utility as Identity Roots

Various studies carried out by the DIES and our own observations show that the evaluation of the SSE refers to three distinct – though sometimes overlapping – registers (namely the institutional register, the identity one and the axiological one) (Trouvé *et al.*, 2006).

The institutional register is mobilized in the relation to the – mainly administrative – norms, in the framework of public policies. The notion of social utility is often designated as an injunction by public actors and legal frameworks. This semantic field is characterized by expressions such as *programme, device and procedure*, frequently associated with the texts written by Thoenig and Duran (1996), Lascoumes (2003) and Rosanvallon (2004). Since evaluation is requested by the funding body with a view to ensuring accountability, what is evaluated is generally the funded programme rather than the organization itself. The immediate results and the direct effects, and even the outputs, are evaluated through quantitative criteria on the basis of which the salaried workers (in the case of employer associations) – in general the executives – provide reports on a yearly basis. In some cases (European funding or local support programme, for example), part of the evaluation must be carried out by an external expert. In this administrative logic, indicators are likely to change from one year to another, for a same activity, in order to meet the priorities of a public entity, and a participative process of evaluation within the associative organization is rarely used.

Variations can be observed depending on whether the evaluation is – or is not – intended directly and exclusively for a funding body. One can easily conceive that funding bodies (and among these, the state and territorial Organizations) are attentive to a "proper use of public funds" and an efficient allocation of resources. The question nevertheless remains of how the efficiency norm is defined and, consequently, on which procedures its elaboration and adjustment are based. There are significant differences between an imposed evaluation, constituting a compulsory counterpart of public funding, on the one hand, and a voluntary evaluation, implemented as a means to produce meaning, debate and maybe even convergences in representations of activity among the various stakeholders.

It is in this perspective that the *identity register* is rooted. Social utility is mobilized by collective actors as a mode of legitimization of a sector of socioeconomic activity through a semantic field built around expressions such as *legitimity, recognition and solidarity-based economy*, which are linked to the works carried out by Laville (1994), Gadrey (2003) and Viveret (2001). The request for evaluation is most often internal to the organization and it is supported both by the salaried workers and by the managers. The evaluation goes beyond a strictly administrative logic: both the programme and the organization are evaluated. It is generally carried out internally by the salaried workers and the managers, in the framework of a co-produced process highlighting the social performance of the organization with a strategic view. The tools and methods of evaluation are diversified (participant observation, interviews, discussion groups etc.) and the indicators taken into account are rather qualitative; they are linked to the societal balance sheet, the measure of public goods, positive externalities or some intangible impacts, such as democracy or social link. Reaching a broad consensus on these social dimensions of economic activities is difficult; and, more importantly, they call for a reflection on the values and principles underlying the action.

Finally, a mobilization of the *axiological register* can be observed. This register refers to actions resulting from compromises between heterogeneous – and even antagonistic – interests, whose goal is to combine individual interests to the benefit of a common interest. Social utility is used here to make the processes of collective action intelligible; it refers to the concept of *agreement* (on the values and goals) among stakeholders and to an enlarged conception of performance. This last semantic field is based on the principles of *mutual consultation, consensus and compromise*, and is linked to authors such as Boltanski and Thévenot (1991) and Enjolras (1999).

The multiplicity of the semantic uses of the social utility crystallises fundamental issues of ideological, normative and political nature (Trouvé, 2007). Its appropriation by the actors is not always easy; this is all the more true that quantitative evaluations of the output persist. Finally, this appropriation largely depends on the practices and values of those who define it and on the territories upon which they operate (Duclos, 2007), i.e. there is no *a priori* definition of the social utility; simultaneously, the issue of a more normative social utility label is regularly raised.

In these various interactions, social utility is thus mobilized both as a justification of public funding, specification of the SSE and opportunity to co-produce new evaluation principles. Sometimes defined as a socio-economic convention of evaluation (Gadrey, 2005), still unstable, its goal would rely on a double dynamic of legitimization (Trouvé, 2005; Fraisse, 2006): a dynamic of recognition of actors and of characterization of the SSE and a dynamic aiming to define new criteria justifying public intervention, regulation of activities and normalization of practices and to make these criteria more objective. The notion of social utility is situated at the crossroads of many issues (reconfiguration of the public action, reconsideration of the value of SSE organizations, relations between the public sector and the SSE); it is currently being consolidated, and it raises controversies which must be allowed to unfold, following the justifications of actors; this might imply both tensions among different action logics and the construction of possible agreements and compromises, more or less stabilized (Richez-Battesti, 2006). One can thus conceive that the notion of social utility is vague enough to manage to fulfil all these functions, jointly or simultaneously, and that it is finally non-consensual (Noguès, 2003), despite the multitude of works, points of view[13] and debates that it has generated.

C. Conflicting Forces: Is Evaluation at the Heart of the Identity Trial?

These evaluation practices still remain experimental and they are not generalized. Indeed, a gap can be observed between the debates and the efforts made to elaborate original evaluation tools, on the one hand, and the practices of SSE actors, on the other hand. In many cases, what is highlighted by SSE organizations is the immediate result (output) rather than the long-term ones (outcome). In the same way, organizational specificities or the processes implemented are little valorized, despite the fact that they constitute one of the specific traits of SSE organizations and condition the modes of production of goods and services (socioeconomic aspect). Voluntary and internalized positive externalities – which constitute the second way to differentiate SSE organizations from public and private for-profit organizations – are sometimes preferred to organizational specificities. Finally, even though the voluntary association of stakeholders appears as a distinctive sign of SSE organizations, the mobilization and management tools of these stakeholders remain little valorized, insufficiently discussed and little taken into account by public authorities.

---

[13] Whereas a report by Lipietz (2001) mentions the notion of community utility, other authors prefer the notion of societal valorization (Fraisse, 2005) or that of societal utility (Bastide *et al.*, 2001). For more developments on this subject, see Trouvé (2004).

In a dialogical perspective, qualifying, assessing and measuring are social acts which constitute *trials* in the framework of which individuals adopt units of measurement, criteria, indicators; some of these are objective, to the extent that they are admitted by the community of individuals and form the subject of lasting conventions, while others generate debates, controversies, disputes because they depend upon contingent, historical, and spatiotemporally determined conventions. Evaluation is thus a trial submitted to rational discussion through the principle of argumentation which formulates validity criteria (true-false, fair-unfair, authentic-unauthentic[14]) always conceived as criticizable, amendable and rectifiable claims, provided that controversies unfold to contribute to the elaboration of an evaluative common world.

Works on the evaluation of the SSE in France also illustrate the tensions linked to the attempts to combine output and outcome. Enjolras (see his chapter in this book) underlines the existence of a paradox: in relation with public policies, evaluation is most often based on immediate results; but the originality of the production of SSE organizations lies simultaneously in their mode of organization (and, consequently, in the modes of production of goods and services), in the positive externalities that they generate, as well as in their goal, which can be social or serve the community. More broadly, this paradox refers to the one which tends to disqualify the economic and social creativity: the latter is not taken into account insofar as it is constituted by the emergence of the unprecedented, which is not listed in evaluation grids. Creativity is disqualified to the benefit of a simple measure of the gaps between the goals and the results (efficiency), and between the allocated means and the means necessary to achieve the goals. The common measure of evaluation is based on this gap as compared to a norm, which is most often determined by public authorities, without taking into account SSE organizations' own intelligence or their negotiations with the buyers. It positions these organizations as subordinate providers. The evaluation process, when it is imposed, is carried out within an asymmetric power relation which minimizes the specificity of SSE organizations (see Eme, chap. 4), and their contribution to social innovation. The negation of the identity of SSE organizations is the corollary hereof, and this constitutes a problem regarding an evaluative recognition which, implicitly, raises the question of the identity of organizations. A tension is thus perceptible in the measure of the gap between a norm prescribed by political and administrative systems and a norm constructed by SSE organizations.

---

[14] The broad distinctions between the theoretical reason, the practical reason and the aesthetical reason (Kant, Parsons, Habermas) can be found here.

Finally, by distinguishing different dominant regulation regimes (Enjolras, 2008), whose mode of evaluation is one of the components, it is possible to characterize the tensions which "irrigate" the evaluation of the SSE, make legible the compromises on which it relies and the consequences on the relations between SSE and public authorities. The choices for combining the four dimensions of evaluation (product, process, impact and performance) of an SSE organization or using only some of these, for co-producing or not the evaluation criteria with the actors carrying out the activity, and for taking into account some criteria and indicators or others are all choices which are linked to the mode of regulation (Richez-Battesti, 2005).

It has to be reminded that tutelary regulation refers to the implementation of a frame for production with a view to avoiding an orientation which would not justify public support. Public authorities are here the guardian of producers (associations) and beneficiaries (users). In this framework, evaluation mainly takes the form of a control of the conformity of the results to the prescriptions In the case of competitive regulation, competition mechanisms guarantee the freedom of consumers and producers (at least to some extent, as public authorities can orientate the market through fiscal advantages, reduction of taxes. Evaluation is here similar as a process of standardization. The partnership regulation bases itself on compromises between public and private actors in construction of common goods, whose results from debates and tensions. In this way, evaluation is negotiated in a democratic process and it is the object of controversies and compromises.

In *tutelary regulation*, social utility is defined, codified and controlled by public authorities. Consequently, it is institutionalized and implies a preliminary agreement of the various stakeholders. The creation of decisional authorities, such as the Departmental Councils for Integration through Economic Activity (*Conseils départementaux de l'insertion par l'activité économique*, or CDIAE), provides an opportunity to build a deliberation space. This mode of governance raises questions; in particular, is it able to guarantee to the stakeholders that they will be effectively represented?

In *competitive regulation*, social utility is the product of the individual and rational actions of each economic actor. The implicit compromise on which this form of regulation is based results from the respective performances of each actor; the responsibility for establishing the legal and administrative rules to which SSE entities must conform is left to state authorities. As underlined by Trouvé (2004a), despite their differences, these two forms of regulation and the conceptions of social utility linked hereto share a common trait: they rely on the responsibility and on the coercive power of state authorities and/or territorial organizations. SSE organizations remain, in both cases, auxiliaries of public authorities.

In *contract-based regulation* (Laville and Nyssens, 2001), also referred to as *partnership regulation* (Enjolras, 2008), social utility would be defined in a democratic way by the organization of public debates, envisaged as places where the values conferred on the actions carried out can be confronted. The political mechanisms of decision-making are based on negotiation and deliberation among the various action logics constitutive of the social utility of associative structures (solidarity, democracy, creation, etc.), likely to lead to *"reciprocal instrumentations"* between the association and public authorities (Eme, 2005a: 49).

Conclusion

We have presented a societal balance sheet with an entrepreneurial dimension, mostly oriented towards an *evaluation of the organization* and of the combination of internal and external social utility; we have also presented an evaluation of associations in terms of social utility, which aims, on the one hand, at an *institutional evaluation* of the efficiency of action and of external impacts and, on the other hand, at an *organizational evaluation*, with a more strategic dimension. The tension between these approaches partly results from the confrontation between the state's will to regulate the public policies that it contracts out and the capacity of SSE actors to influence the regulations affecting them, through the elaboration of conventions which have to be built. This tension also translates a division between the market and the non-market economy; between economic and social dimensions; and even between the services provided to the members or the community and a socially responsible behaviour – a distinction which is often operated in France and is politically structuring in most European countries –, in relation with a conception of social utility as a response to market failures and, through this conception, a limiting vision of the field of the SSE. There is here a risk of locking SSE into a narrow definition.

However, this tension is less marked than it might seem. In both cases, the goal is to elaborate tools likely to allow a characterization of the whole set of productive dynamics within SSE organizations and of the specificities of the latter and, more broadly, a reaffirmation of their identity. The societal balance sheet and social utility also share a reluctance to include aggregated external evaluations and a preference for self-evaluation or participative evaluation processes. But such an orientation makes it difficult to compare the results among SSE organizations and, more fundamentally, between SSE organizations and public and private for-profit organizations.

The debate on evaluation is thus directly linked to the definition of the field of the SSE and its mode of regulation and, consequently, to the legitimacy of its organizations and the conditions for ensuring their long-term survival. This debate, which has been going on for some fifteen years, takes its full meaning in the context of the definition of social services of general interest at the European level. Even though the relation with public policies, and in particular the relation between associations and public authorities, has a structuring effect in the framework of the social utility approach, one can ask oneself whether evaluation could be envisaged as a *tool of competitive regulation* through procedures of labelling, certification and access to public markets, and as a justification for fiscal or regulatory advantages in a market context. In other terms, social utility criteria could be used in the future as the frame for defining general interest services in the European sense of the term and could contribute to the selection of services eligible to compete. The risk in this case would be to confine the SSE to an economy of services for those who are "excluded" (from the labour market, housing, market exchange, civic rights, etc.). But there also exists an opportunity to conquer new modalities of service construction, fully associating all the stakeholders in a partnership governance.

References

Alberola, E., Richez-Battesti, N., "De la responsabilité sociale des entreprises: Évaluation du degré d'engagement et d'intégration stratégique", in *La Revue des Sciences de Gestion*, 211-212, 2005, pp. 55-71.

Alternatives Economiques, "L'utilité sociale", *Alternatives Économiques*, Collection Pratique, 2003.

Attarça, M., Jacquot, T., "La représentation de la RSE: une confrontation entre les approches théoriques et les visions managériales", in *Journée développement durable*, AIMS, Aix-en-Provence, 2005.

AVISE, "La mesure de l'utilité sociale; l'évaluation de l'utilité sociale: bibliographie raisonnée", mars-avril, www.aviser.org, 2003.

Bastide, L., Garrabe, M., Fas, C., "Identité de l'économie sociale et de l'économie solidaire", in *RECMA*, 289, 2001, pp. 19-27.

Boltanski, L., Thévenot, L., *De la justification*, Paris, Gallimard, 1991.

Bruntland, G. H., *Notre avenir à tous, Assemblée générale des Nations-Unies*, 1987.

Capron, M., Quairel-Lanoizelée, F., *Mythes et réalités de l'entreprise responsable: acteurs, enjeux stratégies*, Paris, La Découverte, 2004.

CCE, *Livre vert, promouvoir un cadre européen pour la responsabilité sociale des entreprises*, Bruxelles, 2001.

CCE, *La responsabilité sociale des entreprises: une contribution des entreprises au développement durable*, DG. Emploi et Affaires sociales, Bruxelles, 2002.

Clarkson, M.B.E., "A Stakeholder Framework for Analysing and Evaluating Corporate Social Performance", in *Academy of Management Review*, 20, 1995, pp. 92-117.

CNVA, *L'utilité sociale des associations et ses conséquences en matière économique, fiscale et financière*, Paris, 1995.

Commissariat Général du Plan, *Évaluer les politiques publiques*, Paris, La Documentation Française, 1986.

Commissariat Général du Plan, *Les politiques sociales transversales: une méthodologie d'évaluation de leurs effets locaux*, Paris, La Documentation Française, 1986.

DIES, *Guide de l'évaluation*, Paris, Ministère des Affaires Sociales, du Travail et de la Solidarité, 2002.

Duclos, H., *Guide pratique d'évaluation de l'utilité sociale*, Paris, AVISE et Culture et Promotion, 2007.

Eme, B., "Gouvernance territoriale et mouvements d'économie sociale et solidaire", in *RECMA*, 2005a, p. 42-55.

Eme, B., *La question de l'autonomie de l'ESS par rapport à la sphère publique*, LISE-CNRS/MIRE-DIES, 2005b.

Enjolras, B., "Régimes de gouvernance et intérêt général", in B. Enjolras (dir.), *Gouvernance et intérêt général dans les services sociaux et de santé*, Brussels, P.I.E. Peter Lang, 2008.

Enjolras, B., *Le marché providence: aide à domicile, politique sociale et création d'emploi*, Paris, Desclée de Brouwer, 1995.

Fraisse, L., "La dimension politique de l'économie solidaire", in Laville J.-L. (dir.), in *L'économie solidaire, une perspective internationale*, Paris, Hachette Littératures, 2007.

Fraisse, L., "Utilité sociale et économie solidaire: un rapport ambivalent au cœur de la reconfiguration des régulations publiques", in X. Engels, M. Hely, A. Peyrin et H. Trouvé (dir.), in *De l'intérêt général à l'utilité sociale: la reconfiguration de l'action publique entre État, associations et participation citoyenne*, Coll. Logiques sociales, Paris, L'Harmattan, 2006.

Gadrey, J., "L'utilité sociale", in Laville J.-L., Catani A.D., *Dictionnaire de l'autre économie*, Paris, Desclée de Brouwer, 2005.

Gadrey, J., L'utilité sociale des organisations de l'économie sociale et solidaire: une mise en perspective sur la base des travaux récents", *Rapport de synthèse*, Paris, MIRE-DIES, Dynamiques solidaires, 2003.

Gendron, C., *Envisager la responsabilité sociale dans le cadre des régulations portées par les nouveaux mouvements sociaux économiques*, Chaire en responsabilité sociale et développement durable, Collection Recherche, No. 01, Montréal, UQAM, 2002.

Greffe, X., "L'évaluation des activités publiques", in *Recherches économiques et sociales*, 13-14, Paris, 1985.

Guide de l'Évaluation, *Circulaire du 1er décembre relative aux conventions pluriannuelles d'objectifs entre l'État et les associations*, Paris, DIES, 2002.

Henriques, I., Sadorsky, P., "The Relationship between Environmental Commitment and Managerial Importance of Stakeholder Importance", in *Academy of Management Journal*, 42, 1999, pp. 97-99.

Lascoumes, P., "Gouverner par les instruments ou comment s'instrumente l'action publique", in J. Lagroye (dir.), *La politisation*, Paris, Belin, 2003.

Latour B., *Changer de société. Refaire de la sociologie*, Paris, La Découverte, 2001.

Laville, J.-L., Nyssens, M., *Les services sociaux, entre associations, État et marché: l'aide aux personnes âgées*, Paris, La Découverte, 2001.

Lipietz, A., *Pour le tiers secteur: l'économie sociale et solidaire*, Paris, La Découverte, 2001.

Mitchell, R.K., Agle, B.R., Wood, D.J., "Toward a Theory of Stakeholder Identification and Salience: Defining the Principle of Who and What Really Counts", in *Academy of Management Review*, 22, 4, 1997.

Nogues, H., "Économie sociale et solidaire; quelques réflexions à propos de l'utilité sociale", in *RECMA*, 290, 2003, pp. 27-40.

Perret, B., *L'évaluation de l'économie sociale. Éléments de problématique*, Conférence au Groupe de travail Méthodes et indicateurs d'évaluation de l'économie sociale, Paris, CIRIEC, réunion tenue à l'Hôtel de ville, 10 février 2006.

Perret, B., *L'évaluation des politiques publiques*, Collection Repères, Paris, La Découverte, 2001.

Richez-Battesti, N., "Évaluer la production associative par les pouvoirs publics: du contrôle à la coproduction des critères?", in X. Engels, M. Hely, A. Peyrin, et H. Trouvé (dir.), *De l'intérêt général à l'utilité sociale: la reconfiguration de l'action publique entre État, associations et participation citoyenne*, Collection Logiques sociales, Paris, L'Harmattan, 2006.

Richez-Battesti, N., "Les Régimes d'État-Providence et économie sociale et solidaire en Europe: quelle régulation pour le modèle conservateur français?", Communication à First European Conference of ISTR and EMES, Concepts of the Third Sector: The European Debate, CNAM, Paris, 27-29 avril 2005.

Richez-Battesti, N. *et al.* "ESS, territoires et proximité", in *RECMA*, 296, 2005, pp. 8-25.

Richez-Battesti, N., Gianfaldoni, P., *Réseaux économiques et utilité sociale: évaluation de l'accompagnement et du financement de la création des très petites entreprises en région PACA*, Aix-en-Provence, CEFI, 2003.

Rosanvallon, P., *Le modèle politique français. La société civile contre le jacobinisme de 1789 à nos jours*, Paris, Seuil, 2004.

Rousseau, F., *L'Évaluation de l'utilité sociale: une injonction de la puissance publique*, Working paper, CIRIEC, 2007.

Sainsaulieu, R. (dir.), *L'entreprise une affaire de société*, Paris, PFNSP, 1990.

Sainsaulieu, R., *L'identité au travail*, Paris, PFNsP, 1988, 1re ed. 1977.

Thévenot, L., *L'action au pluriel. Sociologie des régimes d'engagement*, Paris, La Découverte, 2006.

Thoenig, J.-C., Duran, P., "L'état et la gestion publiques territoriale", in *Revue Française de Science Politique*, No. 4, 1996, pp. 580-623.

Trouvé, H., *L'utilité sociale: des pratiques aux représentations – Une étude de cas dans le champ de l'insertion par l'activité économique*, Thèse de doctorat de Sciences économiques, soutenue à l'Université Paris 1 Panthéon-Sorbonne, 2007.

Trouvé, H., Hély, M., Peyrin, A., Engels, X. (dir.), *De l'intérêt général à l'utilité sociale? La reconfiguration de l'intervention publique entre État, associations et participation citoyenne*, Paris, L'Harmattan, Collection Logiques Sociales, 2006.

Trouvé, H., *La dynamique des productions associatives: synthèse des travaux existants*, Dossier d'études de la CNAF, 68, 2005.

Trouvé, H., "Les politiques contractuelles dans le champ associatif: gouvernance et partenariat", in D. Girard, *Solidarités collectives*, Paris, L'Harmattan, 2004, pp. 261-275.

Vienney, C., *Socio-économie des organisations coopératives*, 2 tomes, Paris, CIEM, 1980.

Viveret, P., *Reconsidérer la Richesse, Rapport d'étape de la Mission Nouveaux facteurs de richesses*, Paris, Secrétariat d'État à l'Économie Solidaire, 2001.

Wood, D., "Corporate Social Performance Revisited", in *Academy of Management Review*, 16, 4, 1991, pp. 691-718.

Appendix 1. Synthetic Presentation of the Results from the Grid of Analysis

	Societal Balance Sheet	Social Utility Imposed by the Funding Bodies	Social Utility Evaluated Voluntarily
Request for evaluation	Internal, sometimes encouraged by a group or federation	Imposed by the funding body (or bodies) with a prescribed frame-work which differs according to the funding body (no coordination)	Public actors, federations or sector of activity (external request) Militant organization (internal request)
Carrying out of evaluation	Mixed, in agreement with the methodology of the societal balance sheet	Internal, by the salaried workers (managers) or by an external expert	Internal, by the salaried workers and managers
Participation of the evaluated actors	Participation of all the stakeholders	The actors evaluate, but without a participative process	The stakeholders participate in the evaluation
Level of evaluation	The organization	The funded programme	The programme and the organization
Goal of evaluation	Generating an evolution of the model of governance to combine values and practices: tool supporting decision-making	Immediate results and direct effects, even return	Strategic dimension, medium- and long-term effects and social performance
Tools and method of evaluation	Questionnaire and interviews	Questionnaire	Diversified: participant observation, interviews, discussion groups
Types of indicators	Diversified, mostly quantitative and linked to the organization	Quantitative, diversified and not stable	Rather qualitative
Evaluation criteria	Absence of pre-conceived norms	No evaluation of the gap to the norm, but the prescription can be identical to the norm	No reference to the norm, but identification of specific indicators and verification of their implementation
Periodicity	Every 4 years?	Every year	/

The Evaluation of the Social Economy in Quebec, with regard to Stakeholders, Mission and Organizational Identity

Marie J. BOUCHARD

*Professor and Director of the Canada Research Chair
on the Social Economy, Université du Québec à Montréal (Canada)*

Introduction[1]

Quebec's experience in evaluating the Social Economy is probably not very different from that of other parts of the world that have had a similar type and rhythm of development over the past few decades. The emerging Social Economy is growing substantially with regard to the supply of general interest social services. However, the Social Economy in the more mature sectors of activity is facing strong competition both in the markets as well as in terms of social and environmental responsibility.

The Quebec model, however, stands apart from the rest due to the important presence of the Social Economy within its economic structure, as well as due to support from the State and its partners, particularly unions and financial institutions. Even if the Social Economy seems more established than ever, mutual and public recognition of this economy remains fragmented, much like the compartmentation of public policies *vis-à-vis* these issues and the tensions that exist regarding a model of development. Evaluation, in this context, takes on a new

---

[1] This text was written with the assistance of Valérie Michaud, N'Deye Sine Tine and Sambou N'Diaye, doctoral students at the University of Quebec at Montreal, and Élise Desjardins, a research professional at CRISES (*Centre de recherche sur les innovations sociales*). This research was in part made possible by the financial support of the Canada Research Chairs Programme and the *Fonds québécois de la recherche sur la Société et la Culture*. We wish to thank the members of Ciriec for their comments with regard to the preliminary versions of this text and Karen Simon for its translation to English.

importance, acting as an interface between the sectors of Social Economy and its different stakeholders.

In an attempt to observe current tendencies with respect to evaluating the Social Economy in Quebec, we have chosen those factors that allow us to identify and underline certain specificities of the Social Economy. The cases we have studied show, *a priori*, a variety of evaluation tools almost as vast as the number of sectors of activity. Although we have grouped together the common representations of these different evaluation tools, we can still associate different types of evaluation with different visions of the Social Economy. The evaluation formats information differently according to the institutional context in which it takes place and in keeping with the expectations of those who decide and act with regard to the Social Economy. But the evaluation also influences the definition and the formatting of the Social Economy.

The first part of this paper gives a rapid overview of the state of the Social Economy in Quebec by summarizing some key elements of the context in which it is currently evolving (details are furnished in the Annex 1). The second part describes different practices of evaluation by attempting to identify the principal tendencies. Because our interest is the specificity of the Social Economy, we have concentrated our attention on the evaluation tools of the organizations and sectors of the Social Economy. In the third part, evaluation of the Social Economy is explored in relation to different visions of the Social Economy, according to whether it serves as a palliative for developmental errors, as a predictor and precursor with regard to new social expectations, or as a producer of new standards that could potentially reorient the model of development.

1. Context

The Social Economy has developed in Quebec, as elsewhere, in a vast number of sectors of activity. Mutual associations, *Caisses populaires* (Credit Unions) and agricultural cooperatives have existed for over one hundred years. The Mouvement *Desjardins* is today still the most important and most complete (diversified) financial institution in Quebec. The agricultural cooperatives (ex. the *Fédérée* and *Agropur*) and the forestry cooperatives continue to be strategic actors in the sector, along with numerous other new cooperatives that have appeared over the last thirty years, particularly in the areas of work, housing, schooling, etc. There are many non-profit organizations (NPO), and those that have an economic finality can be found in a diversity of sectors such as social services, leisure and social tourism, culture, housing for the elderly, etc.

In addition, since the 1980s, as elsewhere, numerous small organizations have emerged to answer new needs for services, such as childcare, assisted housing, domestic aid, job insertion through economic activity, community services, etc. These can be in the form of cooperatives or NPOs, the frontier between the two types of organizations being less clear than before as cooperatives develop into multistakeholders organizations and NPOs into social enterprises. In other words, cooperatives, which had been created exclusively in the market world and were principally oriented toward the interest of their members (mutual interest), have been moving toward non-market and general interest activities. A new judicial form, the solidarity cooperative (two or three member categories) can now be found in the areas of health and community services.[2] Large cooperatives and mutual associations have had to adapt to markets that have become very competitive, by working hard to become more socially and environmentally responsible. The NPOs, which were concentrated in the non-market sectors of activity and sought to satisfy the needs of non-members, often economically disadvantaged persons (general interest), are increasingly developing market activities, either to support their social mission or to offer services to target populations. More and more community organizations are functioning with a mixture of resources, including fixing prices to make their services affordable for users. Subsidies for the mission are in part replaced by service contracts with the State (quasi-markets). New solidarity financial tools have appeared to support the development and capitalization of Social Economy enterprises with respect to their organizational form and their values: *Caisse d'économie solidaire, Réseau d'investissement social du Québec, Fiducie du Chantier de l'économie sociale*, etc.

Public policies (of the Canadian and Quebec governments) have, at different times, accompanied the development of the Social Economy. In Quebec, three models of development have been observed at one time or another over the past forty years (Lévesque, 2004). Still, the Quebec model has taken on two principal forms: the fordist or providentialist model (1960-1980), characterized by a *hierarchical and public governance*, and the partnerial model (1981-2003), reflecting a *distributed or simply partnerial governance*. The partnerial model (1981-2003) was the result of a compromise between the State and civil society. Practices then became relatively institutionalized and the model stabilized. Just recently, the current conjuncture has led us to believe that the Quebec model could radically become transformed into a neo-

---

[2] A solidarity cooperative is the Quebec equivalent of the Italian solidarity cooperative (*cooperativa sociale*) or the French cooperative society of collective interest (*société cooperative d'intérêt collectif*).

liberal type model (2004-...), whose method of governance would be based on the market through the PPPs (Public-Private Partnerships) and on consultation with individual citizens randomly chosen to participate in diverse forums, thus challenging the mechanisms of consultation with collective actors. This model tends toward a *competitive market govern-ance* (Bouchard, Lévesque, St-Pierre, 2008; Enjolras, 2008).

This brief overview of the context in which the Social Economy of Quebec has evolved over the last four decades is certainly too sche-matic. Still, it allows us to see that the dynamics at work lead to differ-ent configurations where social dynamics, economic conjuncture, institutional and political environment and the organizational dimen-sions of enterprises all intersect. The configurations influence the processes of creating and developing Social Economy enterprises, but they also influence the expectations of the different parties concerned *vis-à-vis* the Social Economy and the role it must play. Consequently, they influence the "performance" of the Social Economy with regard to these expectations.

2. Principal Tendencies in Evaluating the Social Economy

Observing the different methods used to define and evaluate the So-cial Economy in Quebec reveals the diversity of practices as well as their anchorage in different cultures of evaluation. These cultures may be associated with different characteristics of Social Economy enter-prises, with their activities, the publics they target, the resources they mobilize.

We have examined evaluation tools, guidebooks and manuals, sec-tor-based pictures, social indicator charts, government and university studies.[3] Our first observation is that the objectives covered by the evaluations contrast vastly from one document to the other, each evalua-tion being based on dimensions linked to the nature of the principal activities of the organization or to demands stemming from the deci-sion-making body in charge of the evaluation (usually the funding party). A second observation is that the methodology used is rarely explicit with regard to the hypotheses that underlie the exercise. Al-though this overview of the evaluation of the Social Economy in Que-bec is somewhat rapid, we can still distinguish three categories of

---

[3] This inventory is not exhaustive but has allowed us to consult evaluation documents in 17 sectors of activity: domestic aid, the food industry, communications, early childhood centres, culture, community kitchens, adapted enterprises, reintegration companies, forests, housing, leisure and social tourism, perinatality, waste sorting and recycling, funeral services, business services, schools, workers cooperatives, solidarity financing.

initiatives (or basic models) according to whether the evaluation seeks: to produce an assessment of results, a social assessment, an environmental assessment or an assessment of social responsibility; to equip organizations to be able to promote the specificity of their mission; or to recognize the specificity of the forms of organization and modes of action of the Social Economy. The objectives evaluated, the evaluation indicators, the openness to external evaluation all vary according to the type of activity (production or service, be it principally market or non-market) (Bouchard, Bourque and Lévesque, 2001), the type of resources involved (monetary, non-monetary) (Eme and Laville, 1994), the type of public targeted (mutualistic, altruistic) (Gui, 1991) and the stage of life cycle of the sector of activity or organization (emerging, mature).

2.1 Evaluation in Relation to Objectives

One type of evaluation seeks to provide information with regard to targeted objectives and to furnish explanations to stakeholders outside of the organization. Thus, organizations whose activities are principally market dominant generally produce evaluations of results and impact. Those that count more heavily on monetary resources and whose activity is aimed at their members tend to equip themselves with evaluation tools that emphasize the social dimension of their mode of production or distribution of surplus. Cooperative organizations in mature or growing sectors often produce social and environmental reports whose size and content vary from one organization to the other.

In regard to the activities of primary and secondary sectors (forestry, food industry), assessments are often social and environmental. For example, forestry cooperatives adopt environmental policies in accordance with ISO 14001 certification. Another example, the *Coopérative fédérée*, which groups together 97 agricultural establishments, has an environmental policy and produces a social evaluation that, in particular, shows the economic and territorial impact of its activities in Quebec. It has also recently done a survey on the psychological health of agricultural workers. The same tendency is found in the mature sectors of economic services to members. The *Caisses* and the *Mouvement Desjardins*, the mutual company SSQ Groupe financier, and the *Fédération des cooperatives scolaires du Québec* publish a social responsibility report or a social report. The *Caisse d'économie solidaire Desjardins* (CECOSOL or Desjardins Solidarity Credit Union) produced a report for 2008 inspired by the Global Reporting Initiative (GRI)[4] entitled *Écosolidaire dans la transformation sociale*. In 2008, the CECOSOL

---

[4] See the site of the Global Reporting Initiative http://www.globalreporting.org.

was the instigating force for the first World Social and Solidarity Based Finance Summit.

A more recent stakeholder in the enlarging family of the Social Economy, Fondaction CSN,[5] has recently opted for the production of a durable development report following the standards of the Global Reporting Initiative. In this way, Social Economy financial enterprises could be pioneers with regard to reports on social responsibility and durable and "solidarity" development (Gendron, 2006).

Some initiatives seek to equip *the entire group of SE organizations*. This is with a view toward facilitating reporting on their social performance and showing that they are meeting – or in fact anticipating – the expectations of society, thereby justifying that they are benefiting from public or private support. They seek to develop generic indicators of "social profitability", social impact, involvement in the community, etc. These initiatives come from just about everywhere, ranging from a paragovernmental organization such as the *Comité sectoriel de main-d'oeuvre de l'action communautaire autonome et de l'économie sociale*[6] to an association of cooperatives such as the Canadian Co-operative Association,[7] and including a *Centre local de développement*[8] (local development center) somewhere in the middle. Other initiatives aim to show the structuring impact of a sub-group of social economy enterprises of the Social Economy. For example, in 2004, the *Conseil québécois de la coopération et de la mutualité* created a five-year plan whose principal objective was to reinforce the impact of cooperatives in rural communities affected by demographic decline. In 2009, the five-year plan announced three objectives: demographic change, durable development and occupation of territory. These objectives included the goal that federations would create a durable development policy by 2012, that by 2014, 50% of cooperatives and mutual associations would also

---

5   Fondaction, the *Fonds de développement de la CSN pour la coopération et l'emploi* was created in 1996 by a workers union, the *Centrale des syndicats nationaux* (CSN). This fund seeks to facilitate access to retirement savings while still contributing to maintain or create employment and stimulate the economy of Quebec. The fund also has the specific mission of being available to companies registered in a process of participative management and to Social Economy companies (cooperatives or other). The fund also encourages investment in companies that are concerned with the environment and with more durable development. See the site: http://www.fondaction. com.

6   See the site of the CSMO-ÉSAC: http://www.csmoesac.qc.ca.

7   See their activities concerning community involvement and social responsibility on their site: http://www.coopscanada.coop.

8   Patenaude, J. *La mesure de la rentabilité sociale*, Sorel-Tracy, CLD du Bas-Richelieu, 2004. Available on the site of the RQIIAC: www.rqiiac.qc.ca/fr/liens_outils/doc/rentab_sociale.DOC.

have implemented such a policy, and that the movement would produce an initial "Social Responsibility and Cooperative Report" in 2014.

Among the organizations of *emerging sectors*,[9] we can group together the organizations that offer *support services to economic development* (local development, community development, solidarity financing, support for the creation and maintenance of jobs, etc.). These organizations remain linked to the State but also to the market. They are often supported by a diversity of funders and financial sources: several government levels, a number of ministries, programmes, private donations, the sale of products and services, etc. Although they are subject to public policies, a part of their services or products are charged to users or clients. Their governance is often plural (unions, employers, users, civil society), especially when their activities seek to impact a public external to the organization.

The dimensions evaluated extend from the micro (organizational effectiveness) to the meso (impact on the community). The objectives evaluated generally correspond to measurable results according to pre-established standards, either with respect to quantity (number of actions, participants, networks, jobs created or maintained, subsidies, mobilized capital and human resources, cost of products and services, socioeconomic services of clients reached, socio-economic impact, consulting process, etc.), or to quality (sectors of activity, types of products and services, their complementarity, types of skills and training, organizational performance, type of leadership, regional mobilization, etc.). The evaluation may have a normative finality, serving to identify "good practices", or it may anticipate satisfying new social expectations.

2.2 Evaluation According to Social Mission

A second type of evaluation seeks to furnish organizations with evaluation tools adapted to the specificity of their social mission, in particular those activities that are predominantly non-market. In the area of *collective consumption* (health, social services, education), the organizations enter into a quasi-exclusive relationship with the State, and the way they function is then generally supported by a single funder, such as a government ministry. This government department may dictate standards seeking to homogenize a service and assure its quality (early childhood centres, for example). In other cases of activities complementary to those of the public network, several organizations currently submit to an evaluation procedure implemented by an accredi-

---

[9] Although several of these organizations were born from the changes that took place in the 1970s, when comparing them to companies that have been established for a long time, one often uses the expression "new social economy".

tation agency.[10] This external evaluation procedure is identical to the one mainly used in public establishments, which is based on results (client satisfaction and organizational climate) and on procedure quality (client service and organizational performance). Even if this evaluation is still a voluntary measure, more and more organizations in the sectors of personal services (domestic aid or youth guidance, for example) are moving in this direction.

In the areas of *mutual proximity services* (small work cooperatives, housing, self-help and mutual support groups, etc.) or *interpersonal relations* (pre-employability, socio-economic job reinsertion, cultural integration), the activities depend on a mixture of public, market and non-monetary resources. Tensions may arise between the applicant of the external evaluation and the organization. Even if the evaluation cannot resolve these tensions, it may at lease facilitate the negotiation of the space and objectives evaluated. In the first example, the evaluation tools may be conjointly conceived by the applicant of the evaluation (a public authority) and by a network of Social Economy enterprises or community organizations. This is the case in the sector of job insertion through economic activity, where the development of a tool is created by means of ministry representatives (funders), representatives of integration enterprises and a lead agency specialized in Social Economy. Two categories of evaluated objectives have emerged from this sector: action (short-term evaluation of participants) and activity (evaluation of long-term impact on the community). Four evaluation tools have been developed: an assessment of new entrants or resources (human, material, financial); an analysis of implementation or procedures (quality, conformity, achievements compared to objectives, selection of participants, work climate, etc.); effectiveness (achievement of the short-term objectives); impact (long-term effects, impact on the community). The external evaluator can be chosen by the work insertion enterprise and the participants are included in the evaluation exercise.

Another example is that of community organizations that propose *alternative modes* of meeting social demands. The targets of these non-profit organizations are more global, covering a group of intangible effects ranging from the accession to power of individuals and collectivities (IFDEC, 1992) up to social change (Jalbert *et al.*, s.d.). One of the crucial stakes for these organizations is their autonomy. Here, evalua-

---

[10] For example, the *Conseil québécois d'agrément*, a private non-profit organization created by the establishment of networks (public) and financially supported by them and by the Ministère de la Santé et des Services sociaux. Its board of directors consists, in equal parts, of representatives from professional associations, organizations representing the interests of users and establishment associations. See the site: http://www.agrement-quebecois.ca.

tion is in particular a means to measure how the services offered correspond to the very specific needs of users; it must therefore be carried
out according to the identity of each organization. In Quebec, some of
these organizations identify with an "autonomous community action
movement" that has negotiated a framework of recognition and evaluation with the public authority. This negotiation has led to excluding
certain features from the external evaluation such as the mission, the
relevance of the organization, the models of intervention and the particular practices of these organizations, the soundness of the choice of
needs and populations to be served, internal structure and organization,
the satisfaction of workers and volunteers, implementation in the community, complementarity with the public network (*Comité ministériel
sur l'évaluation*, 1995). It would be the internal evaluation exercise,
then, which would defin – or redefine – the mission of the organization.

If the evaluation in this case deals with the indicators of action efficiency, or an accountability of sorts (quality, impact, user satisfaction,
functioning of the organization), the effectiveness of their method of
intervention, which is the underpinning of their legitimacy, remains
subject to tensions between the organization and the applicant of the
external evaluation. Tensions arise when public institutions develop
partnerships with these groups, bringing into question the scope of their
autonomy when the time comes to report to the public provider of funds.
This is the case of the current reform in the public health system, which
relies more and more on a partnership with community groups but still
leans towards a tighter control of these community groups by public
establishments.

2.3 Evaluation According to Organizational and Institutional Specificity

Several recent studies show the intention to develop "*generic*" indicators for the Social Economy. One of these studies attempts to measure
the specific effects of SE enterprises. The results show that these businesses provide services that could not easily be replaced by other types
of enterprises (public or private), that they mobilize partnerships between stakeholders of civil society and the State and that they adapt the
offer of services to local needs while still falling within the general
objectives of certain public policies (Comeau, *et al.*, 2001). A proposal
for an evaluation tool has also been suggested concerning Social Economy proximity services, which establishes a link between the dimensions of evaluation and theoretic choices relative to the proximity
services and to the Social Economy (Jetté, Comeau and Dumais, 2001).
However, aside from two exceptions, the evaluation tools used by the
organizations and sectors still do not usually place much importance on

the specific dimensions of the Social Economy (Bouchard, Bourque and Lévesque, 2001). The first of these exceptions is the *Bilan de conformité coopérative* (Cooperative Conformity Report) developed by the Québec-Apalaches Cooperative of Regional Development (2006). Based on the seven cooperative principles of the International Cooperative Alliance, the report consists of three types of observations dealing with the collection of information, with decision-making and with the implementation of cooperative principles. The second exception is the Guide for Analysis of Social Economy Enterprises (2003), a tool created to orient the decision making process of social economy financial partners. This guide is based on the double economic and social nature of the Social Economy enterprise. These two examples of evaluation tools target organizational and institutional specificity of the social economy. The Guide is widely distributed in Quebec's social economy milieus and has a structuring potential for the Social Economy in its stages of creation, development and consolidation. One particularity of this type of tool is that *risk* as well as *standardization of evaluation methodology* is *shared* with other financial partners.

Following the Economic and Employment Summit, the *Réseau d'investissement social du Québec* (RISQ) was created in 1997[11] with the aim of providing to Social Economy enterprises capitalization funding that would otherwise not be easily available.[12] Projects financed by the RISQ are also supported by other types of actors, with various missions (public subsidizing, financial services, development capital, consulting expertise) and of diverse nature (Ministry, public enterprises, workers funds, patient capital balanced funds, financial cooperatives, consulting firms). The Guide was created by a collective of solidarity financing experts who often participate in projects but always respect their own logic. These partners discussed pertinent indicators and criteria over a long period of time in order to evaluate risks and identify the principal mitigation factors in Social Economy enterprises.[13]

---

[11] Then called the *Fonds de développement de l'économie sociale*.

[12] The RISQ is a non-profit risk capital funded by underwriters from the private sector and the cooperative movement, and by the government of Quebec. It makes patient capital investments (low interest rate, moratorium on capital, long-term reimbursement), either for start-up, consolidation or growth of Social Economy enterprises. A part of the funds serves to finance training and accompaniment activities for directors. The RISQ is not a financial actor like the others; it supplies "friendly capital", meaning "it accompanies the enterprise and follows it closely" (Élise Tessier, in Rouzier, Mendell, Lévesque, 2003: 34).

[13] Focus group meeting with 5 representatives of these organizations in Quebec City in the offices of the *Caisse d'économie solidaire*, July 2004.

The guide develops a series of indicators that help judge, *ex ante*, the viability of the projects and, *in process*, follow up on the specific indicators for each one by means of an operating report. The indicators are adapted to the organizational form (cooperative or NPO) and the criteria are adjusted to the mission and means of action of the organization. One of the particularities of this tool is the *logical* (or explanatory) *model* in support of the investment decision, in which the viability of the enterprise systematically refers back to associative viability and vice versa.[14] Thus, the 10 indicators used have three dimensions: economic and financial (quality of the asset, financial structuring, long-term viability, operations, market), organizational and managerial (human resources, board of directors, management team), and social (community anchorage, social finality).[15] A case file might thus be recommended for financing on the basis of criteria that would not be taken into account by another financial intermediary.[16]

In addition to financial partners sharing the same tool, a process of *outreach training* has been introduced in supportive living environments for Social Economy entrepreneurships (regional development cooperatives, local development centres, sector federations). Shared utilization by financial partners, by support organizations for enterprises and by public stakeholders, has *structuring effects* on the definition, methods of financing and development, as well as on the practices of Social Economy organizations. Several social economy promoters – solidarity financiers, expert consulting groups – now use the Guide in the evaluation and follow-up of their interventions, particularly those having contributed to the production of the tool: *Caisse d'économie solidaire Desjardins* (whose portfolio is principally made up of social economy enterprises), *Filaction* (a branch of *Fondaction*), *Investissement Québec* (the financial "arm" of the government), diverse community economic development corporations, leading edge groups (*MCE Conseil, Pythagore*), etc. A sort of "community of practice" is thus

---

[14] See C. Vienney, quoted by J.-G. Desforges in his analysis of the cooperative's modalities of development (Desforges and Vienney, 1980).

[15] Social finality is described as corresponding to the "4 Ps": Predominance of the person over the capital; Provision of individual and collective management; Process of democratic decision-making; Production of socially useful goods and services.

[16] For example, even with a relatively weak financial structure, a favourable decision may be rendered by taking into account the quality of the support of community partners (especially follow-up and supervision) and the degree of involvement of the participating members, two mitigating risk factors that the Social Economy enterprise is able to present. The example of the Fonds de solidarité also shows that the social assessment tool becomes a profitability factor for the enterprise, diminishing the risk of social conflict (Lévesque *et al.*, 2000).

created.[17] This experience has contributed to what has recently created another fund of $52.8 million in patient capital for the Social Economy, generated as a result of government financing (federal and provincial) and contributions from financial institutions (*Fonds de solidarité FTQ, Fondaction CSN*).[18] The RISQ has received the mandate for analyzing funding requests for the purpose of recommendation to the board of trustees. Following an experiment of the Community-University Research Alliance (CURA) on social economy research partnering,[19] different Quebec participants decided to form a network of solidarity financing.

3. Evaluation of the Social Economy and Development Dynamics

Evaluation methods and indicators used reveal the expectations the Social Economy in terms of its role in the dynamics of development. Different visions are possible. Without claiming that there is always a correspondence between a modality of evaluation and a vision of the Social Economy, we can still see that some evaluation tools are better adapted for indicating specific positions. We can summarize these positions according to three visions of the Social Economy's place and role in the dynamics of development, according to whether it is palliative for the market and the State, complementary or alternative with regard to the dominant model of development, or whether it constitutes a new framework of development normativity.

3.1. Palliative Social Economy

In the narrow view, the Social Economy serves as a palliative to fill in missing gaps in the market and the State. In other words it counters the effects of "bad development". In the *neo-liberal* view of development governance, the instruments of public policy are contracts or

---

[17] See also examples of international collaboration: the *Bourse aux financements solidaires*, in France (*Partenaires de l'analyse financière pour des outils solaires –* PAFOUS); the Secretariat of the National Association of Workers in Self-Managed Enterprises (ANTEAG) in Brazil (*Partenaires pour des échanges solidaires –* PESO).

[18] The initial capitalization of this trust comes from several partners. Canada Economic Development allots $22.8 million, the *Fonds de solidarité FTQ* invests $12 million, the government of Quebec injects $10 million and *Fondaction*, the *Fonds de développement de la CSN pour la coopération et l'emploi*, contributes $8 million (*Chantier de l'économie sociale, Press release*, January 11, 2006).

[19] The Community-University Research Alliance in Social Economy is a partenarial research infrastructure. One of its partenarial application projects is responsible finance.

quasi-markets (Enjolras, 2008). Evaluation uses relatively standard tools to measure cost efficiency of activities or programmes, without taking into account the specificity of the Social Economy. The representative decision makers of users or citizens have no legal right to participate in the evaluation. The tools are relatively standard and essentially serve to measure the difference between objectives targeted and those achieved. These evaluations are the pending factor of accountability of Social Economy organizations that use collective resources (Perret, chap. 2).

This is also the case of social reports with an instrumental aim. These reports show respect for social obligations or those that, if not respected, would affect the reputation of the organization and/or confidence and loyalty toward it. These are primary stakeholders, in other words those who can directly affect the activity of the organization (clients, suppliers, workers, funding agencies). The evaluation is a strategic issue with regard to external resources on which the organization depends (Spear, 2009), whether these resources be tangible (financing) or intangible (reputation, image).

3.2. The Social Economy as a Complement or Alternative

In the *Fordist-Welfare State* development model, the Social Economy is perceived as complementary to public action and market mechanisms. Public policy contributes toward delimiting the sphere of activity of the Social Economy, and the evaluation exercise reinforces a vision of the Social Economy with regard to objectives targeted (job creation, fight against poverty, development of territory, etc.). The evaluation then serves to orient, supervise or control the activities and practices of the organizations with a view toward reducing the possible gaps between expectations and results, and toward showing their social usefulness (Gadrey, 2005; Richez-Battesti *et al.*, 2006). These tools combine typical approaches of the first, second and third generations of evaluation, which aim respectively at measuring, explaining and contextualizing the results obtained, compared to the objectives targeted (Guba and Lincoln, 1989). The relationships between objectives and results can be found in the explanatory models that presume that links have already been demonstrated between cause and effect (e.g. the creation of jobs reduces poverty, all things else being equal…). The logical models are, as a result, rarely explicit.

The normative aim of the evaluation, often implicit when it is a question of using standard indicators, can on the other hand be part of a deliberate strategy of establishing alternative norms of efficiency and performance or of even creating new standards, showing that the Social Economy organizations could perform better than other forms of enterprises on the social and environmental levels. In this way, the evaluation can outline the particular responses furnished by the Social Economy organizations to new social aspirations, one of these being durable development. The evaluation becomes a tool for individual and collective consciousness of the resources and limits of the organization, an exercise in democracy, and even an exercise in political positioning with regard to external evaluation applicants.

One of the methods often used to achieve these ends is the participative and negotiated evaluation, in particular placing the person (member, worker, user, recipient or citizen) and the community (pertinent environment) in the centre of the evaluation exercise. The decisions concerning the evaluation objectives are made with the relevant actors within an approach where the direction of the action is debated to take into consideration the different points of view. Here the evaluation has a cognitive function and serves to reinforce organizational autonomy. This type of evaluation, called "fourth generation", falls within a constructivist approach where the actors are invited to negotiate the direction of their action in a perspective of pluralism and complexity (Guba and Lincoln, 1989). This method is characteristic of several important experiments in the landscape of Quebec Social Economy and, in general, in evaluation practices developed in Canada (Borys, *et al.*, 2005). The *partenarial* model of development governance in Quebec has been particularly successful (Bouchard, Lévesque and St-Pierre, 2008) since the 1980s.

3.3. The Social Economy Displaying a New Normative Framework

The evaluation can also be a time for the social construction of another normative framework that would be specific to the mission, the organizational forms and the institutional rules of the Social Economy. A third modality of evaluation of the Social Economy aims to establish not so much common indicators as a *logical model* of the interpretation of results according to the specificity of the Social Economy. Although we have only observed several evaluations tools of this type, it remains interesting to analyze it from the point of view of an evaluation grid specific to the Social Economy.

The Guide for Analysis of Social Economy Enterprises (2003) is principally used for judging social economy market projects using criteria that are both part of the world market and the civic world. In the case of capital development funds devoted to the Social Economy (particularly the RISQ and the *Fiducie du Chantier de l'économie sociale*), risk sharing can be done in various ways: between the different funders whose nature is diverse (private, market, public, social economy) or between the solidarity financier and the Social Economy enterprise, since the latter must reimburse capital and interest within a given period of time. In this model, the co-dependency of the social and economic dimensions of given activities leads to arbitration between the criteria of standard evaluation (economic, financial, organizational and managerial) and criteria specifically adapted to the Social Economy (community solidarity, social finality, associative governance, etc.).

This would be one of the characteristics of the "5th generation" evaluation, which is more political and where the evaluation is deliberative (Bouchard and Fontan, 1998). Here it plays the role of *interpreter* for the "common worth" (or *"grandeur"*) (Boltanski and Thévenot, 1991; Thévenot, 2006) of the Social Economy and its relationship with the detailed practices of its stakeholders. The work of the translators consists in laying down a logical model of development for Social Economy enterprises, creating new analysis categories in the world of risk capital, establishing standards, etc. This "form investment" (Thévenot, 1986) is such that solidarity financiers such as the RISQ – or at least its method of evaluation – becomes an almost unavoidable "mandatory pathway" in the world of the emerging Social Economy in Quebec. A community of practice emerges resulting from the socialization of this method among a group of players involved in the development of the Social Economy.

However, the relationship will always remain problematic (Thévenot, 2006), rapidly becoming a source of controversy with regard to the definitions and values of the Social Economy (Eme, chap. 4). Since the Social Economy is a plural and changing reality, the "common worth", instead of evolving, is likely to be eventually contested. The role of interpretation and translation must be able to persist over time through the authorities of *plural governance*, bringing together all parties involved (in this case bankers, workers funds, *Caisse*, subscribers) and also members having no particular interest (experts, other Social Economy entrepreneurs, academics, citizens).

Conclusion

In this text, we have attempted to discover if there are specific tendencies with regard to evaluation of the Social Economy in Quebec. We wanted to see what the evaluation methods and indicators used in different sectors of the Social Economy could reveal with regard to stakeholders' expectations concerning the Social Economy. In this sense, our contribution has more to do with the Social Economy than with evaluation expertise. We have analyzed several evaluation tools and results, but have not made an exhaustive study. Nor have we compared instruments of very different natures and scopes (sector portraits, programme evaluations, social responsibility reports, funding guides, etc.). Nevertheless, our analysis allows us to draw several conclusions.

Our first finding is that the subjects covered by the evaluations contrast greatly from one document to the other. This is due to the fact that in each case the evaluation deals with dimensions linked to the nature of the principal activities of the organization or to demands generated by the party that requested the evaluation. A second observation is that the methodology is rarely explicit, particularly with regard to the hypotheses or logical models that underlie the exercise. This rapid overview, however, still allows us to identify certain common features.

Although the reality is often less contrasted,[20] the evaluation of the Social Economy in Quebec currently seems to follow three principal tendencies: according to objectives, to the mission or to the specificity of the Social Economy. The subjects covered and the design of the evaluation differ according to whether they are directed toward activities whose nature is productive or service-oriented, whether these activities are designed for a public that is internal or external to the organization, whether they are principally market or non-market, whether the type of resources involved are for the most part monetary or non-monetary, and whether the stage of the life cycle of the sector of activity or of the organization is at full development or is emergent. These factors seem to influence not only the subjects and indicators of evaluation but also an openness itself to external evaluation.

The tendencies observed also show different cultures or generations of evaluation. The evaluation is often standardized by means of an established (though often implicit) explicative model that does not really take into account the specificity of the Social Economy. On the organizational scale, self-evaluation and participative evaluation can be used to make the measurements of evaluation correspond to the values put forth by the Social Economy. The evaluation can also be "negotiated" with regard to a sector of activities, whether the demands of evaluation be explicit (programme evaluation) or implicit (social and environmental assessment). Finally, the evaluation can try to translate the general points of reference of the Social Economy into evaluation indicators that are intelligible for the stakeholders and for the parties concerned, allowing it to play a more political role in debates concerning it.

The evaluation also reveals different paradigms or concepts of the role of the Social Economy. At lease three "visions" or ideal types of

---

[20] In some cases, organizations perform several evaluation exercises, one part of which is implicit, often on a day-to-day basis, with the principal interested parties, namely recipients (or users) and workers (employees and volunteers).

the Social Economy can be extracted by observing tools used to evaluate it. In vision number one, it is expected that the Social Economy will help to support economic development in case of market failure or the absence of public intervention. The Social Economy helps to fill market and government gaps (Hansmann, 1980; Weisbrod, 1977). A second role that the Social Economy can play is to serve as a complement to public action and to the market, or even to promote an alternative to the dominant model of development. It can thus reveal new social expectations and "raise the bar" for performance standards by integrating the cost of externalities (Gadrey, 2005; Fraisse, Gardin and Laville, 2001). In a third vision, the Social Economy itself constitutes a specific modality of development, which is different from the market and the State. The evaluation reveals a co-dependency of the social and economic dimensions of the Social Economy's double mission. The evaluation reflects a logical framework of interpretation based on an explicative model of the Social Economy enterprise.

Thus, the evaluation methods and tools are not neutral and are influenced to different degrees by various factors: the nature and type of activity, the sources of financing, the expectations of stakeholders, the specific nature of the Social Economy. The definition of the Social Economy and the vision of its role in the economy and in society condition the referentials of evaluation. Reciprocally, the evaluation conditions the definition of the Social Economy. Obviously, it is difficult to arrive at a consensus with regard to a universal measurement tool to evaluate social dimensions (Perret, chap. 2) or economic dimensions (DiMaggio, 2001) of Social Economy activities. As well, the idea that there can be only one objective concept of performance, independent of the judgement of the different stakeholders is neither tenable nor useful (Herman and Renz, 1998). Finally, since the Social Economy produces at least as many, if not more, externalities than direct results, the evaluation should be able to focus on its impact, even if such an exercise implies considerable difficulties in methodology, particularly because the causal relationships between the objectives pursued by the organizations and the impact indicators have yet to be fully demonstrated.

It therefore appears difficult to think about evaluation tools that would be sufficiently specific to reflect the characteristic nature of the Social Economy, and generous enough to cover the multiplicity of forms and activities. If such a research project seems colossal in size, or even impossible to carry out, it still remains potentially useful to continue pursuing the idea (DiMaggio, 2001). On one hand, its simple implementation would reinforce the reflexivity of Social Economy actors with regard to their own activities. On the other hand, researching the relationships between the indicators of performance (or success) of ing of this form of economy in relation to public powers, funders and public opinion. Therefore, it appears an important priority for future research and should mobilize researchers and contribute toward bringing the actors of the Social Economy closer together.

References

Boltanski, L., Thévenot, L., *De la justification. Les économies de la grandeur*, Paris, Édition Gallimard, 1991.

Borys, S., Gauthier, B., Kishchuk, N., Roy, S., "Enquête sur les pratiques et les enjeux de l'évaluation au Canada", *Bulletin de la Société québécoise d'évaluation de programme*, 18, 2, December, 2005, pp. 5-6.

Bouchard, M. J., Bourque, G. L., Lévesque, B., "L'évaluation de l'économie sociale dans la perspective des nouvelles formes de régulation socio-économique de l'intérêt général", *Cahiers de recherche sociologique*, March 2001, pp. 31-53.

Bouchard, M. J., Fontan, J.-M., "L'économie sociale à la loupe. Problématique de l'évaluation des entreprises d'économie sociale", communication presented at the 67th Congrès de l'ACFAS, Quebec City, May 1998.

Bouchard, M.J., Lévesque, B., St-Pierre, J., "Modèle québécois de développement et gouvernance: entre le partenariat et le néolibéralisme?", in B. Enjolras (ed.), *Régimes de gouvernance et services d'intérêt général dans les services sociaux et de santé*, Brussels, P.I.E. Peter Lang, 2008, pp. 39-65.

Comeau, Y., Beaudoin, A., Chartrand-Beauregard, J., Harvey, M.-E.., Maltais, D., St-Hilaire, C., Simard, P., Turcotte, D., *L'économie sociale et le plan d'action du Sommet sur l'économie et l'emploi*, Ste-Foy, Université Laval and ENAP, Centre de recherche sur les services communautaires, 2001.

Desforges, J.-G., "Stratégie et structure des organisations coopératives", in J.-G. Desforges et C. Vienney (eds.), *Stratégie et organisation de l'entreprise coopérative*, Montréal/Paris, Éd. du jour/CIEM, 1980, pp. 287-311.

DiMaggio, P., "Measuring the impact of the nonprofit sector on society is probably impossible but probably useful. A sociological perspective", in P. Flynn and V. A. Hodgkinson (eds.), *Measuring the impact of the nonprofit sector*, New-York, Kluwer Academic/Plenum Publishers, 2001, pp. 249-270.

Eme, B., Laville, J.-L. (eds.), *Cohésion sociale et emploi*, Paris, Desclée de Brouwer, 1994.

Enjolras, B. (ed.), *Régimes de gouvernance et services d'intérêt général dans les services sociaux et de santé*, Brussels, P.I.E. Peter Lang, 2008.

Fraisse, L., Gardin, L., Laville, J.-L., *Les externalités positives dans l'aide à domicile, une approche européenne*, Projet de coopération France-Québec en économie sociale et solidaire, Annex to the Final Report, May 2001, http://www.unites.uqam.ca/econos/index.htm, site visited May 9, 2007.

Gadrey, J., "L'invention de l'utilité sociale des associations en France: à la recherche de conventions, de régulations, de critères et de méthodes d'évaluation", *Économie et solidarités*, 36, 1, 2005, pp. 7-26.

Guba, E., Lincoln, Y., *Fourth Generation Evaluation*, Newbury Park, Sage, 1989.

Gui, B., "The Economic Rationale for the Third Sector", *Annals of Public and Cooperative Economics*, 62, 4, 1991, pp. 551-572.

Hall, M., Lasby, D., Gumulka, G., Tryon, C., *Canadiens dévoués, Canadiens engages: Points saillants de l'Enquête canadienne de 2004 sur le don, le bénévolat et la participation, Ottawa*, Ministère de l'Industrie, June 2006.

Hall, M. H., de Wit, M.L., Lasby, D., McIver, D., Evers, T., Johnston, C., McAuley, J., Scott, K., Cucumel, G., Jolin, L., Nicol, R., Berdahl, L., Roach, R., Davies, I., Rowe, P., Frankel, S., Brock, K., Murray, V., *Force vitale de la collectivité: faits saillants de l'Enquête nationale auprès des organismes à but non lucratif et bénévoles*, 2003, Ottawa, Statistique Canada, 2004, 61-553.

Hansmann, H., "The role of the nonprofit enterprise", *Yale Law Journal*, 89, 2, 1980, pp. 835-898.

Herman, R.D., Renz, D.O., "Nonprofit Organizational Effectiveness: Contrasts Between Especially Effective and Less Effective Organizations", *Nonprofit Management and Leadership*, 9, 1, 1998, pp. 23-38.

IFDEC, "Le développement économique communautaire et les CDÉC Montréalaises". *Colloque d'orientation/ évaluation*. Cahier du participant, Colloquium held at the Université du Québec à Montréal, Institut de formation en développement économique communautaire, 1992.

Jalbert, Y., Pinault, L., Renaud, G., Zuñiga, R. Epsilon. *Guide d'auto-évaluation des organismes communautaires*, Montréal, Centre québécois de coordination sur le sida, s.d.

Jetté, C., Comeau, Y., Dumais, L., *Guide des dimensions évaluatives des organismes et des entreprises oeuvrant dans les services de proximité*, Projet de coopération France-Québec en économie sociale et solidaire, Annex to Final Report, May 2001. http://www.unites.uqam.ca/econos/index.htm, site visited May 9, 2007.

Lévesque, B., *Le modèle québécois et le développement régional et local: vers le néolibéralisme et la fin du modèle québécois?*, Montréal, Université du Québec à Montréal, Cahier du CRISES, 0405, 2004.

Monnier, L. Thiry, B., *Mutations structurelles et intérêt général. Vers quels nouveaux paradigmes pour l'économie publique, sociale et coopérative?* Brussels, De Boeck, 1997.

Perret, B., "Evaluating the social economy: clarifying complex rationality", in M.J. Bouchard (ed.), *The Worth of the Social Economy, An International*

Perspective on the Evaluation of the Social Economy, Brussels, P.I.E. Peter Lang, 2009.

Richez-Battesti, N., Trouvé, H., Rousseau, F., Eme, B., Fraisse, L., "Evaluating the social and solidarity based economy in France. Societal balance-sheet, social utility and identity trial", in M.J. Bouchard (ed.), *The Worth of the Social Economy, An International Perspective on the Evaluation of the Social Economy*, Brussels, P.I.E. Peter Lang, 2009.

Rouzier, R., Mendell, M., Lévesque, B., Symposium sur le financement de l'économie sociale, Montreal, Community-University Research Alliance on the Social Economy, T-06-2003.

Spear, R., "Social accounting and social audit in the United Kingdom", in M. J. Bouchard (ed.), *The Worth of the Social Economy, An International Perspective on the Evaluation of the Social Economy*, Brussels, P.-I.-E. Peter Lang, 2009.

Thévenot, L., *L'action au pluriel. Sociologie des régimes d'engagement*, Paris, La Découverte, 2006.

Thévenot, L., "Les investissements de forme", in Thévenot, L. (dir.), *Conventions économiques*, Paris, PUF, Cahiers du Centre d'Étude de l'Emploi, 29, 1986, pp. 21-71.

Vienney, C., *Socio-économie des organisations coopératives*, Paris, CIEM, 1980.

Weisbrod, B. A., *The Voluntary Nonprofit Sector*, Lexington, MA, D. C. Heath, 1977.

Annex 1

Definition of the Social Economy in Québec

"Economy" refers to the concrete production of goods or services, where the enterprise is a type of organization that contributes to a clear increase in collective wealth.

"Social" refers to the social profitability of these activities, which is not purely economic.

This profitability is measured according to its contribution to democratic development, through the support of active citizenship and the promotion of values and initiatives by individuals and the collectivity. Social profitability therefore contributes to the quality of life and wellbeing of the population, particularly by offering the greatest number of services. Just as in the public sector and the traditional private sector, this social profitability may also be evaluated according to the number of jobs created.

Taken as a whole, the Social Economy is a group of activities and organizations resulting from a collective entrepreneurship that functions according to the following principles and rules:

- The Social Economy enterprise has as its goal to serve its members or the collectivity, rather than simply generate profits with a view toward financial profit;
- It is managed autonomously with respect to the State;
- It includes in its statutes and ways of functioning a democratic decision-making process which involves its users;
- It defends the primacy of persons and work over capital in the distribution of its surpluses and revenues;
- It bases its activities on the principles of participation, empowerment and individual and collective responsibility.

Source: Working Group on the Social Economy, 1996.

There are over 3,000 cooperative businesses and 39 mutual organizations in Quebec. They include more than 7 million producers, consumers and workers. Quebec also has more than 46,000 non-profit organizations (NPOs) (Québec, *Registraire des entreprises*, 2004). Among all of these, it is estimated that between 4,000 and 10,000 non-profit organizations could be considered part of the Social Economy.[21]

[21] Hall *et al.* (2004) estimate at 10,000 the non-profit organizations that have employees and produce goods and services (without being quasi-governmental or religious organizations nor advocacy or professional groups). The estimate made by the *Bureau*

The Canada Research Chair on the Social Economy has identified no fewer than 15,000 establishments in Quebec whose sector-based and territorial (regional and local) stakeholders define them as part of the Social Economy.

In Quebec, 70% of the French-speaking population is a member of a cooperative. This is the highest rate in Canada (Co-operatives Secretariat of Canada, 2006). Compared to the rest of Canada, there are more cooperatives and associations in Quebec than in the other provinces: with 23.6% of Canada's total population, Quebec has 39% of its cooperatives and 29% of its associations (all NPOs). It is interesting to note that Quebec is the Canadian province whose average annual donation and volunteer rates are the lowest (Hall, *et al.*, 2006) but whose volunteer and non-profit organizations draw 60% of their revenues from the governments (contrasted with the NPOs in Alberta, which only draw 33% of their revenues from government) (Hall *et al.*, 2004). Along with several other regions in the world, the Social Economy in Quebec is growing. The economic activity of the "basic" non-profit sector (excluding hospitals, universities and colleges) increased 7.1% in 2001, compared to 6.1% for the whole of the Canadian economy (Statistics Canada, 2005). Moreover, between 2000 and 2004, the turnover of non-financed cooperatives in Quebec increased 26% (Quebec's Direction des cooperatives, 2006). By way of example, Quebec's GDP increased 17.6% during the same period (Institut Statistique du Québec, 2006).

There are two principal Social Economy networks in Quebec and one government agency that recognizes autonomous community organizations. The *Conseil québéquois de la cooperation et de la mutualité* (CQCM), founded in 1939, includes cooperative federations and mutual associations. The *Chantier de l'économie sociale*, formed from the *Groupe de travail sur l'économie sociale* (Working Group on the Social Economy), was created as a non-profit organization in 1999 and brings together association and cooperative networks, development support organizations and representatives of social movements. The "autonomous community organizations" may be recognized by the *Secrétariat à l'action communautaire autonome* (SACA) of the *Ministère de l'Emploi et de la Solidarité sociale*, created in 1995 by the Government of Quebec. Most of the autonomous community organizations are non-profit associations, but some of them are philanthropic foundations and cooperatives.

---

de l'économie sociale et la Direction des coopératives du ministère in 2002 is 4,000 Social Economy NPOs. These were still the same figures published by the *Chantier de l'économie sociale* in 2006. See the site: http://www.chantier.qc.ca/

Social Accounting and Social Audit in the UK

Roger SPEAR

Senior Lecturer, Chair Co-operatives Research Unit, Open University, Milton Keynes (United Kingdom)

1. Context

There are many different types of evaluation. But evaluative frameworks are becoming increasingly elaborated: accountancy frameworks to include social/environmental accounting; public sector priorities now objectified and measurable with advent of New Public Management (NPM e.g. Hood, 1991). Thus social economy (SE) organizations are increasingly required to play this game. But the way they need to play it is conditioned by the sub-sector they operate within and the governance systems that operate therein; and taking a resource dependency view, by the resources that they are most concerned with acquiring.

The structure of this paper is as follows: the next section reviews the changing and increasingly influential nature of evaluative frameworks. Section 3 goes on to examine the nature of the different governance contexts for social economy organizations. Then in Section 4 the different resource frameworks associated with different sub-sectors in which social economy organizations operate are examined; the Section goes on to show how different social economy evaluative frameworks are utilised by social economy organizations to exploit the resource contexts they inhabit. The paper concludes in Section 5.

2. Trends: Approaches to Evaluation and Social Accounting

As noted above in the Context, evaluative frameworks are becoming increasingly elaborated. We see accountancy frameworks being extended to include corporate social and environmental responsibility and associated dimensions of social/environmental accounting. And in the public sector, for a variety of reasons, performance measurement and performance indicators are being developed and are extending their role in more and more domains of services. With the advent of NPM more priorities have now become transformed into measures and indicators.

There are several reasons for this. Both *internal* reasons to improve management's capacity to improve efficiency and effectiveness, but more usually for *external* reasons: so that accountability to diverse stakeholders can be made more transparent. By improving awareness by diverse stakeholders (especially consumers/users) of the performance of a service provider operating to deliver a "public" service, pressure can be brought to bear on the board to ensure management is better directed. However assessing outcomes is not an easy matter, nor is making comparative judgements about other service providers – since different objectives may be being pursued, in different socio-economic environments, using different accounting methods, and with different levels of management efficiency (Smith, 1993). Thus there are competing tensions due to the different functions that indicators play:

accountability vs
managing performance (effective management control) vs
organizational learning vs
marketing.

This also raises questions about the role of *intermediaries* in assessing value for money. Intermediaries play roles of external evaluators, facilitators of internal evaluations, and independent assessors of evaluations – and so play key roles in constructing practices. Until the field becomes professionalised and methodologies standardised there is considerable scope for variable practices. Similarly given the complexity of the situation, it is clear that there are potentially distorting effects of measurement systems in any specific context – Smith (1993) specifies seven:

- –Tunnel vision
- –Sub-optimization
- –Myopia
- –Convergence
- –Ossification
- –Gaming
- –Misrepresentation

Paton (2003) develops some of these themes in depth when examining evaluation systems and social enterprise. He emphasises the gaming theme where unintended consequences arise from the way actors and organizations adapt to manipulate favourable outcomes in the measurement systems used to assess them. On the other hand, there can be strategic value in promoting evaluative systems that measure the social economy difference, since such systems may lead to changes in behaviour both of social economy organizations, and their competitors in public and private sectors.

And Nicholls (2006) argues that the difficulties faced in establishing performance metrics in this area is considerable, as they: "inhabit a no-man's land between rationalist/positivist interpretations of outcomes and outputs, and a more social constructivist view of social impact and influence."

2.1 Social Accounting and Social Audit

In the social economy we have seen the development of universalistic measures (ISO 9000, Key Performance Indicators (KPIs)), as well as more customised measures linked to the specific needs and contexts of individual SE organizations.

Different types of evaluation have different origins: they may be statutory, i.e. externally imposed by government. They may be linked to a specific sector, and there may be an element of voluntary self evaluation for different reasons. There are several different types of social accounting methods with different origins and purposes;

Social return on investment (e.g. Nichols, 2004), as the name indicates, this approach is more relevant to assessing the social and economic value of investing in projects, run by SE (or other) organizations. It involves developing measures for economic and social value, assessing "deadweight" or the comparable effect of doing nothing, and ultimately monetising the social impacts, so that an overall assessment of investing in the project can be established. As such it bears comparison with cost-benefit analysis.

Social Balance Sheets which attempt to develop a balance sheet approach (similar to the financial one) to an organization, both for internal and external purposes. Several co-ops in Italy have used this approach. The French system of Bilan Sociétal is an approach which focuses on the return to workers (benefits to them). The Italian system is more developed, particularly in its recent developments for application to social co-ops.

Performance indicator based methods to allow comparability with other organizations in the same and different sectors (for example measures of return to labour, measures of relative rewards (pay differentials) at different levels in the organization. "Key Performance Indicators" (KPIs) are social accounting indicators which have been strongly promoted recently in the co-operative sector, where they are based on co-operative principles (see Appendix).

Social audit – this typically provides a report on the social (and environmental) performance of the organization, based on a portfolio of qualitative and quantitative measures, which are related to strategic objectives (linked to values, principles or stakeholders). These complement conventional accounting measures to provide an overall profile of the socio-economic performance of the SE organization. It is covered in some depth in the Section below.

2.2 Social Audit

There are two main forms of social audit although a variety of methodologies have been followed. The development of social audit has been associated with several distinct aims, which have been differentially emphasised by adopters and promoters:

a) To monitor and manage the social and ethical impact and performance of the organization

b) To provide a basis for shaping management strategy in a socially responsible and accountable way, and to inform marketing strategies

c) To facilitate organizational learning about how to improve social performance

d) To inform the community, public, other organizations and institutions in the allocation of their resources (time and money) – this links with issues of accountability and ethics (e.g. ethical investment).

The two main forms of social audit that have been applied are:

– *Values and principle approaches* – where a range of measures which relate to the social economy (sometimes specifically to co-operative) values and principles. The UK Co-operative movement adoption of KPIs could be seen as a simple version of this. The French "Bilan Sociétal" is the most highly developed of such approaches. It was developed by the Centre des Jeunes Dirigeants de l'Économie Sociale, and is based on 15 criteria relating to values underlying different logics (or motivations) of socio-economic action – ranging from: economic activity, security/health, environment to ethics, aesthetics, and solidarity. It has been used in social economy organizations in France (Capron and Gray, 2000; see Richez-Battesti *et al.*, in this book).

– *Stakeholder based approaches*: this involves examining the performance of an organization from the perspective of different stakeholders (members, shareholders, managers, the community, customers, trade unions, etc.). Studies have been done of co-ops in the UK, ethical organizations, and voluntary and community organizations, as well as third sector support organizations.

Leading organizations in the UK field have promoted stakeholder approaches. The New Economics Foundation was an important organization promoting such approaches, and developing a self-help manual (Pearce, Raynard, and Zadek, no date, but approx. 1990), and has continued this work with participatory methodologies like "Prove it" (Walker et al, 2000). And the Social Audit Network (SAN) is contributing to a professionalization of practices with a register of approved practitioners, and a manual and CD (see website: http://www.socialauditnetwork.org.uk/). There are a number of other influential organizations, including the more broadly based Accountability (initially, 1996, the Institute of social and ethical accounting) which has promoted the AA1000 assurance standard, which is designed to guide good practices in reporting on wider organizational performance for sustainable development. [The Co-operatives Research Unit (CRU) was an early promoter of a social audit for co-operatives (CRU, 1982)].

The current methodologies for social audit share a few basic stages in a stakeholder based approach:

1. Negotiation of scope of social audit, purpose (strategy, marketing, learning, etc), and the level of involvement of client

2. Identification of stakeholders and determination of their involvement (workers, community, lenders, suppliers, customers, general public, etc.)

3. Identification of Objectives and Measures of Performance for each stakeholder

4. Collection of data relevant to each measure

5. Reporting to client (and stakeholders)

6. Action planning based on findings.

Social Audit experience – The numbers of social economy organizations that have used social audit is not high. 78 are listed on the SAN website, but these do not include some of the highest profile social audits such as those of the Co-operative Bank or Co-operative Insurance Services (now combined in one organization: Co-operative Financial Services, which produces an annual "Sustainability Report"). This number compares with an upper estimate of 900,000 SEOs in the UK (*The UK Voluntary Sector Almanac*, NCVO 2006). Part of the reason for this may be that the benefits of conducting a social audit are not seen as overwhelming, but it may be the barriers are more significant: the costs in terms of staff time and external consultants, technical difficulties in applying methodologies, difficulties adapting information systems, and survey/publication costs (Butler, 2005).

Nonetheless, social audit has quite a high profile possibly because one of the three key planks in the government strategy for social enterprise is to: "establish the value of social enterprise" (with specific mention of social audit as a means of achieving this).

And partly because organizations like the Co-operative Bank have been so successful in tapping into or helping to create ethical markets, with social audit being a key part of their strategy for demonstrating distinctiveness.

The growth of corporate social responsibility (CSR) linked to strong brand marketing has muddied the waters; and some of the methodologies employed look remarkably similar to those used in social audits. Thus the distinctiveness of SEOs is more difficult to demonstrate, despite the fact that some consultants sell "reputation assurance" rather than social audit, more as a way of safeguarding the corporation from negative news rather than promoting the positives.

3. Governance Context: Competing Frames of Reference

Increasingly we are seeing a move from government to governance, with a greater role for non-governmental actors, in complex state-society relationships in which networks rather than hierarchy dominates the policy making process (Bache, 2003).

Different aspects of governance play different parts in different sector. From a resource acquisition perspective, organizations will need to act differently depending on the sector and the resources they seek to acquire.

3.1 Modes of Governance

With the advent of the Blair Government (New Labour) we have seen some attempts to develop the idea of a Third Way which combines the benefits of efficient market style operation with an attempt to develop active citizenship and community. Newman (2001) argues that there are competing models of governance which co-exist, some more dominant in some public service subsectors than others. She identifies 4 governance models:

- Self-governance (partnership with active citizens)
- Hierarchy (bureaucratic, standardization, accountability)
- Open systems (network system of interaction)
- Rational Goal (managerial, targets, measures).

And the *market system* of governance (or more precisely quasi-market) may be added.

This framework elaborates the markets, networks and hierarchies approach, by refining the conceptualization of how hierarchy operates (hierarchy and rational goal system), together with refining the network concept (self-governance and open systems) – and these operate in a quasi-market context.

Newman argues that New Labour has been trying to shift the balance between some of these models. Whilst inheriting the Rational Goal model (embodying much of NPM), it values this as a force for reform, it has sought to move towards the open systems and self-governance models – emphasising decentralization, partnership, capacity building, public/community participation, and democratic renewal. But that the picture now is complex with a market system for contracting, together with structures of community/citizen/partnership governance that guide and regulate the system.

This rich approach encapsulates the diversity and ambiguities that operate in governance systems, where as Martin (2002) argues "the result is a combination of multiple drivers of change and paradoxical "operating codes" which reflect both the politics of the modernizing agenda and our current lack of understanding about which approaches will prove most effective in enabling performance improvement in the public sector."

These different governance systems (partnership, bureaucracy, networks, target regimes, and markets) shape the contexts within which social reporting operates. Social reporting plays different roles for SEOs, allowing them to negotiate different systems of influence within these contexts. Thus taking each in turn: partnership requires stakeholder engagement where legitimacy is important, and revealing similar values facilitates the development of relationships; bureaucracy (state) typically requires that value for money is demonstrated, or at least the SEO can show it understands the rules of the game; networks have similar requirements to partnerships, but have are likely to involve an orientation to diverse (multi) stakeholders; target regimes require discourse on quantified impacts and policy outcomes; markets require mechanisms for comparative assessment of performance.

4. Resource Dependency Perspective

In this section it will be argued that there are 5 different types of resources, that are more or less prominent in 4 sectors which are the major ones for social economy activity. Then the role of social accounting/auditing will be examined in relation to each resource.

Five resource frameworks

– subsidies/grants (state/philanthropy)
– quasi-market (state)
– private markets (business/consumer)
– ethical values market (business/consumer)
– social capital (solidarity networks)

Four distinct sectors

– regeneration/exclusion
– public service provision
– markets (business/consumer)
– ethical markets (fair-trade)

4.1 Resource Dependency and Resource Acquisition

This section examines resource related themes which influence the operation and performance of social economy organizations:

– different ways of conceptualising the resource dynamics of social economy, largely based on the organizational level;
– different resource contexts from which social economy organizations typically developed an appropriate mix of resources
– strategic considerations regarding resource acquisition;

There is a large amount of literature on the social economy, but the themes addressed in this paper draw selectively on a few important research studies at the inter-organizational level. And this is complemented by an institutional perspective which focuses on legitimacy. It is argued that resource dependency of social economy organizations strongly influences the way they act – in order to secure their resources and reduce uncertainty.

Polanyi has made a major contribution to understanding resource contexts. This work has been drawn on by the French Solidarity Economy and taken up by the EMES European research network and used in its studies. His approach emphasised three types of exchange:

o redistribution (through the state or philanthropy)
o market exchange
o reciprocity (social capital).

But here his approach is developed further by differentiating the market exchange to include *public contracting (quasi-markets), and ethical values markets* such as for ethical services, and fair-trade, as well as more purely commercial market exchange; using a resource dependency perspective to explore strategies employed by organizations, and considering the nature of the different resources required – resources such as legitimacy and expertise, information, etc.

The reason for arguing for the distinctive nature of public contracting is that with increasing contracting out of public sector services to private sector and third sector providers, it has become clearer that redistribution often only plays a small part (or in some cases no part) of the service provision. Historically, the state has often played a collectivising monopoly role with regard to certain types of services. Thus for example utilities were state monopoly services in many countries but are now contracted out. There is often little or no redistribution element in the supply of utility services; similarly for waste collection and recycling, and so on. And where there is a redistributive element,[1] for example in public transport, this may be handled differently by for example changing the system of redistribution to subsidise the individual directly rather than the service; so for example providing free bus passes to older people and funding this separately from a general contract for bus services.

In many countries, public service markets are also typically quasi-markets with the state contracting on behalf of the consuming taxpayer; and this changes resource dependency relations and the nature of resource acquisition strategies.

The reason for arguing for the distinctive nature of ethical values markets is that in many cases they have emerged from social economy innovation (for example in fair-trade), and the character of both resource relationships and resource acquisition strategies appears different – though isomorphic pressures may reshape such characteristics over time.

Thus the elaborated Polanyi resource framework becomes 5 resource frameworks:

– redistribution (through the state or philanthropy)

– market exchange (commercial)

– quasi-market

– ethical values market

– reciprocity (social capital)

These will be discussed in more depth in the following sections.

---

[1] Note that the concept of *general interest* in service provision has become a key part of current reviews of the redistribution element of public service provision (ref to SHSGI study).

4.2 Managing Resource Dependencies and Legitimacy

This section adopts a resource dependency perspective to examine the effect of different resource contexts on social economy organizations.

The resource dependency perspective (Pfeffer and Salancik, 1978) argues that organizations are externally constrained and that they need to respond to those organizations that control critical resources; but that organizations seek strategically to manage these dependencies in their environments, in order to gain more autonomy and enhance their capacities of survival. Resource dependencies include political support, legitimacy, as well as economic inputs.

Three factors are critical in determining resource dependency:

– the importance of the resource for survival
– the extent to which the external group/organization has discretion over resource allocation/use
– the extent of alternative resources

The capacity to manage such dependencies is partly a function of size, but smaller organizations can band together to create more power in dependency relationships – for example through joint ventures, mergers, various forms of interfirm coordination (interlocking directorates, movement of senior staff between firms, see Galbraith, 1973), and co-operatives.

The theory is quite complex, but some simplifying principles will be used here: firstly just the consideration of external actions to reduce dependency will be considered; and secondly the general principle of high dependency leading to greater coordinative activity will be examined. There are essentially 2 types of interdependence:

The first type is "competitive interdependence" where firms are competing with each other but where the potential for collaboration is related to concentration: it is low at the extremes – with many firms and low concentration since each firms actions do not have significant consequences for another; and low when concentration is high, since a few large firms may tacitly coordinate; thus the intermediate position where uncertainty is highest has the highest coordinative activity between firms.

The second type of interdependence is "symbiotic interdependence" between buyers and sellers; here as one might expect if there is a high level of transactions there is greater linkages between buyers and sellers. And with regard to government purchase: high dependence is associated with a propensity to favour government policies, and strategies of co-option, etc. to reduce dependency.

It is also important to analyse resource contexts, by considering how the resource acquisition process is different in the different resource contexts, in particular consider the following factors:

a) Unit size of the resource – small increments of resource will be less risky than large lumpy ones.

b) Extent of alternative sources (Pfeffer and Salancik's framework); risk will be reduced if there are many alternatives.

This may be particularly important in quasi-markets where the state has monopoly purchaser power. This will influence resource acquisition (e.g. building many/few funding relations) and growth strategies. And there will be different organizational process for single vs multiple alternative sources which will need to be balanced against reducing risk/dependency, such as transaction costs and modes of engaging/marketing/relating with single vs multiple funders.

The importance of legitimacy issues (3 types, see box) will also vary according to context.

Legitimacy – an institutional perspective
Dart (2004) and Nyssens (2006), argue that in institutional theory, legitimacy is a central resource for social enterprise. Dart discusses pragmatic, moral and cognitive legitimacy: pragmatic legitimacy is where an organization delivers some outcomes (including quality) of interest to stakeholders. While moral legitimacy is supported because the organization operates in a way that accords with a framework of values that is in the ascendant (for example the business model as a way of doing things). And cognitive legitimacy "feels right", or accords with the world views and perspectives that have become culturally embedded. Thus cognitive legitimacy goes along with an institutionalization of a particular form of organization in a specific sector.

These issues may reduce the opportunities for small non-legitimate organizations to emerge, and may be partially addressed through various strategies including co-operative strategies to reduce uncertainty (cf. Galbraith for other possible coordinative actions).

To summarise: dependency, legitimacy, and resource type combine to influence strategy. In the next section we try to develop an analysis of the implications of taking this perspective on the actions of social economy organizations.

distinct sectors where the social economy typically plays an important role:

Main Polanyian resource (elaborated)	Social Economy Sector	Resource controlling agent
Redistribution – subsidies/grants	Regeneration/ exclusion	State/philanthropy
Quasi-market	Public service provision	State
Market	Markets (consumers and business)	Consumers/business
Ethical values market	Ethical markets (fair-trade)	Ethical consumers/business
Reciprocity: social capital [Key secondary resource]		Solidarity networks of individuals/organizations

Each main resource will be more or less important for social economy organizations in each of the different social economy sectors; the controlling agents of those resources help shape the contexts of resource dependency. Of course this is a general argument, and the precise nature of resource dependency will require a detailed consideration of the empirical reality. The historical institutional development of each sector will shape the mix of resources available to social enterprise. Thus for example in the UK, even in the regeneration/exclusion sector there has been a trend away from subsidies and grants towards quasi-market contracts for services.

For the purpose of this analysis it is simpler to consider the 5 different resource frameworks and the resource controlling agent, in order to examine the consequences for social economy organizations. These (elaborated Polanyian) 5 resource frameworks (and resource controlling agents) will be addressed in turn in the next section: looking at strategies to reduce resource dependency in each case and the role of social accounting/audit methods.

- Redistribution: subsidies/grants (state/philanthropic foundations)
- Quasi-market (state)
- Private markets (business/consumer)
- Ethical values market (business/consumer)

- Reciprocity: social capital (Solidarity networks of individuals/ organizations)

The main *strategic options for dependency and uncertainty reduction* are:

- Coordinative or collaborative actions between providers/suppliers (competitive dependency)
- Building relationships between purchaser and provider (symbiotic dependency). With regard to this resource relationship, the balance between the following will change: marketing vs networking vs brand vs values/ethics (trust as differentiator).
- Hybridization: one of EMES contributions has been that social enterprise combine (or hybridise) resources to help meet such challenges.
- Improving legitimacy via institutionalization and social capital
- Growth: for example small organizations in quasi-markets have big legitimacy/resource challenges which means they will have difficulties surviving unless they can collaborate or grow fast – one route to growth is by developing an alternative source of resources such as the market for private services – this can be seen for example in the UK amongst homecare co-ops.

As we shall argue, social accounting/audit methods can play important roles in several of these strategies particularly those associated with legitimacy, building relationships, and collaborative action.

4.4 Resource Dependency Strategies and Social Accounting/Audit Methods

We now examine each type of resource in turn, and consider the effect of the resource context on social economy organizations, and strategies that might be employed to manage dependency and acquisition of resources.

4.4.1 Redistribution: Subsidies/Grants (state/philanthropic foundations)

In contexts such as in regeneration, or exclusion sectors, where subsidies and grants are critical or major sources of resources, typically it is the state that is in a dominant resource provider position. Key strategies are:

a) Social economy organizations may reduce dependency by seeking similar resources (from other state bodies) or different resource types (market or philanthropic funding).

b) A central part of strategic responses to this type of resource is: gaining and maintaining legitimacy; this operates firstly within the governing elite and bureaucrats, and secondly with the community of service users (though in practice this is not as important, and many organizations have been successful without expending effort on this).

c) Social capital may fulfil a dual purpose of improving legitimacy as well as providing a complementary resource.

d) Turning now to the role that social accounting methods might play in any resulting coordinative action: the state typically operates with its own performance indicators in this area, so the extent to which social accounting methods fit with these is important. And the extent to which SEOs can coordinate a standardised methodology will reduce their dependency.

4.4.2 Quasi-market (state)

In these contexts (typically for public service provision), the state is the major player (quasi-market), and it may be more difficult for small social economy organizations to negotiate other types of resources. Key strategies are:

a) Collaboration for example via consorzi (Italian social co-ops) or sub-contracting partnerships with larger organizations.

b) Hybridization: small homecare co-ops have sought to access private markets and private customers to balance dependency on municipal contracts;

c) Growth may be crucial in strategies for avoiding dependency – larger social economy organizations are more likely to have contracts with different municipalities.

d) There are important legitimacy issues in this sector, and progressive institutionalization may overcome these issues, as can be seen in the social cooperatives in Italy, and in the WISE (work integration social enterprise) studied by the EMES group.

Turning now to the role that social accounting methods might play in any resulting coordinative action: similarly to the above, the state typically operates with its own performance indicators in this area, so the extent to which social accounting methods fit with these is important. However the SEOs may have more difficulty in standard public services in showing their distinctiveness, since they will generally be minor players.

4.4.3 Private Markets (business/consumer)

In this context the level of concentration in the sector is the key factor in determining dependency and uncertainty. Key strategies are:

a) For small social economy organizations it seems less likely that they will face contexts where coordinative actions are likely to reduce dependency.

b) However in niche markets, some coordinative actions with like-minded social economy organizations might prove fruitful.

c) Brand and quality are more important than legitimacy (except in ethical markets – see below)

d) Turning now to the role that social accounting methods might play in any resulting coordinative action: in the general market, it is not apparent that anything is to be gained from going beyond standard CSR practices.

4.4.4 Ethical Values Market (business/consumer)

In ethical or value-based markets such as fair-trade social economy organizations may have inherent legitimacy. Key strategies are:

a) Strengthen legitimacy

b) Exploit opportunities for utilising the socio-political embeddedness of these kinds of markets and

c) Exploitation of social capital.

d) But large business organizations investing in their brand can be very strong competitors.

Role of accounting/audit methods: with regard to fair-trade/ethical markets, it may be argued that social accounting strengthens the purchaser relationship, and helps reduce competitive dependency. This is particularly the case if a collective dimension can be established – as can be seen in fair-trade securing niche segments of established markets.

4.4.5 Reciprocity: Social Capital (Solidarity Networks of Individuals/Organizations)

This resource is unlikely to be the main resource in most contexts. However in some contexts (regeneration or ethical markets), it may be an important secondary resource and considerably assist social economy organizations. Thus one might expect some kind of coordinative action to help support this.

Turning now to the role that social accounting methods might play in any resulting coordinative action: this resource is particularly important with regard to two sectors under consideration here: regeneration/exclusion where it provides an additional resource thereby reducing dependency on other resources; and in relation to niche ethical markets where it can lead both to greater loyalty and price margins.

5. Conclusions and Recommendations

There are many different types of evaluation, and evaluative frameworks are becoming increasingly elaborated; this includes conventional accountancy frameworks being extended to include social/environmental accounting. This paper has been more concerned with a variety of contexts including public sector related contexts where NPM has led to priorities becoming more measured and replete with performance indicators. And social economy organizations are increasingly required to play this game. But the way they need to play it is conditioned by the sector they operate within and the governance systems that operate therein; and taking a resource dependency view, by the resources that they are most concerned with acquiring.

The paper has argued that a closer examination of governance and the adoption of a resource dependency perspective can reveal those resources and contexts where social accounting methods can play important roles for the organization: including in relation to solidarity networks, ethical markets. It is argued such methods may only be able to play limited roles in regeneration contexts, and they may struggle in quasi-markets unless collective action is undertaken to create legitimacy for social accounting (beyond the measures already in existence). This leads to a view that sectoral initiatives to develop processes of institutionalization may be more important to develop rather than merely promoting the growth of individual SEO actions.

References

Bache, I., "Not Everything that Matters is Measurable and Not Everything that is Measurable Matters: how and why local education authorities 'fail'", *Local Government Studies*, 29, 4, 2003, pp. 76-94.

Ben-Ner, A., Hoomissen, T.V., "The Governance of Nonprofit Organizations: Law and Public Policy", in *Nonprofit Management and Leadership*, 4, 4, 1994, pp. 393-414.

Butler, T., *Social accounting and audit: barriers, benefits, and future support, MSc dissertation*, Sheffield Hallam University, 2005.

Capron, M., Gray, R.., "Accounting in Europe: Experimenting with assessing corporate social responsibility in France: an exploratory note on an initiative by social economy firms", *The European Accounting Review*, 9, 1, 2000, pp. 99-109.

CRU, *Co-operative Working 3. Co-operatives Research Unit*. Open University, Milton Keynes, 1982.

Hood, C., *The Art of the State: Culture, Rhetoric and Public Management*. Clarendon Press. Glocs, UK, 1998.

Jackson, M., *Systems Methodologies for the Management Sciences*, Plenum 1991.

Laidlaw, A.F., *The Social Auditing of Co-operatives*, from the CUC report, Ottawa, 1985, 1992.

Martin, S., *The Modernization of UK Local Government: markets, managers, monitors and mixed fortunes*. Public Management Review, 4, 3, 2002, pp. 291-307.

Mayo, E., *Strategies for Socialising the Economy*, New Economics Foundation, London, 1994.

Newman, J., *Modernising Governance*, Sage. London, 2001.

Nicholls, A., *Capturing the performance of the socially entrepreneurial organisation (SEO): and organisational legitimacy approach*, ISERC Book, 2006.

Nichols, J., Social Return on Investment: valuing what matters, New Economics Foundation. London, 2004.

Paton, R., *Managing and Measuring Social Enterprises*, London, Sage, 2003.

Pearce, J., Raynard, P., Zadek, S., *Social auditing for small organisations: the workbook*. New Economics Foundation, London, (s.d.).

Pestoff, V.A., *The Market, The State and Civil Society*, School of Business Stockholm University, Sweden, 1994.

Pfeffer, J., *Organizations and Organization Theory*. Pitman. Mass, 1982.

Pfeffer, J., Salancik, G. R., *The External Control of Organizations: A Resource Dependence Perspective*, New York, NY, Harper and Row, 1978.

Smith, P., "Outcome-related performance indicators and organisational control in the public sector" *British Journal of Management*, 4, 3, 1993, pp. 135-151.

Spear, R., "Governance in Democratic Member Based Organisations", in *Special issue of Annals of Public and Co-operative Economics: Governance in the social economy*, 2004, pp. 33-60.

Spear, R. Cornforth, C., Aiken, M., *For Love and Money: Social Enterprise and Governance, Governance Hub*, London, 2007. See: http://www7.open.ac.uk/ oubs/research/pdf/For_Love_&_%20Money_Full%20Report.pdf.

Strube, M., Ramsbottom, H., *The Assessment of Democracy*, Paperback Ltd, London, UK, 1994.

The New Economics Foundation, *Social Audit*, London, 1993-1994.

Traidcraft plc, Social Audit 1993-1994, *New Economics Foundation*, London, UK, 1994.

Ulrich, W., *Critical Heuristics of Social Planning*, Verlag Bern, 1983.

149

Zadek, S., *Socialising the Accounting Process*, New Economics Foundation, London, 1993.

Zadek, S., Evans, R., *Auditing the Market, Traidcraft Exchange*, Tyne & Wear, UK, 1993.

Zadek, S., Gatwood, M., Transforming the Transnationals: Social Auditing or Bust?, in M. Edwards and D. Hulme (eds.), *Beyond the Magic Bullet: NGO Performance and Accountability*, Earthscan, London, 1995.

Appendix: Key Performance Indicators used in UK Co-op Movement

Indicator 1: Member economic involvement.

Indicator 2: Member democratic participation.

Indicator 3: Participation of employees and members in training and education.

Indicator 4: Staff injury and absentee rates.

Indicator 5: Staff profile – gender and ethnicity.

Indicator 6: Customer satisfaction.

Indicator 7: Consideration of ethical issues in procurement and investment decisions.

Indicator 8: Investment in community and co-operative initiatives.

Indicator 9: Net carbon dioxide emissions arising from operations.

Indicator 10: Proportion of waste recycled/reused.

Evaluating Nonprofit Organizations in the United States Welfare System

Charles Patrick ROCK

Professor of Economics, Rollins College,
Winter Park, Florida (USA)

Introduction

Over the past fifty years, demands for accountability have spread throughout both the pubic and nonprofit sectors of the United States. For over a decade, all programs funded by the federal government are legally required to be assessed for effectiveness. And the non-governmental intermediary organizations supporting nonprofits are equally interested in seeing the results of their funding.

To provide context, this paper describes the financial and inter-organizational linkages among the US public sector, nonprofit organiza-tions (NPOs), and the citizen-beneficiaries of the system. It looks at the variety of ways that evaluation has been made to take place in this complex system. In some cases, it is a traditional cost-benefit or cost-effectiveness analysis focused on quantifiable effects, while in a grow-ing number, it involves looking more broadly – at the changes in the knowledge or behavior of beneficiaries, using a variety of quantitative and qualitative components. One also sees occasional evaluation proc-esses in part focused on developing the NPO itself, or more unusually, on creating popular citizen activism in social movements.

As several authors have noted – in both the theoretical and empirical articles of this volume – the demand for evaluation often disguises a political purpose. The actual practice of evaluation is never perfectly neutral, and correlates highly with the source of the funding for NPOs. So, this paper also traces the financial flows, seeing how those who control them often determine if evaluation occurs, what objectives it sets, how it is carried out, and which 'masters' it must answer to. Since the funders of NPOs are quite diverse – all levels of government and a variety of government agencies plus a large and highly diverse set of other NPOs, businesses, individuals, and other intermediaries) – the ways in which evaluation occurs or is used varies significantly. In some cases, even a single funder may promote, or at least accept, varied evaluation strategies. Generalizing about evaluation patterns in the US is risky business.

The paper is organized, I hope, in a way that clarifies the role of NPOs and evaluations. First come very brief overviews of the nonprofit sector and the early history of program evaluation. Second are some basic descriptive facts and figures of the nonprofit sector and the NPOs that constitute its subsections. Throughout the paper, the sizes of financial flows are compared to the size of the economy (gross domestic product, of GDP). Third is a look at the non-governmental sources of financing the US welfare regime. Heavily financed by public funds, often through complicated channels, NPOs are the primary organizational delivery mechanism of most social services. A brief discussion follows of NPO governance and the financial power of all types of funders over NPOs. A look at the dominant role of governments in demanding the institutionalization of program evaluations follows, along with some other causes for the increased attention on evaluation among NPOs. In recent years, evaluation seems to be spreading everywhere, perhaps even a self-sustaining 'movement' throughout the nonprofit sector. The paper ends with the positive and negative effects of nonprofit evaluation.

The Nonprofit Sector and NPOs in the US – rarely the 'Social Economy'

Because the US 'welfare state' is complicated – at least when it is compared to most other developed countries – it is useful to describe the institutional structure and flows of financing. The nonprofit sector itself is neither uniform not unified. Nonprofit organizations are divided into many formally or informally associated subgroups: by economic sector, by type of activity (e.g. financing, providing services, advocacy), by size, by region and state, by the human groups who are the targets of their work, and by ideological commitments. All NPOs get special (favorable) tax treatment and most are interested in convincing people of their important contributions to improving society.

Nonprofits receive their funding from three main sources: governments, fees charged for their services, and private grants and donations. Because of the federal nature of the US political and welfare systems, welfare-related nonprofits may receive funds from more than one level of government. NPOs may also receive grants, loans, or payments from other nonprofits, as well as from private individuals.

Most Americans have no idea what 'social economy' refers to. It never appears in writings about nonprofit organizations in the US. Nevertheless, most of the organizations that would be part of the 'social economy' in other countries would be found in the US nonprofit sector (Rock and Klinedinst, 1992).

Nonprofits, Finance & Creating the US Welfare State Regime

In the USA, relatively few government agencies provide services directly to citizens. Governments – at the federal, state, county & municipal levels – do, however, provide the majority of financing for social welfare programs in the USA. Additional funding comes from the private sector, from a diverse set of institutions and individuals. NPOs actually deliver most welfare-related services (e.g. health, human services, training and employment assistance, etc.). These legally autonomous nonprofit 'corporations' target individuals with needs inadequately met through market earnings or direct government income transfers. In years since the conservative revival since 1980 in the US political system, more and more frequently, the organizations providing these services and goods have come to include a rising percentage of for-profit businesses and purely religious organizations that have been publicly financed to do the same work as secular NPOs. Thus, the basic flow of financing occurs most often along the following path:

Government/Private funds→ NPOs' services → Citizens/beneficiaries

Since 1980, except in health care, an increasing percentage of total revenues of NPOs has come from fees, charged for services and goods and paid by beneficiaries, or, indirectly and directly, by governments. Fees represent over 70% of total revenues of the entire sector: about two-thirds of the total for NPOs in education, about half in health NPOs, and a smaller percentage in other domains. For all nonprofits in the US, private charitable donations represent slightly more than 10% of revenues, but only 5% in health care.

In 2007, the gross federal (national) government tax receipts were about $2,600 billion (or about 20% of GDP). Of these revenues, some are passed along to each of the fifty state governments as 'grants-in-aid' or 'block grants' (NASCSP, 2007). In 2007 the total of intergovernmental transfers was about $300 billion (over 2% of GDP). Two-thirds of these federal-to-state transfers are dedicated to health services for low-income families (in 2007, $191 billion for the Medicaid program) matched by an equal or larger amount of money from each state itself (OMB, 2008).

State and local governments also raise taxes. In 2007 their total receipts were about half the size of federal taxes (about $1,420 billion, or 10.4% of GDP). State governments also pass along funds to subsidiary local governments for a variety of programs. In 2007, this was almost equal to the federal funds received (nearly $300 billion, 2% of GDP). In some states (e.g. New York), funds will originate from all four levels of government (federal, state, county, city) to subsidize a subset of NPO services providers. Beyond health care, the funds that are transferred have required uses, mainly for different kinds of social welfare program purposes. This multilayered transfer system makes the US welfare regime even more difficult to comprehend and measure with precision.

A final caveat: One of the bizarre peculiarities of the US accounting and tax systems is that it is impossible to calculate precise shares of government and private aid to any single nonprofit from publicly available data sources. Naturally, this has major implications for attempted evaluation assessments of the efficacy of public spending (Salamon, 1999 and private communication, 2008).

Beginnings of Program Evaluation Research in the USA

Evaluation research in the USA has its origins in early 20th century public health and education studies, debates about Roosevelt's 'New Deal' programs of the 1930s, and manpower planning needs during WWII. Increased attempts at evaluation came with the expansion of government's role in society and the greater interest in social problems, analytical and statistical developments in the social sciences, and their increased professionalization. Program evaluation had become 'commonplace' by the 1950s.

Evaluation research boomed in the 1960s, along with the large expansion of social programs. A desire for applied quantitative science was dominant within public administration. Mainframe computers supported this development. The critique of this expansion of government by conservatives stimulated the search for more 'scientific' results that could defend publicly provided social welfare and community development programs. During the 1960s, scholarly writing about "evaluation research grew dramatically" and during the 1970s, "evaluation research emerged as a distinct specialty field in the social sciences" (Rossi *et al.*, 2004: 9).

Although social science researchers and users set most of the agenda for evaluation studies before the 1970s, later, there was a "qualitative change" so that evaluation is "now sustained primarily by funding from policymakers, program planners, and administrators who use the findings and by the interests of the general public and the clients of the programs evaluated" (Rossi *et al.*, 2004: 9-10).

Brief Overview of the US Nonprofit Sector

There are an estimated 1.4 to 2+ million NPOs in the US. Most of our information about them comes from federal tax authorities (IRS) and from general employment surveys. NPOs are required to register with the IRS for preferential tax treatment. Of the 1.6 million NPOs that are legally registered, less than one-third actually 'reports' (i.e. files a tax return) yearly. The missing 1+ million NPOs have either not earned the minimum $25,000 annual revenues that require reporting, or have ceased operations entirely but never notified the tax authorities; still others are some of the approximately 350,000 religious congregations not required to report annually, but which may have registered in the past.

These half million reporting NPOs received a total of $1,361 billion in revenues in 2004 (equaling about 10% of GDP) and spent slightly less ($1,255 billions) increasing their assets. In total they own a significant amount of wealth; their assets are valued at $2,967 billion (equaling over 20% of GDP but a very small share of all US wealth). This Most is held by educational institutions (30%), health NPOs (41%), human services NPOs (11.5%), and 'public and society benefit' NPOs (10.4%).

Of the nearly half-million reporting NPOs in 2004, about 300,000 are 'public charities' – they serve the general interest of society (e.g. arts & culture, education, health, human services), getting special tax treatment. Another 75,000 'foundations' get this special tax treatment because they also serve the public interest, but indirectly, by accumulating donations and then distributing a small portion of their wealth each year. Another 100,000 get some favorable tax treatment but not so generously, since they mainly serve their memberships and not the general public (NCCS, 2008).

The 300,000 'public charity' NPOs have revenues of $1,050 billions (equaling 7% of GDP). In this subset, the main sources of income are: fees charged (70.9%), direct government grants (9.0%), and private contributions (12.5%) (NCCS, 2008, Figure 2). However, this distribution gives a misleading picture since much of the total in fees paid originates in governmental transfers for payments (fees) for services. Governments are probably the source of at least one-third of all the revenues of 'public charities' and may account for more. Health care NPOs represent 60% of total revenues and expenses in this 'public charity' group. Thus, we have this summary of the main NPOs that make up the whole sector:

All NPOs (Registered & Unregistered): 2 million (estimate)
Registered NPOs: 1.4 million
Reporting NPOs: 486,982
Reporting 'public charity' NPOs: 299,033
Reporting 'foundations' (NPOs): 75,478
Reporting other NPOs: 112,471

Foundations gave away $30 billion (equaling 0.2% of GDP) to other NPOs in 2004 that was only ten percent of the total of private philanthropy of $260 billion (equaling 2% of GDP) in 2004. (GivingUSA.org) Except for the one-third to religious congregations, virtually all the rest goes to NPOs (NCCS, 2008).

The nonprofit sector has a highly unequal size distribution. A small number of NPOs accounts for a very large percentage of revenues, expenditures and assets. Philanthropic donations are concentrated among a minority of the very wealthy who give the majority of donations. The size distribution of 'clients' or beneficiaries are also relatively unequally distributed among NPOs. For example, a small number of the largest foundations (1% of them) hold nearly 70% of all foundations' assets. Similarly, only 1.1% of all 'public charity' NPOs account for 61.5% of total assets and 65.6% of total revenues of all 300,000 'public charity' NPOs (NCCS, 2008, figure 1; Salamon, 1999: 28).

Private Sector Financing of the American Welfare State

There are myriad private-sector organizations and individuals that contribute additional funding to NPOs for various social services. The major players here are 'foundations' despite their small share (about 2%) of total financing of NPOs, but a larger percentage share of grants. Foundations are NPOs set up as separate entities by various individuals, related family members, groups of unrelated individuals living in the same community or region, and for-profit corporations. These are essentially 'pass-through' financial intermediaries and they carry out few if any services themselves, but do pass on funds for many of the nonprofits working with the most needy and most socially excluded Americans (and new immigrants). Thus, in the USA we can have simultaneously all of the following types of foundations financing one or more social policy areas: individual, family, city, regional, county, state, national, and business (corporate foundations) and single-purpose foundations. Special statutes in the federal tax code regulate foundations. They are mandated to give away a minimum 5% of their net assets each tax year. These foundations may have a legally restricted focus to their activities (set into the articles of incorporation or in their corporate by-laws) or they may have more flexibility and only set out their goals and focus in their evolving organizational 'mission' statements. Since foundations receive money (contributions and investment earnings) and their sole function is often to give away their wealth to other (mostly) nonprofit organizations, they are essentially 'pass-through' financial organizations. They provide financial grants to thousands of NPOs – in social welfare services; in education and health care; in arts & culture & advocacy.

Individuals may donate directly to any NPO or they may donate to a 'pass-through' organization that is similar to a foundation, except that it immediately will pass along the funds to a NPO. This is the indirect private donation channel:

Contributors→Pass-Through NPOs→Other NPOs'→Citizens

The best-known pass-through NPO, and largest in terms of money-flows, is the United Way (UW). The 1,300 local UW organizations collect money through public campaigns each year involving solicitation of at workplaces in cooperation with employers. In 2007 they raised a total of $4 billion nationwide (about 1.5% of total private philanthropy). The 1,300 local UWs are affiliated into a national organization (United Way of America) that regulates who may use the 'United Way' name but has no direct control over the local UWs. In recent years, the United Way organizations (both the national umbrella organization as well as many of the affiliated locals) have engaged in significant work promoting standards and criteria for evaluation and monitoring addressed later in the paper.

Control Within Nonprofit Organizations (including Foundations)

In all nonprofit corporations, control is established under the specific articles of incorporation and the by-laws of the (nonprofit) corporation. The Board of Directors of a nonprofit foundation may be an individual, or small group, or a much more diverse and larger group, often representing different stakeholder interests. They are normally self-selecting boards; this means that the current Board members choose all new members of the Board. This 'self-selection' of controlling decision-makers is one constant across almost all NPOs. This control feature can be diagrammed:

Existing NPO Board (Self-selecting new) Members→Control Rights→NPO

For-profit companies may set up autonomous NPOs (these are usually called 'corporate foundations') and larger companies have set them up to remain controlled by the company officers and executives. Increasingly, over the past 25 years, for-profit companies buy 'corporate image' advertising to communicate about the good works funded by their foundations and generally to enhance the public's image of their being 'good corporate citizens' and 'socially responsible' businesses.

Even governments can establish nonprofit corporations (e.g. 'community development corporations' begun by local governments in the 1960s) to create options that the private sector has failed to provide (e.g. economic development in places that business finds unattractive).

Follow the Money – Paying to Play in the Evaluation Game

People, governments, and nonprofit organizations that provide financing can and have demanded accountability from the recipients of their funding. If organizations or individuals do not comply with formal or informal requirements of the funders, they may be 'de-funded' in the future. Hence, among NPO recipients, 'money talks,' and it speaks very loudly. Funders – both governments and non-government entities – are usually the initiators of evaluation practices in the US.

An NPO may have many 'funding partners' to whom it must answer. The NPO may be accountable to multiple levels of government. They may also be subject to different sets of specialized laws (federal and state) creating the programs and funding, and in some cases, subject to general laws as well (e.g. non-discrimination) that are also often a prerequisite for government funding. Funders' power in evaluation comes from funding and potential future funding as in this diagram:

Funders→Financing→Required Evaluation→Recipient-NPOs' Activities

In addition to governments, NPOs also must consider the desires and goals of their private sector funders. Hence, an NPO may need to fulfill obligations, carry out self-evaluations, and meet criteria established by NPO-foundations, other pass-through funders like the United Way, and even private individuals whose donations are critical to the organization's operations. In numerous cases, awareness of these multiple types of accountability tends to come with experience, often through the implied threat of 'de-funding' by a source of financing.

The complexity of these potential obligations and outside criteria means that many people working or managing in the nonprofit organization remain unaware of the full scope of accountability. United Way organizations in many regions (as well as many NPO-foundations) have been among the leaders helping nonprofit service providers to develop their knowledge about accountability, evaluation methods, monitoring, and developing explicit goals for the organization. For example, in central Florida, the local United Way is addressing this challenge with specially assigned UW 'evaluation staff' members who proactively provide evaluation training (and implicitly require attendance of staff from recipient-NPOs) for local NPOs.

Governmental Role in the Rise of the 'Evaluation Movement' in the US

Nearly all welfare-related NPOs can trace at least some of their financing back to government (and most often to the federal government). In the last 15 years, since the beginning of the Clinton administration, when Vice President Al Gore became the symbol of 're-inventing' government, there have been a series of federal initiatives that have led to a large rise in evaluation activity throughout government agencies, and through most of the nonprofit sector.

A very large stimulus to evaluation came with the passage of the Government Performance and Results Act of 1993, or, GPRA (US Congress, 1993). It required all federal organizations to engage in performance measurement within 5 years. Although it originally focused on national governmental agencies at the beginning, through additional legislation and through spillover demonstration effects-on lower level governments, private foundations, key federated funders (e.g. the United Way locals), and other nonprofit organizations-the legislation unleashed an avalanche of developments in evaluation practices.

The 1998 Community Services Block Grant Reauthorization Act also promoted this review of evaluation methodology across the country. The act required any state administering programs in certain social services to implement a management and evaluation strategy that measured and reported the outcomes of community action: 'Results Oriented Management and Accountability'. It was required of every state. The plan called for state visits to every one of the 1,000 local community action agencies (NPOs with Board governance shared among public officials, client representatives, and private business). The state officials had to propose their own methods of evaluating the local program for the regular reports (back to the federal government agency) about success or failure in community development. However, an assessment of the implementation of the law showed that during the 2002-2005 period, very little of this 'required' activity occurred in most of the states studied (US GAO, 2006).

It is hard to trace out precisely the effects of the 1993 GPRA, but hundreds of 'outcomes' evaluations are done each year (with the largest quantity in education and health). The main trend appears to be the replacement of measurements of 'activities' or 'units of service' somehow related to goals and missions, with the active intention to measure 'outcomes' or the changes that occur among the 'clients' of services and programs. Despite the haze of jargon that makes evaluation training so formidable, the basic idea is to measure what has changed among the people being helped, with less focus on what the helpers are doing. And more precisely, more important than just counting how many people were served is analyzing what those people could now do themselves that they could not do before.

In its first term the Bush administration paid minimal attention to evaluation studies of innovative social change programs like the 'community action agencies' and their community development goals. In recent budget proposals from the president, they were completely unfunded and only congressional action kept them alive. In recent years, Bush has pushed for 'using evidence' to make decisions on cutting or retaining federal programs. This 'Program Assessment Rating Tool' (PART) was used to justify reductions in social programs as 'ineffective' (OMB, 2006). Large tax cuts in 2001 put significant fiscal (deficit) pressure on the federal government to reduce overall spending. The PART approach supposedly allows evidence-based decisions. However, PART has engendered widespread criticism from Congress and others, not for its theory or fundamentals, but rather because the administration's current program-cutting proposals seem completely uncorrelated with the actual performance rankings of funded or de-funded programs (OMB Watch, 2005).

Nevertheless, the federal push for measurement of outcomes has spread into many other state and local levels of government, and even into the corporate world (e.g. Total Quality Management and other consultant-terms referring to performance changes), as well as into schools and higher education (i.e. quantitatively measurable faculty/student 'objective' performance indicators with a baseline from which to observe changes over time).

Evaluation is perhaps most solidly entrenched in the fields of education and health care. This is mainly due to the large-scale public funding of education and health care from all levels of government. This is mostly for schools below university (and mainly public schools) although the federal government is a crucial indirect funder of university level education through loans and grants to individuals. In recent years (since 2001), below the university level, the emphasis has been on evaluation by examining comparative standardized test results, with potentially serious penalties for lack of improvement in test results year-by-year. However, the federal government decentralized some crucial decisions about which tests to use so that most states have manipulated the success requirements by selecting tests that will ensure that they meet most of the minimum mandated outcomes.

Health care financing and monitoring became important after 1965 with the passage of national health insurance for elderly or disabled and the very poor (i.e. Medicare and Medicaid, respectively). In order to assess the outcomes and impacts of such programs, governments have mandated and subsidized evaluation research, partly due to the rapid rise in health care costs over the last 30 years, leading to a variety of programs for monitoring costs, as well as outcome and impact assessment. The federal health coverage programs have required study of prices and quality measures for cost effectiveness analysis, and this also applied to NPO health providers. Many states do the same. Thus nearly all the thousands of NPOs engaged in health care services have been subject to government-mandated research and reporting requirements, just as public and for-profit providers are. The flows of money and the power to exercise demand for evaluation by governmental funders can be traced:

Federal Gov.→Money→State Govs.→Money/Evaluation→NPO-Recipient

A final governmental effect on NPO evaluations came through the taxation laws. In part, due to perceived conflicts-of-interest of NPO administrators and Boards of Directors, the tax authorities (IRS) mandated the public availability of a limited amount of tax-related information. This basic information (provided to tax authorities on the official form, the IRS Form 990) must be available to anyone who asks for it. The Internet now makes it available worldwide simply by going to www.guidestar.org. Several other Internet sites use this tax information about NPOs to create guides and quality rankings for potential private donors.

Origins of the 'Program Evaluation Movement' in the Nonprofit Sector

Over the past quarter century, a large number of NPOs have also become more focused on promoting evaluation research and other structured attempts to gauge the effectiveness of both social programs and NPOs as providers of services. There is much greater pressure today to demonstrate the net benefit of such programs and the efficiency of the nonprofit providers in creating improved outcomes. Some NPO staffers see evaluation research as one possible means of defending continued public financing in an anti-government culture, and combating ideologically driven criticisms of welfare spending.

Besides the pressure coming from federal and state and local governments, there are other reasons for this greater attentiveness to careful evaluation research, to regular monitoring of providers, and to trying to substantiate the positive contributions of programs and providers. Some of these reasons are quite negative.

Cases of financial mismanagement and program failures have put some organizations – and by implication, the entire publicly subsidized social economy – on trial in the public square. A series of well-publicized cases of outright corruption by leaders of nonprofit organizations have put the sector under the spotlight (e.g. the corrupt head of the United Way of America was a particularly egregious example about 15 years ago) and even led to legislation that requires all nonprofits to include the total salary compensation of the five highest-paid staff members in their annual tax returns (these appear on NPOs' tax returns – the publicly available IRS Form 1990s). In the late 1990s, conservative congressional leaders proposed harsh anti-NPO tax legislation (e.g. an amendment that would have changed the tax-privileged status of nonprofits) and other measures that would significantly diminish the freedom of operations of multi-activity nonprofits. Research that showed the positive effects of nonprofits would help defend the sector from other attempts at harmful legislative or tax-law changes.

Two other events have also raised calls for tighter regulation of NPOs. In the aftermath of the World Trade Center attacks of September 11, 2001 and Hurricane Katrina flooding New Orleans, the American Red Cross aggressively advertised and played on people's emotions receiving large contributions from sympathetic citizens. Then, the media discovered that this very large NPO had taken in $100 million extra that it intended to keep for future uses. Several media pundits made the Red Cross misrepresentations a symbol of hypocrisy among NPOs in general. This made it politically easier for critics of NPOs to generalize about the need to better regulate the whole universe of NPOs to avoid this abuse of the public's trust in the future. Evaluation, especially the kind that measures their accomplishments, could be helpful in regaining trust.

Corporate scandals and legal trials in the for-profit sector since 2001 caused closer regulatory monitoring and laws. This spilled over onto NPOs. Out of these business scandals came new corporate governance laws increasing the liability of Board of Directors. These regulations require comprehensive reporting of complete compensation packages of directors and executives. The tightened regulation most explicitly affects for-profit companies. Nevertheless, board members at nonprofits are worried about their legal liabilities, since board members at all types of 'corporations' including NPOs are required to be more aware of the operations they govern. (There are, of course, significant differences between unpaid board members at nonprofits and well-paid board members at for-profit businesses, but conflicts of interest do exist.) Since 2001, many outside equity owners of for-profit businesses have been pursuing lengthy and costly legal actions against corporate board members and executives. Apart from funding organizations, nonprofits do not have such a clear class of motivated outside interests who might sue them. Stakeholders do not have a legal property stake in NPOs. For social service NPOs the outsider beneficiaries are 'clients' and the 'general public' whose legal standing in relation to the nonprofit governance is legally ambiguous. According to some thinking, these concerns among board members made them likely to support more evaluation research so board members could show they are pursuing the goals in their mission statements and making good-faith attempts for transparency in performance.

Evaluation's Autonomous Development in the Nonprofit Sector

The most influential private organizations in developing new evaluation programs are foundations, despite their relatively small amount of money funnelled to NPOs. Most foundations require recipient-NPOs to report back to them. Each foundation may have developed their particular set of criteria that must be met or reported on. In recent years, many nonprofit service organizations have asked for more efficiency in these requirements, since, for example, an umbrella nonprofit (i.e. one that has several sub-activities and even several other NPOs within its 'umbrella') may face a formidable task of reporting to numerous funding foundations as well as governments. Ever since the 1960s, when major private foundations were able to set a new agenda in 'community development' through significant funding of innovative nonprofit or hybrid (public and private for-profit & nonprofit) partnerships, many foundations have desired to become leaders in promoting 'social innovations'. One of the potential negative effects of this desire to continuously 'innovate' is that it may be quite easy to get private or foundation funding for a new program, but it may be quite difficult to obtain financing after the programs are no longer 'new'. Many nonprofits have had to allocate a great deal of energy to simply acquiring new sources of funding, rather than giving more effort to the program services that they would like to focus on. The largest foundations can, nevertheless, set whole new agendas in areas of social policy (e.g. the Gates Foundation large scale support for many non-public innovations in basic education).

A second influential source of change in evaluation comes from the United Way affiliates. Many local UWs have been leaders in promoting program evaluation over the past dozen years. Although these developments were mainly for local nonprofits that the UW local organizations helped subsidize, the Internet has allowed the dissemination of 'best practices' and other ideas more rapidly than in the past, when ideas mostly spread through networks of the staff members who were able to attend regional and national meetings of affiliated UW organizations. Since the UW has given a lot more attention to evaluation recently, there are many sets of criteria available on the internet for others to review, learn from, or borrow wholesale (e.g. UW – Greater Twin Cities, 2008).

Over the past two decades, a variety of NPOs, academics, researchers, and community activists have increasingly created community surveys of unmet social needs, often in only one major area (e.g. health services). Often these needs-assessment studies are produced by informal coalitions of individuals from these organizations along with citizen-activists and academics. The methodologies are diverse but the focus is on identifying families, individuals and children in need of more income, health insurance and health care, childcare services, early child (pre-school) development programs, nutrition, housing and housing financing, or job training and other forms of education in specific communities and regions. In a handful of cases, initiatives for social service and community enhancement have come from corporate-NPO partnerships. The UW of Minneapolis-St. Paul is probably the best-known metropolitan region that has done this extremely well (Nocera, 2007).

Foundations and philanthropists have often been the origin of major innovations in program development and evaluation use. The digital revolution has created a sizable number of extremely wealthy (and often quite young) people in the US. They are a major reason that prestigious educational institutions like Stanford University (itself an NPO created more than a century ago by Leland Stanford and family) and its business school have recently begun to devote time and money to new ideas like 'social enterprises' and 'venture philanthropy'. Some commentators think we are on the verge of a revolution in philanthropy that can bring about massive and revolutionary – 'wholesale' – social change in the US, and even in the entire world (Hecht, 2008).

Evaluation Trends in the US – The Good

Rather than just 'counting beans' of how many people attended such-and-such workshop or training program or came into the social service agency, the new evaluation movement puts much more focus on how their knowledge and behavior changes – mainly focused on individuals and their increased self-sufficiency in economic and social life.

The new evaluation movement asks service providers (and often various 'stakeholders') to identify the most relevant indicators that truly move the nonprofit and the communities they serve toward their goals – individual self-sufficiency so that the nonprofits will no longer have any job left to do. Improvement (or not) in performance indicators compared with baseline measures shows what is not working, promoting positive organizational change. This formative assessment becomes embedded into the ongoing process of managing the NPO.

Evaluation has stimulated some private nonprofit funders and foundations to review their pre-existing strategies of community aid. It has shaken up some of the previous inertia of just funding the same organizations year after year. It has led some funders their process of funding, by first reviewing what their most important goals are and by considering what should be priorities in creating 'healthy communities' (Nobles, 2007).

All this ferment appears to have revived and re-stimulated the debate within the 'evaluation community' (see, e.g., the American Journal of Evaluation or New Directions in Evaluation, 2002-2007) about what evaluation ought to be about, what evaluation processes are appropriate for what things, who ought to be involved in part or in whole (e.g. 'stakeholders') and how evaluation itself can relate to the broader political changes and social goals people desire – what is the 'good society' and how can evaluation play a role in helping us see how to promote changes toward it?

Evaluation Trends in the US – The Not-So-Good

The new evaluation movement is costly. It is very hard to create these new sets of indicators and to measure them regularly; it takes a lot of training of staff, a lot of time to develop and, hence, a lot of resources to keep it up (Poole *et al.*, 2000).

Yet more 'stakeholders' are now identifying ways to measure and evaluate success, thus enriching and stimulating collaboration among various 'partners' in the process of addressing America's most pressing social needs. This is the upside. On the other hand, it may also 'co-opt' people and groups who, instead of evaluating, might have been more active in advocating for more governmental generosity or organizing to elect politicians who would ensure more government resources were forthcoming. There is an opportunity cost to 'participation', and the cost is different when one gets involved in a very time-consuming process, even if, *ceteris paribus*, it is for a highly commendable short-term goal.

The new evaluation movement with its focus on measurable indicators is particularly well suited for some activities and not so much for others. Health care and education are traditionally measurable at the individual level. But exclusionary social behavior and practices are the really tough challenges to overcome, so that even if an individual is shown to be more competent as a result of NPOs services, the inclusion of that individual into the mainstream of US society may not be allowed.

The American ideological tradition of 'rugged individualism' and the 'self-sufficiency' fits quite nicely with this new evaluation movement since it emphasizes new capacities, behaviors, and knowledge mainly at the individual level. But there is a downside to this micro focus. It means that many social welfare professional staff and workers must pay attention to indicators that measure individual change, thus neglecting community/regional institutional features and structures that may be generating the problems.

The focus on measurable indicators that are evident in individuals and families has led to a plethora of these indices. People developing the new evaluation processes at agencies and those working with funders can be inundated with dozens, hundreds, or even thousands of indicators (e.g. especially if they fund nonprofits in several different sectors, like the United Way). This apparent incoherence of hundreds of 'indicators' measured and reported make it difficult to focus on broader goals, drowning NPO researchers in the details, stealing the energy to devote to the (desired) overall goal. This has led some foundations and other groups to propose more attention to developing easy and cheap measured indicators.

Like most organizations, NPOs want to prosper and survive. The new evaluation movement of measurable 'outcomes' indicators means another costly, time-consuming hurdle for the organization to leap over. Enlightened funders want their grant recipient organizations to be able to see what is working and what is not. When it is not working, they want the organization to correct course and not simply repeat failures or use resources inefficiently. For this is supposedly the point of the exercise: continuous and real improvements. But the recipient-NPOs and workers who carry out the evaluation of their work will often see the new evaluation procedures like those of the past: you need to show some success in order to retain funding in the new year. Hence, there is a strong incentive to manipulate the results to show regular improvements, even when there may be none.

Individualistic Focus Neglects Institutional Structures in an Anti-State Political Culture

Several contributions to this research project have addressed important issues neglected in this paper. Many of these trends found elsewhere (devolution/subsidiarity; the privatization of social services; new evaluation debates, methodological proposals and new indicators, and contests over defining the purpose and process of 'evaluation'; etc.) have also appeared in the US. One of the major divisions among the countries being studied here is the traditional one (among scholars of the 'welfare state' at least): What kinds of institutional features and public policies describe each of the respective national polities? When comparing already 'rich' countries, the US is usually on one end of the typical spectrum: it is the classical 'liberal' (or, 'neo-liberal') welfare regime that prioritizes (for 'efficiency' reasons) not helping those who do not have great needs. Because of this, compared to most of Western Europe or Canada, a broader and deeper array of economic and social needs go unmet in the US (Goodin *et al.*, 1999). When there will be unmet needs even in the best of economic times and despite great voluntary effort, it is important to know what works best – what does most when faced with the inadequate resources provided by the combination of the state, the market, and the other 'social economy' activities and financing.

The current renaissance in the US of 'evaluation' of 'objectives' (or, more specifically measurable 'outcomes') appears to be beneficial. But how much is the focus on individual outcomes in evaluation causing the US to pay less attention and effort to transforming US political life, to tackling the structural and institutional features that regenerate dire needs in each succeeding period of American history? Are the results of all this evaluation a tragic redirection of energy in the US, so that we are even more unlikely to increase our overall collective efforts (money, resources, time, personnel) dedicated to eliminating the structural causes of ever-increasing individual and social problems facing us?

References

American Evaluation Association, "Guiding Principles for Evaluators July 2004". http://www.eval.org/Publications/GuidingPrinciples.asp (accessed April 6, 2006).

American Journal of Evaluation, American Evaluation Association journal, miscellaneous volumes and articles, 1999-2007.

Giving USA, 2007, http://www.givingusa.org.

Goodin, R. E., Headey, B., Muffels, R., Dirven, H.-J., *The Real Worlds of Welfare Capitalism*, New York, Cambridge University Press, 1999.

Issel, L. M., *Health Program Planning and Evaluation: A Practical Systematic Approach for Community Health Programs*, Sudbury, MA, Jones & Bartlett, 2004.

Jacobs, P., Rapoport, J., *The Economics of Health and Medical Care*, 5th ed., Gaithersburg, MD, Aspen Publishers, 2002.

Joint Committee on Standards for Evaluation, http://www.wmich.edu /evalctr/jc/ (accessed May 3, 2007).

Joseph S. W., Hatry, H. P., Newcomer, K. E. (eds.), *Handbook of Practical Evaluation*, San Francisco: Jossey-Bass, 2004.

Mathison, S. (ed.), *Encyclopedia of Evaluation*, Thousand Oaks, CA, Sage, 2005.

NASCSP (National Association of State Community Services Programs), "Community Services Block Grants", NASCSP, Washington, D.C., 2007. http://www.nascsp.org/csbg.htm.

NASCSP (National Association of State Community Services Programs), Performance Measurement Reports from States Administering the Community Services Block Grant Program: FY 1998, (by Glenn Kambler), Washington, D.C., September 2000. http://www.nascsp.org/ROMA/ Roma_ docs/report-1.pdf.

NCCS (National Center for Charitable Statistics at the Urban Institute), Nonprofit Sector in Brief: Facts and Figures from the Nonprofit Almanac 2007, 2008. (Accessed Feb. 8, 2008), http://www.urban.org/ uploadedpdf/311373_nonprofit_sector.pdf.

New Directions in Evaluations, Jossey-Bass and the American Evaluation Association, miscellaneous special numbers.

Nobles, M. E., "Focus On Community Impact Has United Ways Changing", *The Nonprofit Times*, March 1, 2007. http://www.nptimes.com/ 07Mar/npt-070301-3.html.

Nocera, J., "Emerald City of Giving Does Exist", *New York Times*, Dec. 12, 2007.

Office of the President, US Government. http://www.whitehouse.gov/omb/ budget/fy2009/pdf/hist.pdf.

OMB (Office of Management and Budget), *Budget of the United States Government, Historical Tables, Fiscal Year 2009*, 2008.

OMB (Office of Management and Budget), *Program Assessment Rating Tool website*, Office of the President, US Government, 2006. http://www.whitehouse.gov/omb/part/

OMB Watch, Senate Investigates PART, 2005. www.ombwatch.org/ http://www.ombwatch.org/article/articleview/2889/1/369?TopicID=1

Rock, C. P., Klinedinst, M., "In Search of the Social Economy in the USA", in J. Defourny and J. Monzon-Campos (eds.), *Économie Sociale/Social Economy*, Bruxelles, De Boeck, 1992.

Rossi, P. H., Lipsey, M. W., Freeman, H. E., *Evaluation: A Systematic Approach*, 7th edition, Sage Publications, 2004.

Salamon, L., *America's Nonprofit Sector: A primer*, (2nd edition), Wash., D.C., The Foundation Center, 1999.

Trattner, W. I., *From Poor Law to Welfare State: A History of Social Welfare in America*, 6th edition, 1999, NY, Free Press.

United Way (Greater Twin Cities), News Release: "United Way Announces 2007 Health & Independence Goals – Comprehensive Plan Focuses on Most Vulnerable Citizens", Minneapolis-St. Paul, 2007. MN, January 25, 2007.

http://www.unitedwaytwincities.org/newsandevents/documents/HealthI ndependenceReleaseFinal_001.pdf (Accessed 4 May, 2007).

United Way (Heart of Florida), Interviews with Joan Nelson, Evaluation staff member at the Heart of Florida (Orlando region) United Way, January 26, 2006 & May 9-10, 2007, Orlando, FL, 2007. (Organizational website: http://www.hfuw.org).

United Way of America, "Community Impact: A New Paradigm Emerging, A White Paper on Change in the United Way Movement", Item No. 0120, United Way of America, Alexandria, VA, 1998. http://national. unitedway.org/files/pdf/soc/2001/CIParadigm.pdf (6 May 2007).

US Congress, Government Performance and Results Act [GPRA] of 1993 Public Law 103-62, Washington, D.C., 1993. http://www.sc.doe.gov/ bes/archives/plans/GPRA_PL103-2_03AUG93.pdf.

US DHHS, Office of the Assistant Secretary for Planning & Evaluation, *Program Evaluation Activities of the US Department of Health and Human Services [DHHS]: Performance Improvement*, US DHHS, Washington, D.C., 1995. http://aspe.hhs.gov/pic/loginhttp://aspe.hhs.gov/pic/perfimp/index.html.

US GAO (General Accounting Office), (June), *Executive Guide: Effectively Implementing the Government Performance and Results Act* [of 1993] (GAO/GGD-96-118), Washington, D.C. 1996. http://www.gao.gov/archive/ 1996/gg96118.pdf.

US GAO, Government Auditing Standards: 2003 Revision, Office of the Comptroller General, GAO, 2003. http://www.gao.gov/govaud/yb2003. pdf; http://www.gao.gov/govaud/ ybk01.htm.

US GAO, Community Services Block Grant: HHS Should Improve Oversight by Focusing Monitoring and Assistance Efforts on Areas of High

169

Evaluation of the Social Economy in Brazil
An Analysis of the Practices in some NGOs

Maurício SERVA, Carolina ANDION,
Lucila CAMPOS & Erika ONOZATO

*Full Professor at the Universidade Federal de
Santa Catarina – UFSC (Brazil), President of the CIRIEC-Brazil
Full Professor at the Universidade Estadual de Santa Catarina –
UDESC (Brazil), Researcher at the CIRIEC-Brazil
Full Professor at the Universidade do Vale do Itajaí – UNIVALI
(Brazil), Researcher at the CIRIEC-Brazil
Professor at the Faculdade Internacional de Curitiba – FACINTER
(Brazil), Researcher at the CIRIEC-Brazil*

Introduction

The objective of this article is to offer an overview of how evaluation is being dealt with by organizations that work within the Social Economy in Brazil. Over recent years, the subject of evaluation has come to occupy a prominent position on the agenda of discussions between political actors in Brazil, being seen as an instrument capable of increasing the transparency of organizations in the social economy and of giving society a means of controlling them. This article will not be assuming that this interpretation is a given. Just the opposite, we seek to discover what meaning is attributed to evaluation, how it is being used and what the consequences of the practice are. We understand evaluation to mean the determination of the value or merit of the object evaluated (Worthen, Sanders and Fitzpatrick, 2004: 35). From this perspective, evaluation will *be examined* as a *translator* that expresses the view of the social economy held by society and which reflects the prevailing methods of regulation or governance (Bernier; Bouchard and Lévesque, 2003).

In order to proceed towards this objective, it is necessary to first delineate what we understand by the term Social Economy. This expression does not have the same meaning in Brazil as that often used in Europe and French-speaking countries. One definition sums up well what these countries understand by this "New Social Economy" – to use an expression from Quebec – is that provided by Favreau (2005). According to this author, these organizations (whether associations and cooperatives or mutuals) represent initiatives, manifestations of collective action, that aim to achieve "enterprise in another form". Favreau states that this definition considers the three dimensions of these initiatives without conceding priority to any of them. These dimensions are the social dimension (collective action), the economic dimension (enterprise) and the political dimension (in another form). Collective action refers to the need to work together that is a product of social expedients, whether these be socioeconomic, sociopolitical, sociocultural or socioenvironmental. Enterprise is linked to the economic character of these initiatives, which go beyond the market, although without excluding it; here hybridization of economic regulation mechanisms is considered together with the different forms of enterprise. The expression "in another form" means that these initiatives are the fruit of a multitude of sociopolitical projects designed to promote social transformation.

In the case of Brazil, there has historically been a very clear separation between the universes occupied by cooperatives (of varying types) and by the other not-for-profit organizations (especially foundations and associations) that are part of the Social Economy. So, there is a predominant conception of the second of these groups as being a "Third Sector", which primarily focuses its actions on the social and political spheres, putting economic functions in the background. Parts of the reason for this split can be found in the genesis and growth trajectory of the field itself, where the primary structure was based on a social welfare network and which later, during the years of dictatorship, came to take a position of "opposition" to the State. In both cases, the influence of Christian ideology and of pro-third-world political currents was decisive, meaning that economic questions were relegated to the background or simply forgotten (Revel and Roca, 1998).

For these reasons, when one speaks of a social economy in Brazil, the first thing that comes to mind is the activities of the not-for-profit organizations, although the description "not-for-profit" does not mean that they do not play a relevant economic role. In 2004, the Brazilian Institute of National Statistics and Geography (IBGE – Instituto Brasileiro de Geografia e Estatística) published a survey of not-for-profit associations and foundations which promote collective interests in the country. According to IBGE (2004), there are around 276,000 organizations of this type and, between 1996 and 2002, the number of jobs in these organizations increased by 48%, from 1,039,925 to 1,541,290.

The jobs created in this sector of the economy account for 5.5% of all jobs created in the country.

Having explained this peculiarity of the Brazilian context, in this article we will be focusing on the group of organizations that are known in the country as NGOs. It is important to point out, however, that this is not a homogenous group, this space is shared (and fought over) by many different groups that strive to gain recognition and to claim their positions. There are many different typologies attempting to explore the composition of the field of Brazilian NGOs. For the purposes of this chapter we will adopt the typology developed by Andion (2007) who identifies five principal groups:

- older NGOs, the majority founded during the military dictatorship (1964-1985), and linked with the traditional social movements (trades union movement, neighbourhood associations, or ecclesiastical communities and pastoral organizations belonging to the Catholic Church);
- more recent NGOs, linked with the "new social movements" (feminist movement, ecological movement, black movement, etc.);
- more recent NGOs created by technical and professional people and which are not affiliated with social movements;
- foundations and institutions, the majority of which were created by companies or which are linked with the private social investment movement;
- philanthropic organizations, many of which are also linked to the Church and whose objective is to promote social welfare activities

In the case of this research, fieldwork was carried out with a sample comprising eleven organizations: eight associations and three foundations. Four of the associations can be characterized as the older type of NGO, two as the newer, more professionalised type, with no links to social movements, while the last two are philanthropic. One of the three foundations was created by a group of citizens, while the other two were set up by large companies (one private, the other public) with the objective of developing private social investment in the context of the corporate social responsibility movement. All of these organizations have been established for more than 10 years and their central headquarters are in the South and Southeast regions of Brazil. We believe that the diversity of the types of NGO included in this selection makes it representative of the universe being considered, although we are conscious of the limits to generalization of this research.

Since the focus is an analysis of the methods of evaluation employed by these NGOs, its meaning and the ways in which they are applied, the questions that guided this study were the following. What are the principal methodologies and instruments of evaluation employed within these organizations? What are the objectives of this evaluation? What influence do the stakeholders involved have on this process? What effect does this evaluation have on increasing the accountability of these NGOs? In summary, the intention is to investigate the theoretical concepts that are expounded in the literature and disseminated in the institutional context of the social economy in Brazil and the manner in which evaluation is perceived and utilized by the members of these organizations.

In order to achieve this, the study was designed in two phases. First, a review was carried out of secondary data on the evaluation models used in the field of NGOs in Brazil, since there is no single standard that has been adopted countrywide. The results were used to choose four models,[1] based on the following criteria: (1) the representativeness of the institutions that published and recommended the models; (2) the range of the organizations' sectors of activity that are affected by the models; (3) the extent to which the models are utilized in the country's different regions. Analysis of the models made it possible to determine the dominant evaluation standards and gave the opportunity to raise some of the assumptions made by the study, which were then revisited during the analysis of the eleven cases investigated.

The following text presents the results of this research in three sections. The first part discusses the peculiarities of the way in which the field of NGOs in Brazil has arrived at its current position, by the analy-

---

[1] The first model (Roche, 2000) was published by OXFAM and recommended by the Brazilian Nongovernmental Organizations Association (ABONG – Associação Brasileira de Organizações Não Governamentais). Since 1958, OXFAM has supported and financed the implementation of social projects in all of Brazil's regions, establishing partnerships with organizations from civil society. The second was published in three volumes (Nemes, 2001, Sessions, 2001 and Spink, 2001) by the Brazilian Multidisciplinary AIDS Association (ABIA – Associação Brasileira Interdisciplinar da AIDS). This association comprises a network of organizations whose goal is to exert social control over public policies for AIDS prevention on a national level and it has a significant influence on NGOs working in the area of healthcare in Brazil. The third model (Marino, 1998) was published by the Instituto Ayrton Senna. This institute was founded in 1994 by the sister of the motor racing driver Ayrton Senna (who died in 1994) and its mission is to support and finance social projects, primarily in youth education. The institute supports NGOs throughout the country and has become a model of excellence in the area of youth education. The fourth model (Chianca; Marino and Schiesari, 2001) was published by the Instituto Fonte, which provides services geared towards institutional reinforcement of associations and foundations by means of NGO management training programmes throughout Brazil.

sis of the relationship that has been established between the State and civil society. This preamble is necessary, since it attempts to understand the influence of governance standards on the meaning of evaluation and on the ways in which evaluation has been applied in the national Brazilian context. The second section consists of an examination of the models described above, indicating similarities and differences in their concepts, in their aims and in the actual design of these models, making it possible to demonstrate the different ways in which evaluation is conceptualized. In the third and last section, an analysis is made of the principal applications of the prevailing evaluation practices in the NGOs investigated. This is in order to better understand the meaning and the praxis of evaluation in these organizations, how it is used and to what extent it can meet the challenges that are faced by the Brazilian Social Economy today. Thus, the intention is to use this examination, of what NGOs understand by and practice of evaluation, in order to demonstrate that the strategies and mechanisms employed do not only have a technical and functional role, but also express the importance, position, and value that the Social Economy has come to assume in Brazilian society today.

1. Historical Standards of Governance and Evaluation Practices in the NGO Sector

In Brazil, the relationship between the State and the Third Sector, as the NGO field is often called, has historically been organized on the basis of a range of different regimes of governance. We understand governance as a configuration of laws, structures, resources, administrative rules and institutional standards which program and condition public services and their regulation (Bernier; Bouchard; Lévesque, 2003). Here, the definition of public service is wider than just the State, since it includes other actors that act in, and have influence on, the public sphere. We attempt, therefore, to demonstrate how the transformation of these standards of governance over time has impacted on the concepts and forms of the evaluation methods used within the field of NGOs.

From colonial times onwards, the *regime of "assistance"* predominated in Brazil, where public services were ineffective and community services were not financed by the State, but on a clientelistic basis. It was during the period of the First Republic (1889-1930, also known as the Colonels' Republic) that first philanthropic entities were created to provide spontaneous and disinterested help to the poor. The Blessed Houses of Mercy (*Santas Casas de Misericórdia*), the Sisterhoods (*Irmandades*) and the Third Orders (*Ordens Terceiras*), together with other non-Catholic religious institutions, took a prominent part in caring for the majority of the population who were beyond the boundaries of the basic social policies. It could therefore be considered that the idea of civil society was interwoven with notions of philanthropy and charity, by which the poor (the greater part of the population) were seen not as citizens with rights, but as the objects of their benefactors' goodwill. During this period the issue of evaluation did not even exist as a value, since the services provided were in the form of spontaneous assistance (benevolence) motivated by a feeling of solidarity, on the part of society, with the excluded.

The *welfare regime* was institutionalized from the 1930s onwards, during the administrations of President Getúlio Vargas, when the first social welfare laws were created in Brazil, and the great majority of these are still applicable to this day. Decree number 525 of 1938 defines the objective of social service as, "to reduce or overcome the want or suffering caused by poverty or destitution". This legislation did not break with the tradition of social work as charity; on the contrary, as Landin (2002) points out, it helped to define the role of the associations as being complementary, thereby legitimizing the concept of a civil society guided by the State.

This is made clear by the creation of the National Social Welfare Association (CNAS – *Conselho Nacional de Assistência Social*), the objective of which was to delineate the "institutions of a private nature" responsible for these services and to study their situation for the purposes of State-awarded grants. In this manner, the government recognized the existence of these institutions and made itself the principal arbiter of their regulation. This was reinforced by the law number 3,071 of 1935 which recognized the public utility of these organizations. In order to maintain the title it became compulsory to submit an annual report detailing the services provided to the public. This was the first attempt at an instrument to evaluate these organizations, requiring them to account for themselves to the government.

In another way, a non-mercantile character became an essential part of the definition of such initiatives (since they could not remunerate their board of directors) and was also essential to establishing the fact that the State was financially renouncing these organizations. In 1959, law number 3,577 exempted philanthropic and social welfare entities from making social security contributions, which was to be confirmed by the Federal Constitution of 1988. However, in order to qualify for this exemption, organizations had to meet the requirements set out in law, i.e., they could not be involved in any type of mercantile enterprise, could not distribute proceeds from their economic results or share profits and they could not transfer ownership of shares in their assets. It is therefore clear that, from the first moment on, the welfare regime has had a very strong influence on the composition of the Brazilian "Social Economy", which may be one of the reasons why the economic sphere, and even any concern with management, is absent from its actors' agendas. It is interesting that this concept has remained up to the present, as can be observed in the Brazilian civil code itself, which came into force in 2003. This defines associations as "legal entities subject to private law, with non-economic objectives, being defined as associations or foundations (depending upon their terms of constitution)".[2]

However, at the end of the 1970s and during the 1980s, tensions began to appear with relation to this "social economy of welfare", at a time when other regimes of governance began to emerge in Brazil. During this period it is possible to trace two simultaneous movements which reconfigured the dynamics of the relationship between State and civil society, creating the basis for a *participatory regime* (Paes de Paula, 2005). First, a social mobilization movement began to appear which was characterized by the emergence throughout the country of the new type of social movements. The most important of these include the: Grassroots Ecclesiastical Communities (CEBs, *Comunidades Eclesiais de Base*), neighbourhood associations and groups that are part of what are known as the "new social movements" that operate in rural areas (the family agriculture movement, the landless people's movement, etc.) and in urban areas (environmentalist movements, the black movement, the feminist movement, etc.). This phenomenon has been identified by many authors as a milestone of democratic transition and of the growing strength of Brazilian civil society. Scherer-Warren and Krischke (1987) describe these organizations as collective initiatives that fight against traditional ways of conducting politics. They distinguish themselves from the old social movements by their struggle for the recognition and social inclusion of the "Brazilian people"; a term that is used here in a wider-ranging sense than the concept of the working class. This "people" will seek its affirmation as citizens who have rights. For Dagnino (2002), the appearance of these movements redefined the concept of citizenship and made it possible to construct a truly public dimension within Brazilian society, proving that everyone has the right to have rights.

It was at this point that NGOs of a new type began to be created, different from the philanthropic and welfare organizations that had predominated up until that point. In the beginning, these organizations did not see themselves as NGOs, just as centres for assisting the newborn movements: "their members did not demonstrate any sense that they

---

[2] Translated from the Portuguese.

belonged to a unique institutional class"[3] (Landim, 2002: 18). In addition to being supported by the new social movements, the majority were maintained, in financial terms, by international cooperation. International NGOs were in need of local partners who were capable of planning projects and monitoring their execution, in order to promote development in South American countries. The local NGOs were "mediators" between the movements, the popular organizations and the foreign financers, which allowed these organizations a relative degree of autonomy from the government. This relationship reinforced the influence of the international NGOs, both in terms of ideology and management of the local organizations. This fact is relevant to understanding the origins of the adoption of evaluation models and methodologies developed by international NGOs such as the Kellogg's Foundation, OXFAM, Avina, and Misereor, among others, which are widely used in Brazil to this day.

Another prominent feature of this process of mobilization is the growing involvement of the private sector in social issues, starting during the 1990s. This brought with it the adoption of practices such as private social investment, corporate volunteering and social responsibility, which up until then had been rarities in the country's private sector. Within the institutional dimension, this movement resulted in the creation of many foundations and institutes by large private companies with the aim of carrying out social projects, very often in partnership with the NGOs. Furthermore, it has engendered the foundation of representative institutions with national and even international circles of activity, such as the Group of Institutes, Foundations and Enterprises (GIFE)[4] and the Ethos Institute for Social Responsibility.[5]

The other relevant movement during the 1990s relates to changes in the institutional framework (legal, organizational and decision-making) of the State that resulted from the new Constitution of 1988. Important mechanisms were inserted into the new Constitution in order to guarantee public participation, such as plebiscites and referendums, public audiences and councils. These last will make it possible for civil society

---

[3]   Translated from the Portuguese.

[4]   GIFE is a not-for-profit entity created in 1995 in the form of an association by 25 organizations set up by major private economic groups that carry out social investment in Brazil. Nowadays, GIFE is a network of 81 associated entities, all affiliated to major national or multinational economic groups.

[5]   The Ethos Institute was founded in 1998 by a group of businessmen and executives from the private sector with the objective of deepening the commitment of their companies to corporate social responsibility. It now has 1,049 associate companies, which account for a volume of business that corresponds to around 30% of Brazilian GDP and which employ around one million people.

to participate in the conception and implementation of public sector policies and in defence of rights. Furthermore, the Constitution makes municipalities into autonomous federative entities and increases the proportion of federal taxes passed to the states and municipalities by the Union. Increasing their political and fiscal autonomy, the municipalities took on functions in terms of public policies, on their own initiative or by joining programmes proposed by a level with wider scope. All of this stimulated decentralization and increased the responsibilities and powers of local organizations (Arretche, 1999).

All of these mechanisms have widened the possibilities for control by society. In this sense, evaluation of civil society organizations that work within the public sphere is no longer just a function of the government and has come to be a function of society itself. In spite of the advances brought about by the Constitution, it is known that there are many limits to the application of such mechanisms,[6] with respect to achieving real change in evaluation practices. In the majority of cases, the councils can claim little representativeness, their members have little training and they do not have the real instruments (neither financial nor institutional) necessary to act more proactively.

Towards the end of the 1990s, this tendency toward consolidation of a more participatory regime controlling the relationship between State and civil society was to meet with a movement to implement a *new regime of governance, inspired by neoliberal principles*. During this period, which coincided with President Fernando Henrique Cardoso's two terms of office, there was a restructuring of the State in Brazil, which was institutionalized in the form of the Master Plan for the Reform of State Apparatus (*Plano Diretor da Reforma do Aparelho do Estado*), and which had been made possible by the constitutional amendment of 1996 (Bresser Pereira, 1998). This reform involved fiscal adjustments, in addition to "modernization" of public administration, by means of decentralization. The reform drove the transfer of exclusive activities of the State to the private and nongovernmental spheres through privatizations and the creation of new legal public institutions such as: the Regulatory and Executive Agencies (*Agências Reguladoras e Executivas*), Social Organizations (*Organizações Sociais*) and Civil Society Organizations of a Public Nature (OSCIPs – *Organizações da Sociedade Civil de Caráter Público*). The guiding principle of this reform was that only strategic activities were to be preserved for the State, while the remainder (especially social and scientific services) would be passed to the nongovernmental sphere. This strategy was seen as a way to reduce costs and to amplify the efficiency of public services.

---

[6] For greater depth on this discussion see Arretche (1999) and Fauré (2005).

The emphasis here is on the operational efficacy of the organizations in the "Third Sector".

The OSCIP Law 9,790 of 1999 was passed in the same spirit, and is considered the first step towards a "new legal standard" in the field of Brazilian NGOs, since it resulted in a series of changes to the way that these organizations were perceived and to their relationship with the State. According to the new rules, organizations can be classified as OSCIPs if they work in the traditional areas of philanthropy (social welfare, education and health), and also in other areas such as: cultural activities, conservation of national historical and artistic heritage, preservation and conservation of the environment, promotion of volunteering, and others. However, classification as an OSCIP also distinguishes those organizations whose objectives are truly public from those whose goal is to benefit only their own members. This being so, the title of OSCIP both amplifies and qualifies the range of organizations that can be legally recognized as working to promote public interests.

Another change made by this law was the possibility of remunerating management. This illustrates recognition of the way in which the field has become professionalised and to a certain extent breaks with the previously dominant vision of a sector motivated purely by spontaneous help. The state is therefore accepting for the first time that this sector is also an economic sphere, to the extent that the board of directors can be paid for their work. However, it is important to point out that classification as an OSCIP makes no reference to immunity or exemption from taxation, and is no substitute for a Federal Declaration of Public Utility, issued by the Ministry of Justice, nor for a Certificate of Philanthropic Status (*Certificado de Fins Filantrópicos*), which is issued by the National Social Welfare Council (CNAS – *Conselho Nacional de Assistência Social*). Therefore, in order to take advantage of fiscal benefits, these organizations cannot remunerate management, consultants, members, founders, benefactors or equivalents.

Finally, another essential feature of this law was the introduction of a new legal instrument which regulates the relationship between the State and organizations classified as OSCIPs, the Partnership Contract.[7] This instrument introduced new ways of administrating the partnership between the State and the organizations, increasing audit mechanisms and modifying the traditional evaluation methods. In order to win a

---

[7] Prior to Law 9,790 of 1999, individual covenants were the primary mechanism for effecting transfer of public resources to civil society organizations and it was compulsory that these be registered with the CNAS. The alternative was via contract, which had to fulfil the strictures of Law 8,666, of 21st June, 1993 (The Public Tenders Law).

Partnership Contract, organizations have to submit a working plan containing: (1) the goals and results predicted, with execution deadlines and a spending schedule; (2) objective performance evaluation criteria; and (3) a forecast of revenues and costs. The law also requires organizations to submit accounts directly to their partner body, in the form of a report on the execution of the objectives of the Partnership Contract, which must contain (1) a comparison between goals and results; (2) a cash flow statement indicating revenues received and payments made; and (3) a published statement of physical and financial activities carried out. Furthermore, Public Policy Councils (*Conselhos de Políticas Públicas*) must be consulted before the Partnership Contract is signed and must participate in the commission that evaluates the results (Castro, 2008).

This concern with changing the legal standard did not proceed much further once the government changed and, during the mandate of President Luiz Inácio da Silva (from 2003 to now), the policy was not continued. This aspect was also reflected in the weak take-up by civil society organizations, with relatively few of them opting to be classified as OSCIPs.[8] However, the discussion about the need for regulatory instruments that increase the transparency of the sector remains in the centre of the agenda under debate. For example, at the start of 2008, the federal parliament set up a Parliamentary Commission of Inquiry (*Comissão Parlamentar de Inquérito*) on NGOs, charged with investigating financial operations between the federal government and certain NGOs during the period between 2003 and 2006.

The historical analysis carried out above allows us to conclude that the composition of the field of NGOs in Brazil has taken on different outlines over time. These transformations are reflected by the different identities that these organizations have taken on over time, by the roles that they have assumed for themselves and the relationships that they have nurtured with other social spheres. In the case of Brazil, these transformations have been guided by the different regimes of governance that have developed over time (assistance, welfare, participatory and neoliberal). The more recent regimes have not substituted the traditional ones, they continue to cohabit today, colliding at many different points and resulting in a confused regulatory standard, in addition to institutional standards that are very distinct between different NGOs. This analysis is reflected in the evaluation published by the

---

[8]   According to official statistics from the Ministry of Justice, in 2005 3,334 not-for-profit organizations had successfully obtained the title of OSCIP. When one considers the survey carried out by IBGE, which identified 276,000 organizations in 2002, those that have been classified as OSCIPs so far account for just 1.2% of the entire sector.

Brazilian Nongovernmental Organizations Association itself (ABONG – *Associação Brasileira de Organizações Não Governamentais*).[9]

> The legal framework that regulates the functioning of civil society organizations is complex and fragmented. It does not meet the demands of the organizations involved, nor does it meet the demands of government. It does not strengthen the involvement of organized civil society, nor does it establish a transparent relationship with the State which would allow civil society to control public policies and achieve truly democratic access to public resources (Da Paz, 2005: 23).[10]

This entire process will influence the way in which evaluation is understood and applied in Brazil. As has been examined earlier, evaluation will come to be valued in this field primarily on the basis of a concept of hierarchical control by the State and other donors. Although mechanisms for social control by civil society have been created, in practice, these are little used and ineffective. Over time the importance of evaluation has increased, but this importance is primarily linked to the notion of controlling results. This tendency is more evident during the last few decades, with professionalization and institutionalization of the field and a greater demand for transparency on the part of the NGOs. However, is this perception also projected by the practice of the NGOs themselves? We believe the answer is yes, and in order to verify this hypothesis, we carried out research that took account of both evaluation models and the NGOs' practices. The results of this research are presented below.

2. Analysis of the Evaluation Frameworks and Research Assumptions

In evaluating the four models studied, we perceived that there is no homogeneity either in terms of methodologies or in terms of the combinations of indicators proposed for evaluating NGOs, notwithstanding the few similarities that were detected. The "culture of evaluation" is a recent appearance on the scene and has been very much influenced by the demands of the donors, the majority of which are both the sponsors and executors of these evaluations. Therefore, we believe that it is important to illustrate two features of the way in which the models under examination were developed: the point of view from which the models were conceived and their institutional origin.

---

[9] This is a not-for-profit civil society which aims to, "represents and promote exchange between NGOs working to strengthen citizenship and to win and represent social rights and democracy" (ABONG website, 2005). Founded on 10th of August 1991, in 2004 ABONG had 277 associates.

[10] Translated from the Portuguese.

Although all of the models analyzed declare that both internal and external actors demand evaluation, it is clear that all of the models are, in general, conceived from an external point of view. The logic that presides over the choice of evaluation scales is that which most interests the sources of finance (whether the State or businesses) rather than the other actors involved, including the members of the organizations themselves.

The programme is the privileged level of the evaluation process, and approaches that are centred on management[11] and on objectives[12] are the most common (Worthen; Sanders and Fitzpatrick, 2004). The organization and measures to strengthen it only appear in one model and, even in this model, the programme is indicated as the principal level of evaluation. The financial backers provide resources to the organizations in order that they execute specific programmes, and so they attempt to control the efficiency, efficacy and effectiveness with which these resources are employed during implementation of these programmes. The logic of this is that the way in which the organization functions and even the effects of its actions on communities may remain beyond the scope of the evaluation process. The primary subjects of evaluation are the activities, effects and yield defined by the initial programme (which is very often used as the evaluation and monitoring instrument).

In terms of the institutional origins of the models, we found that three of them had been developed by NGOs (two are Brazilian and one is international) which are financial backers or play a formative role in the sector. Although the State is entering into ever more partnerships with associations and foundations – creating mechanisms to regulate this relationship – public institutions do not yet appear to play a role as protagonists in the production of widespread NGO evaluation models. One reason for this may be the strong influence still exerted in the field by the international donor institutions.

Despite the good intentions expressed in the models being studied, the predominance of the unilateral perspective of donors could restrict their potential for application. Evaluation can therefore be seen as something outside of the requirements of the organization itself and of its target public, and as something they have not taken ownership of. Based on these findings, we now come to certain research assumptions that we have defined as reference points for our analysis of the data obtained from the organizations investigated:

---

[11] The central interest is to identify and meet the needs for information of the managers who are taking decisions.

[12] The focus is on specifying goals and objectives and on defining measures that make it possible to verify whether they have been achieved.

- Since the formal models of evaluation are conceived from a point of view that is external to the organization, the evaluation resulting from their application may not necessarily engender a revision of the NGO's practice, probably because it is carried out much more in order to meet external demands than organizational needs.

- In addition to the formal models of evaluation proposed by the donors, it may have other social spaces, other practices and other instruments used by NGOs in order to reflect on their practices, and also to evaluate them.

- The application of the formal models of evaluation does not appear to demand real participation by actors from the communities affected by the organization's activities (the public). Therefore, application of these models does not necessarily contribute to increasing the accountability of NGOs.

3. The Meaning and Practice of Evaluation of the NGOs Studied

As has been stated earlier, we analyzed data relating to the evaluation processes of eight associations and three foundations. Appendix 1 provides a brief characterization of each of the organizations investigated, describing their origins and activities, in order to provide readers with a better idea of their institutional dynamics. We will present the results of the analysis with relation to the three research propositions laid out above, attempting to give a general view of the evaluation processes being examined.

In 10 of the organizations, the primary demand for formal evaluation is external to the organization and it is the donors who are the most interested in the results of the evaluation. Just a single NGO was not in this situation since it does not receive incomes from external organizations. In this case evaluation is demanded by the management. For all of the other organizations, the process of systematic evaluation is established by the financial backers who also impose their specific model. These models primarily aim to evaluate the programme financed by each agent providing resources, and whose priority interests are to analyse activities (management-centred approach) and results (goal-centred approach). Each evaluation is carried out according to the procedures established by the sponsor: there are cases in which evaluation is performed entirely by representatives of the financial backer, in other cases it is carried out by members of the organization and in some cases there are both external representatives and internal members involved.

In five cases there is provision for the community affected by the organization's activities to take part in the data collection stage. In these cases the communities participate in processes to evaluate projects/activities, but almost never take part in the final stage of analysis and feedback of the data collected. Data are collected by the donor or by the organization or by the two together, and then these data are sent directly to the programme's sponsors and very rarely returned to its beneficiaries. Retransmission of evaluation results to organization members is not systematic and in many cases there is no retransmission of information to the community, which results in weakness in terms of the degree to which results are utilised in a wider process re-evaluating the organization.

The processes of evaluation investigated here are very often of a cumulative character (Scriven, 1967), focusing on assessing the merit of projects/activities with relation to criteria considered important (primarily by the sponsors), by means of testing the results against what had been forecast. There is, therefore, less emphasis on evaluation of processes or evaluation leading to learning, emphasising the creation of information useful for improving management. It is important to point out that in all of the cases there are internal management evaluation mechanisms, such as; a system for rendering accounts, annual reports and indicators of more consolidated results. However, utilization of this information remains restricted, since it is primarily communicated to external backers.

On the other hand, it was observed that this tendency is combined with more utilitarian evaluations (House, 1983), where value is attributed to the overall impact of the programme on those affected by it. From this perspective, the "greatest good is that which will benefit the greatest number of individuals" (Worthen, Sanders and Fitzpatrick, 2004: 109). This means that greater weight is given to objective indicators and to those which illustrate the "quantities" affected rather than the "quality" of the programmes. This being so, even when indicators are mixed, priority is given to quantitative indicators that illustrate the results achieved in the most objective form possible. The evaluation instruments most often used are document analysis and questionnaires. In cases where there is more obvious engagement with the community, interviews and discussion groups are also employed for data collection. The period evaluated is generally the same as the programme duration. For certain longer programmes, sponsors may require three-monthly or six-monthly data collection, but in general evaluations are annual.

The analysis of the data collected from the organizations therefore contributes to confirmation of the first research proposition: the evaluation that results from applying formal models established by the donors does not appear to engender any systematic review of these organization's practices. In certain organizations (two older associations, one more recent association and one foundation), the members are already conscious of the gap between the requirements of sponsors and those of the organization. They make it clear that it is necessary to develop and practice other forms of evaluation of their organizations' actions. Nevertheless, this does not mean that these organizations have already implemented more consistent evaluation processes. This finding brings us on to the second research proposition.

All of the NGOs studied, to a certain extent, carry out an internal evaluation of the impact of their actions. However, these evaluations are not systematic and could be characterized as "spontaneous". Furthermore, with the exception of the single NGO which does not have any external body demanding evaluation, all of these processes are still centred on final activities and do not focus on a more systemic vision of the organization or of its planning.

In one older NGO, affiliated with urban social movements and which has entered into a dynamic of professionalization and role changing, we observed a process of construction of an evaluation model which corresponds to its specific sector of activity. This construction is based on qualitative indicators related to the different strands of its activities. Taking the indicators as references, this organization intends to evaluate the results and the impact of its actions. This is the most advanced effort to develop a method for impact evaluation that we encountered during our research, made on the organization's own initiative.

In addition to programme-centred evaluation, the "spontaneous" processes involved holding periodic meetings (in general, weekly or monthly) between organization members. This was a practice that was generalized throughout the NGOs. At these meetings actors discuss ongoing activities, the difficulties and problems encountered, etc. However, the absence of systematization and cascading of information and the fragmentation of the subjects dealt with (in general more operational) make it difficult to achieve deeper reflection on the organizations' actions. One member of a more recent NGO, which works to develop family agriculture, stated that, "the evaluation that is carried out at these meetings has a weak effect on the group, because of the lack of systematization, and it does not contribute to the transparency of our activities, since the results of our discussions and also of the data analysis that we send to our external sponsors are not transmitted to the community as they should be."[13] On one hand, a lack of systematization

---

[13] Translated from a transcript in Portuguese.

means that it is unlikely that members will grasp the full depth of information that is being dealt with; on the other hand, the effects of discussions and evaluations do not often reach the users. It should also be pointed out that certain NGOs are resistant to the implementation of systematic internal evaluation, and also to divulging some of the results of their evaluations.

At two of the foundations (one set up by a business and the other by citizens) significant efforts are being made to carry out internal evaluations that result in learning, with strong interaction between organization members and the community. In both these cases, organization members respond to their financial backers' impositions (primarily businesses) sending all of the information demanded and, at the same time, have constructed a specific space based on their own values in which evaluations leading to learning are carried out.

Therefore, with reference to the second research proposition, it can be stated that – beyond the formal evaluation models proposed by donors – other practices are indeed also employed by organizations to reflect on their actions, but these mechanisms appear to still be limited in terms of consolidation, systematization, communication and utilization of information.

With relation to the third research proposition – which suggests that there is a relationship between participation by community actors in evaluation and the accountability of organizations – the data analysis demonstrated that application of the formal models of evaluation does not contribute to any significant increase in the accountability of the organizations studied. When the evaluation models are applied, community actors primarily take part in data collection as information providers. The analysis of this information and, as a consequence, its interpretation, is not very often retransmitted. Of the 11 organizations analyzed, just four (two foundations and two older associations) carry out evaluation with any true community participation. These organizations take advantage of evaluation to promote strong interaction between their members and community actors, providing an incentive for discussion of the activities defined by the programmes. These are initiatives taken by the organizations themselves, independent of the models established by their sponsors. Nevertheless, these initiatives continue to be centred on the evaluation of programmes.

In the light of these findings, we can conclude that in the majority of the cases investigated evaluation is still seen, and practiced, much more as an external instrument for controlling the organization than as a means for promoting learning. Few organizations take ownership of evaluation and translate the models proposed by their financial backers, using them as a means of institutional reinforcement. It can, therefore, be perceived that the meaning of evaluation and the evaluation types and instruments employed in the field of NGOs reflect the tendencies brought up by the standards of governance analyzed earlier. Next, we will explore this interface a little more, reaching the final comments of this text.

4. Final Considerations

We believe that the issues raised above are crucial to a better understanding of the challenges that currently characterize the process of evaluation of Brazilian NGOs. This subject has taken on a crucial importance in a national scenario in which NGOs are gaining ever more influence, being considered as active agents in the management of public policies and promotion of public services. In this context, there is an increase in the social controls and pressure on NGOs to become more transparent and to account for their actions. The question that society generally asks is: are the regulatory mechanisms in existence today, both internal and external to the sector, sufficient to ensure this transparency?

Two opposing views predominate within public opinion with relation to this question.[14] The first claims the positive character of these organizations as an a priori fact, based on their values and purposes, as though the simple fact of belonging to civil society was a guarantee of effectiveness. The second is suspicious of NGOs in general – particularly of those sponsored by the State – and sees them merely as apparatus created in order to take advantage, in a dishonest manner, of public resources. Both views suffer from a lack of rigour and, more than anything else, reflect the lack of a wider discussion about the relationship between the State and civil society in a democratic project.

We have tried to approach this discussion in this text, expounding two principal pieces of evidence: the first is the predominance within the sector of standards and models of evaluation imposed by donors. The second, linked to the first, is the lack of consistent initiatives, on the part of the NGOs themselves, to implement methods of evaluation,

---

[14] A debate in the press occurs on this subject. For more information see: ONG não é governo. In O Tempo. Belo Horizonte: 16/08/2007; Associação de ONGs defende "regras claras" para convênios com governo. In A Tarde, Salvador: 22/10/2007; Fortes rebate crítica de Dulci e defende CPI das ONGs. In A Tarde, Salvador: 16/11/2007; Ministro defende ONGs e critica CPI. In Diário do Nordeste, Fortaleza: 16/11/2007; Oposição quer CPI investigando fraudes. In Diário do Nordeste, Fortaleza: 17/07/2007; CPI das ONGs investiga mais de 100 autoridades. In Última Hora, Campo Grande: 13/04/2008; CPI pede que Banco Central investigue ONGs suspeitas. In Última Hora, Campo Grande: 16/04/2008; PF vai intimar dirigentes de 60 entidades filantrópicas. In Última Hora, Campo Grande: 14/03/2008.

whether formal or informal, which would permit them to increase the accountability of their actions.

With relation to the first piece of evidence, we have seen that the evaluation standards of this sector have historically been constructed, "from the outside in", with no conciliation between the different actors involved. In other words, the ways in which evaluation has been perceived and practised reveals the interplay of forces that have influenced the configuration of the field of NGOs itself (affected more by governments and financial backers and less by beneficiaries and communities).

It is perceived that the regulatory standards within the field were conceived historically from a perspective of "hierarchical control" exerted by the state on the NGOs. On the other hand, the majority of the evaluation models utilised were developed and proposed by sponsors, with the object of ensuring that results will be achieved and the resources employed will be better utilized. In both cases, the NGOs are seen much more as "executors" of programmes than as active participants in the planning and formulation of these programmes. Evaluation can therefore be interpreted here as a means for revealing the importance, the merit and the value of the object evaluated (Worthen, Sanders and Fitzpatrick, 2004), being a translator of the vision that society has of the field of NGOs. This appears to still be seen more as a space where the inefficiencies of the State (and the market) are compensated for, than as a self-justifying sector that generates wealth (both monetary and non-monetary) and produces social innovations.

We believe that, to the extent that this vision is transformed, and this depends to a great extent on the configuration that the NGO sector takes on over the coming years; the concept of evaluation itself and its practice may be redefined. If concern is no longer solely with the "functionality" of a Third Sector – towed along by the State and the market –, evaluation will come to be seen not just as an instrument of control, but also as a means for constructing and communicating learning about the sector. In such a scenario, actors would also be concerned with using evaluation as a means to delineate the impact that these organizations actually have on society, because they would consider their activities as indispensable to the development of that society.

We come therefore to the second piece of evidence which is the non-existence of any motivation that could propel the NGOs towards deepening their accountability. We believe that such a process would demand collective effort – more than the individual initiatives existing today – in order to create systems of regulation that are shared by different social actors and which can be linked to incentive mechanisms and an institutional support structure[15] (Lloyd; Las Casas, 2005). Although it has its limitations, as demonstrated above, the OSCIP classification was developed in this spirit and created new mechanisms aimed to make the practices of evaluation of NGOs and achieving accountability more effective.[16]

> However, as has been described by Lloyd and Las Casas (2005) – who investigated a variety of experiments with self-regulation in NGOs all over the world – external variables alone are not enough to increase the accountability of these organizations. It is important that evaluation experiments take into account the requirements and expectations of all the different stakeholders involved: private sponsors, governments, partners, management, technical and professional staff, volunteers, beneficiaries and communities. Evaluation must make sense to all the different actors involved with an organization, in particular the members of the NGO itself and its users, who, in the majority of cases, have seen the least benefit from its effects. This implies real dialogue between interested parties, both at the level of the NGOs and of the sector as a whole.

From this perspective, evaluation is not merely an instrument for responding to external demands and becomes an instrument for promoting institutional reinforcement both of the organizations themselves, and of the entire field. Evaluation is conceived as an important vector for determining the value of the actions of NGOs. It can aid in identification of the "results achieved" and also their true impact on social, economic, political and environmental changes in the regions. We believe that this is a crucial aspect for the development of the sector, given the importance that the issue of the transparency of NGOs has taken on in current Brazilian public opinion.

References

Andion, C., *Atuação das ONGs nas dinâmicas de desenvolvimento territorial sustentável no meio rural de Santa Catarina: os casos da APACO, do Centro Vianei de Educação Popular e da AGRECO*, Tese de doutorado defendida no Programa Interdisciplinar em Ciências Humanas, Florianópolis, Universidade Federal de Santa Catarina, 2007.

---

[15] Examples of incentive/reinforcement include the use of certification as a criterion for distributing funds, offering tax incentives or even audits by competent bodies (Lloyd; Las Casas, 2005).

[16] It is important to point out that none of the organization which is investigated as part of this research is classified as an OSCIP. It would, therefore, be interesting to draw parallels between the cases studied here and NGOs that have been classified as OSCIPs in order to determine whether there are any relevant differences in their evaluation practices.

Arretche, M. T. S., "Políticas Sociais no Brasil: descentralização em um Estado federativo", in *Revista Brasileira de Ciências Sociais*, 14, 40, São Paulo, junho de 1999.

Bernier, L., Bouchard, M. J., Lévesque, B., "Attending to the general interest: new mechanisms for mediating between the individual, collective and general interest in Québec", in *Annals of public and cooperative economics*, 74, 3, September 2003.

Bresser Pereira, L. C., *Reforma do Estado para a cidadania: a reforma gerencial brasileira na perspectiva internacional*, São Paulo, Editora 34, 1998.

Castro, L., *Entidades Filantrópicas*, www.uff.br/direito/artigos, 2008.

Chianca, T., Marino, E., Schiesari, L., *Desenvolvendo a cultura da avaliação em organizações da sociedade civil*, São Paulo, Instituto Fonte, 2001.

Dagnino, E., "Sociedade Civil, Espaços Públicos e a Construção Democrática no Brasil: Limites e Possibilidades", in E. Dagnino (org), *Sociedade Civil e Espaços Públicos no Brasil*, Rio de Janeiro, Paz e Terra, 2002.

Da Paz, R. D. O., *Organizações não-governamentais. Um debate sobre a identidade política das associadas à ABONG*, São Paulo, Cadernos ABONG, 33, junho de 2005.

Fauré, Y. A., "Des politiques publiques décentralisées: entraves au développement local. Expériences brésiliennes", in *Revue Tiers Monde*, 181, janeiro-março 2005.

Favreau, L., "Qu'est-ce que l'économie sociale? Synthèse introductive", in *Cahiers du Crises*, Collection études théoriques. ET0508, mai 2005.

House, E. R., Assumptions underlying evaluation models, in G. F. Madaus, M. Scriven, D. L. Stuffebeam (Eds.), *Evaluation Models: ViewPoints on Education and Human Services Evaluation*, Boston, Kluwer-Nijhoff, 1983.

IBGE – Instituto Brasileiro de Geografia e Estatistica, *As fundações privadas e associações sem fins lucrativos no Brasil*, Brasília, IBGE, 2004.

Landim, L. "Múltiplas identidades das ONGs", in S. Haddad (dir.) ONGs e Universidades, São Paulo, Peirópolis, 2002.

Llyod, R., Las Casas, L., NGO *self-regulation: enforcing and balancing accountability*, Alliance Extra, December 2005.

Marino, E., *Manual de avaliação de projetos sociais: uma ferramenta para aprendizagem e desenvolvimento de sua organização*, Belo Horizonte, Instituto Ayrton Senna, 1998.

Nemes M., *Avaliação em saúde: questões para os programas de DST/AIDS no Brasil*, Coleção ABIA, 1, Rio de Janeiro, ABIA, 2001.

Paes de Paula, A. P., *Por uma nova gestão Pública*, Rio de Janeiro, FGV, 2005.

Revel, M., Roca, P.-J., "Les ONG et la question du changement", in J. P. P. DELER *et al.* (org.), *ONG et développement. Société*, économie et politique, Paris, Karthala, 1998.

Roche, C., *Avaliação de impacto dos trabalhos de ONG*, São Paulo, Cortez, ABONG, OXFAM, 2000.

Scherer-Warren, I., Krischke, P. J. (orgs.), *Uma revolução no cotidiano? Os novos movimentos sociais na América do Sul*, São Paulo, Brasiliense, 1987.

Scriven, M., "The methodology of evaluation", in R. E. Stake (Ed.), *Curriculum evaluation, (American Educational Research Association Monograph Series on Evaluation)*, 1, Chicago, RandMcNally, 1967, pp. 39-83.

Sessions, J., *Avaliação em HIV/AIDS: uma perspectiva internacional.* Coleção ABIA, 2, Rio de Janeiro, ABIA, 2001.

Spink, P., *Avaliação democrática: propostas e práticas*, Coleção ABIA, 3. Rio de Janeiro, ABIA, 2001.

Worthen, B. R., Sanders, J.R., Fitzpatrick, J.L., *Avaliação de programas: concepções e práticas*, São Paulo, Editora Gente, 2004.

The Evaluation of Social Solidarity Organizations in the Portuguese Context

Isabel NICOLAU & Ana SIMAENS

Associate Professor, ISCTE-IUL,
Lisbon University Institute (Portugal)

Senior Teaching Assistant, ISCTE-IUL,
Lisbon University Institute (Portugal)

Introduction

The relevance social economy organizations have in economy and in society is well recognized, but the way their activities are managed and evaluated is under discussion. The organizations are facing issues of a different nature, such as competition for limited resources, the governance challenge and the role of the government in the area of social solidarity services. Besides, having different principles from those of public and private organizations, traditional management practices are not always adapted and other alternatives are needed to combine the principles with the management instruments. Evaluation is an important area to be developed and can have an important contribution to overcoming these major issues. The role of evaluation in the progress of social economy organizations as well as in building legitimacy and credibility is more and more recognized. However, evaluation practices and procedures differ according to the activity, the type of organization and the juridical framework, as well as the social pressure for accountability and transparency (Bouchard, chap. 1).

The recent evolution of the social economy in Portugal, the major issues social solidarity organizations face, as well as the role of evaluation in this context will be highlighted. Finally, the main trends in methods and indicators of evaluation in the social solidarity organizations will be analyzed in order to come to conclusions on the major consequences of evaluation on organizations' practices.

1. Context

1.1 Recent Evolution of the Social Economy Sector and Organizations

The emergence of social economy in Portugal is not recent, but in the last three decades there has been an evolution in its social and economic roles. This evolution has been mainly shaped by three major factors: the change of the political regime in 1974, the globalization phenomenon and the adhesion to the European Community.

At the national level, the major change occurred in 1974 when the revolution replaced the dictatorship with a democratic regime, opening the society to new values and collective behaviors. At the world level, globalization has promoted the openness of political borders, liberalization of markets and the intensification of competition of firms and territories, which has transformed the world economic and social landscape. Finally, the adhesion to the European Community accelerated the internal reforms and allowed a much deeper integration to the worldwide wave of change. As a consequence, in Portugal, during this period the political, social, economic and institutional contexts underwent a profound transformation with consequences in the scope and role of social economy sector.

In fact, freedom of speech and association gave a crucial push to new forms of organization within civil society. New legal and institutional frameworks were designed and public policies concerning social economy were deeply modified, offering a more propitious environment. The new Constitution established public support for cooperatives and for the first time, defined explicitly three sectors in the economy: public, private and cooperative. The public institute for the cooperative sector INSCOOP was created in 1976 to mediate the relationship with the government.[1]

The explosion of the associative movement led to the creation of numerous social organizations with several juridical forms, mainly cooperatives, associations, mutual benefit societies, foundations and charitable institutions. In spite of this boom, the first decade of democracy was marked by strong instability with high creation and destruction rates of organizations, sometimes due to the lack of management abilities or financial support, in line with what was happening in the whole economy. A more flourishing period began with the admission of Portugal to the European Community in 1986. The available funding

---

[1] INSCOOP – *Instituto António Sérgio do Sector Cooperativo.*

gave a new push to cooperation and association which contributed to the increase and consolidation of the Portuguese social economy.

This civil movement was a result of the political openness and an answer to the new social needs created by a changing society. The allowance of divorce for Catholic marriages, the increasing participation of women in the working force, the aging of the population, as well as the transformation of social values, had consequences in the families' organization. Moreover, the globalization phenomenon, changing the world location of activities, modified the economic and social regional landscape. The incapability of the State to satisfy new needs had consequences on the number of social organizations, and on their scope and role. In spite of the maintenance of the fundamental principles, cooperatives became very different from those of the end of the 19th century or even of the middle of the 20th century. The modern cooperative movement is no more circumscribed to the proletariat, farmers or peasants. Its social base was enlarged and we can find cooperatives of service workers, technicians, artists, liberal professionals or even small enterprises (Namorado, 1995). Also, the social solidarity enlarged the restricted concept of charity which was focused on poor people's needs, as was the tradition of Catholic Church, to a more inclusive way of thinking of the social problems. The cooperative movement was progressively engaged in this area and, as a consequence, the 1989 revision of the constitutional text redefined the third sector, becoming cooperative and social. Their role had also been enlarged. Social economy organizations have had a fundamental role in the improvement of social cohesion, especially in local communities. Sometimes they represent the sole possibility of economic survival in a region as is the case of some agricultural cooperatives; in other situations, they are the only viable way to solve a social problem. For instance, social solidarity organizations that support elderly people keep them near the community, and at the same time, avoid the desertification of some little villages offering jobs to younger people. Otherwise, as globalization has been promoting the change of location of activities, some of the lesser competitive regions are losing the most important firms which cause a lot of problems for the survival of local populations. Organizations emerging from civil society are frequently an alternative for the generation of locally grounded income, less vulnerable to the global rationality.

However, social economy in Portugal is still a diffused concept. The existing studies and data comprise only parts of it, which makes it difficult to identify it as a whole.[2] The social solidarity action is one of

---

[2]   Portuguese cooperatives, mutual benefit societies, charitable institutions and some foundations, accounted for around 2.2% of the total workforce and in 1997, the co-

the most important areas in which social economy organizations act. In 2006, they represented about 70% of the existing offer of the Social Facilities Network, i.e., kindergarten, day care centers, domiciliary support, education, health care, for instance (GEP/MTSS, 2007). Those not-for-profit organizations have different juridical forms such as associations, foundations, mutual benefit societies or cooperatives. Most of them are qualified as private institutions of social solidarity, named IPSS.[3] According to their specific statute, they are constituted not-for-profit, by private initiative, with the purpose of giving organized expression to the moral duty of solidarity and justice among individuals.[4] They pursue a set of objectives through the concession of goods and provision of services and cannot be managed by the State or by a local public authority. The government gives them financial support, considering that they have a relevant action in solidarity. The principle behind this is the subsidiarity, meaning that the government should perform only those activities which cannot be performed effectively by the IPSS that are closer to the social problems of the communities.

Due to the relevance of social solidarity in the context of social economy, the following analysis will be focused on social solidarity organizations (SSO).

1.2 Major Issues Faced by Social Solidarity Organizations in the Present Context and the Role of Evaluation

In the last thirty years, SSO have faced increasing challenges due to the social and economic evolution. Because they are often dependent on external resources to survive, SSO are challenged to adapt to the present context in the provision of services and in the capture of the needed resources. Nowadays current debates on the field indicate that they face three major issues: the increasing competition, the changing role of government and the governance challenge. The role of evaluation must be analyzed in this context.

Competition and the Role of the Government

In the social solidarity sub-sector, competition is more and more intensified. Organizations compete not only for customers but also for

---

operatives (excluding the credit cooperatives) generated about 5% of the national GDP (Nunes, Reto and Carneiro, 2001). Otherwise, according to Franco *et al.* (2005) the nonprofit sector in Portugal represents 4.2% of the economically active population, and the social service represents almost 50% of the workforce in the whole Portuguese civil society.

[3]   IPSS – *Instituições Particulares de Solidariedade Social.*

[4]   Law-Decree No. 119/83, 25th of February.

employees, volunteers, investors, donors, locations, ideas or any other resources to pursue their purposes (Post, Preston and Sachs, 2002), such as public recognition and media attention (La Piana and Hayes, 2005). This competition comes both from similar not-for-profit organizations, and increasingly from for-profit organizations, which have had an increasing role in the Social Facilities Network.[5] In fact, the lines between public, social and private sectors are more and more diffused. Social services are increasingly attractive for for-profit initiative and the government leaves the main role to private organizations, for-profit or not, acting as a complement.

Nevertheless, the public role is much more important than this could suggest. The government subsidizes the IPSS, through cooperation agreements, and is mostly their main funder.[6] The government expressly reinforces the intention of establishing a truly social public partnership with these organizations. As Ferreira (2005: 8) refers, in the social security budget for the social action sub-sector "the amount of transfers to nonprofits through cooperation agreements is greater than the amount the State spends providing its own services".[7] The amount of funds are negotiated once a year, in cooperation protocols, signed at a national level and negotiated between the Ministries and peaks associations of IPSS.[8] As is the case of the United States (Rock, chap. 8), also for-profit organizations are not completely excluded from access to public funds, since they can be subcontracted to provide social services (health, for instance). So, in the near future, it is predictable that private sector, besides funding in the context of social responsibility, will be a serious competitor in the provision of social services, as well as in the demand of public funds.

This relationship could apparently fit in the partnership governance type of regime which is in line with the typology developed by Enjolras (2005). However, the extent to which the institutional coordination for policy making is both formal and pluralist, i.e., includes a balanced power of the providers of social services, may be questioned. The government has an increasing determinant role as a regulator and funder because it establishes the rules, defines the eligible activities and pro-

---

[5]   In 2006 they provided around 27% of social services and facilities, compared to 20% in 1998 (DEPP, 2001; GEP/MTSS, 2007).

[6]   Specific norms regulating the cooperation were established later in 1992 with the Normative Dispatch No. 75/92, of 20th of May.

[7]   About 70% on average between 1997 and 2001 (Pereira, 2002; 2005).

[8]   Afterwards, regional services of the Ministry establish specific cooperation agreements with each organization giving the money according to the number of individuals served in each area of intervention.

vides funds. These terms are the main references to the organizations that may apply for support.

For the IPSS, this model of funding may reduce its financial vulnerability, but there are not only advantages for them. Despite being autonomous, when they rely too much on public funds, they act as an extension of public offer of services since their action is restricted by the conditions imposed by the government with the use of the given funds. Some argue that this raises some constraints on innovation capability and limits their autonomy and flexibility (Evaristo, 2004; Equal, 2004). Besides, the uncertainty of the amount obtained from the Portuguese Budget Law for the following years as well as the reliance on these funds may have a negative impact in the strategic management of these organizations. The fact that organizations have to plan on a year-to-year basis puts the stress on the survival rather than in the development of these organizations, inhibiting organizations initiatives and innovation.

The Governance Challenge

The corporate governance has been widely debated in the literature (Keasey, Steve and Wright, 1997; Collis and Montgomery, 1998; António, 2001; Dess, Lumpkin and Taylor, 2004; Davies, 2006). The more restricted definition describes corporate governance "as the system by which companies are directed and controlled" (The Cadbury Committee Report, 1992: 14), whereas some others extend the scope of the definition to include "the entire network of formal and informal relations involving corporate sector and their consequences in the society in general" as referred by Keasey, Steve and Wright (1997: 2). Thus, corporate governance is related to the management practices of organizations as well as the relationship with their stakeholders and the evaluation and control organizations are submitted to. Because SSO have special missions, they transform several stakeholders such as clients, funders, suppliers, government, partners, staff, members and community, as part of their responsibilities. So, it is important to identify the ones that are more relevant by analyzing how they evaluate the organization, how they can influence it and what the organization needs from them (Bryson and Alston, 2005).

This situation can be analyzed in the context of resource dependence theory. The underlying premise is that "organizational activities and outcomes are accounted for by the context in which the organization is embedded" (Pfeffer and Salancik, 1978: 39). So, the organization's behavior is influenced by the external actors with which they transact and, consequently, "organization must attend to the demands of those in its environment that provide resources necessary and important for its continued survival" (Pfeffer, 1982: 193). This means that, on the one hand, organizations must respond to the demand of actors in the environment that control critical resources, and, on the other hand, boards must manage the external dependencies to ensure the survival of the organization and more autonomy and freedom from external constraints.

One of the major problems for SSO is to get funds for their activities. In accordance with their missions, these organizations are not mainly generators of funds, but users. Funds may come from private donors, public subsidies or self revenues. Usually, this last source is not the most important and the funds coming from other sources may be more or less concentrated on one specific funder (sponsor, government, for instance). This causes a strong dependence from external forces with implications on governance practices. In fact, the organization must comply with the funder's objectives, as well as its evaluation criteria. Boards are challenged on the one hand, to respond to these requests, on the other hand, to avoid an adverse behavior. As Wheelen and Hunger (2004: 330) alert, "because the effectiveness of the not-for-profit organization hinges on the satisfaction of the sponsoring group, management tends to ignore the needs of the client while focusing on the desires of a powerful sponsor". When the funder is mainly the government, as what frequently happens in Portuguese SSO, sometimes they tend to structure themselves to support the demands of public funding, being caught in a "subsidiary trap", as called by Brooks (2000: 452). This may mean that there can be a mission creep, "a pernicious process of moving further and further away from the core mission" as stated by La Piana and Hayes (2005: 6).

Besides the reactive behavior, as stated by resource dependence theory (Pfeffer, 1982; Greening and Gray, 1994; Hodge and Piccolo, 2005; Spear, chap. 7), organizations must attempt to reduce the dependences to keep their autonomy. Thus, it is up to SSO to undertake strategies and actions that help them cope with the environment, for instance diversifying the funding sources (Froelich, 1999). Piggybacking strategies and strategic alliances are possibilities (Wheelen and Hunger, 2004). A piggybacking strategy consists of investing in or developing unrelated businesses, which are considered safe investments and compatible with market opportunities (Nielsen, 1982). As La Piana and Hayes (2005: 33) explain, "the successful competitor not only gains immediate resources, but in the longer term, it positions itself to attract a variety of additional resources. As it differentiates itself, it is more likely to grow more than the others". Strategic alliances can be pursued especially to attain self-funding objectives of the organizations, and are also ways of reducing costs in a collaborative perspective (Wheelen and

Hunger, 2004). This shows that strategic management is then one relevant aspect of the governance challenge.

Asides from funders, organizations have become more scrutinized by other stakeholders (workers, technicians, users, community, etc.) and SSO are increasingly confronted and compared with private providers of similar services, having to prove their social superiority. Issues like the quality of services, efficiency, participation and commitment of workers with the mission are fully recognized and, as a consequence, improvement of managerial practices, are crucial. However, some lack of professional competences in this area is an obstacle to the improvement of practices both in the day-to-day operational activities and in strategic management (Veiga, 1999; Carvalho, 2005).

One question is how to adapt the traditional management tools to social economy organizations that are mission-driven and preserve and enhance their fundamental values and characteristics. Yet the big issue is about the use of management tools in the creation of a governance model complying with the diversity of internal and external stakeholder's expectations, satisfaction and commitment.

The Role of Evaluation

In this context, what is the role of evaluation?

Evaluation means giving value to something. However, the concept of evaluation may be applied to very different situations. It can designate an isolated action (judgment of results, for instance) or, on the contrary, a systematic process, that is, as stated by Idáñez and Ander-Egg (2002: 31), "a way of applied systematic, planned, and focused social research, in order to identify, get and provide in an accountable and valid way data and information which is enough and relevant to support a judgment about the merit and value of a program or an activity". Evaluation in this broad sense is different from measuring, monitoring and controlling, terms that are often used interchangeably. Measuring is the process of determining the extension and/or quantification of something; monitoring is the continuous and periodic examination, with the purpose of assuring activities' schedules, avoiding discrepancies with planned objectives and controlling is the verification of the results. A consistent evaluation is only possible when we can measure data, monitor the achievement of successive goals and control the results. Then, measuring, monitoring and controlling are all parts of the evaluation process.

SSO are permanently evaluated by their stakeholders according to the expectations they have regarding their activities. Due to their diversity of interests, evaluation may take different forms according to the objectives. Within an organization, evaluation may be done at different levels, such as individuals, programs, projects, departments, or the organization as a whole. The object of evaluation may be inputs, processes, outputs and outcomes depending on the objectives and available resources.

In addition, the process of evaluation that SSO are submitted to depends on who is asking for the evaluation and its intended use. Thus, it can take a relevant role on the development of the organization or be a *pro forma* without a meaningful impact. Depending on the process, evaluation may act as:

– a transparency factor in the relationship with the stakeholders;

– an enabler of legitimacy and credibility, since these organizations depend on public and private funding, evaluation methods and indicators can help organizations create a good reputation that allows them to prove their social utility and leverage fundraising;

– a learning process and a management tool because better management practices can be enhanced by evaluation routines. In this sense, evaluation has an "instrumental utility" (Ferrão, 1996: 31) and must be seen as a learning process, not as a simple obligation to satisfy the request of any internal or external demander. In this perspective, the process must consist of a clarification of the mission; definition of the objectives and plans of action; establishment of measures and indicators, and the attribution of responsibilities. The gap between what was planned and what was achieved can then be evaluated, the corrective measures are taken, allowing the organization to learn from the past errors. The results in terms of innovation, quality of services, efficiency on the use of resources, satisfaction of the users can be improved. This requires more than running a process of evaluation, it needs a culture of evaluation that must be embedded in daily management practices. This may not always be clear to everyone since there is often some resistance to being evaluated, mainly if it is seen as verification and control, rather than a learning process;

– a mean to reinforce the principles of the social economy. The development of the evaluation process may be an opportunity to involve the workers in decisions, creating a more democratic internal environment and strengthening their commitment to the mission. A culture of systematic evaluation can also put stress on ethical procedures and promote a responsible social solidarity. In addition, by revealing the outcomes and externalities to the community, evaluation reinforces the role of social economy as an alternative to the market economy.

The issues these organizations face and the way they will overcome them will be determinant for their future development.

2. Main Trends in Evaluation of the Social Solidarity Organizations

As mentioned before, there is a great diversity of organizations acting in the social solidarity field of social economy sector, not only in terms of juridical forms (for instance, cooperatives, foundations, associations), but also in the developing activities (kindergarten, daycare centers, domiciliary support, professional training, for example). So, the methods of evaluation as well as the indicators may diverge according to the specificities of each organization, the context they act and the intended use of the demander. The intention is not to present an exhaustive list of practices but instead, reveal some examples based on empirical research, documentary research and professional experience.[9]

Evaluation of these organizations is an increasingly important issue in Portugal. However, besides the theoretical discussions claiming the benefits of transparency, legitimacy, credibility and learning of better practices, it is not difficult to realize that evaluation has not yet become part of the agenda of many organizations and, when it has, often it is shaped and used in a limited way. In fact, in general, evaluation is still synonymous with accountability in a limited sense, i.e., as "a mean by which individuals and organizations report to a recognized authority and are held responsible for their actions" (Edwards and Hulme, 1996: 967). These organizations are responsible before a lot of stakeholders – funders, users or clients, government, workers, community in general. However, there is an asymmetry of power and, as stated by Ebrahim (2005), because the accountability is a relational concept, the accountability mechanisms are shaped to satisfy the dominant actors. Considering the relevance of the public funding (the Portuguese government and the European Union), in general, one can say that the institutional and political frameworks have a determinant influence on evaluation methods and often evaluation is little more than the accomplishment of some compulsory procedures. However, there are also examples that reveal some interest in doing evaluation for management purposes, especially those organizations that are engaged in becoming more efficient and recognize the need to imbed a culture of evaluation in their daily practices, as is the case of some SSO that are planning to adapt the balanced scorecard as a management tool.

In order to have a better understanding of the evaluation methods and indicators, as well as the impact they have on organizations, evalua-

---

[9] A questionnaire to twenty-five social solidarity cooperatives helped develop the diagnosis of methods and indicators of evaluation used in these organizations.

tions according to the internal or external stakeholder's initiative will be presented.

2.1 The Evaluation of Internal Initiative and its Impacts

Evaluations solicited by internal stakeholders usually take the form of internal auditing or monitoring procedures with managerial objectives. In fact, there are more and more organizations that feel compelled to develop these evaluations which may be developed by internal staff or by externals. The purpose is to achieve an extended understanding of how the organization functions in order to produce some useful recommendations. Several dimensions can be the main focus of these evaluations. The development of the relationships with external stakeholders, the financial performance, the quality of services and the performance of human resources among others, are usually taken into consideration. Some indicators have been used in order to treat these subjects more objectively:

– Links to external entities and institutional cooperation are very important in the development of networks through which organizations are inserted into society, pursuing their missions. The evaluation of these links is usually done using indicators such as the number of companies the organization works with; the number of companies coaxed into professional insertion and the number of retained relationships. These indicators tend to be merely quantitative. They do not measure neither the quality of the links nor its relative importance to the network, indicating only the extension of the network;

– Financial performance is perhaps the dimension most often monitored due to the financial constraints that most of them have. Indicators concerning the level of budget execution; investment executed and self-funding capacity are used, among others;

– Quality of the service provided. As mentioned earlier, this is recognized as a challenge SSO face and this is also visible in internal auditing. The indicators depend on the type of activity. Some are widely used, such as the number of claims; others are more specific, for instance, in professional training the approval rate; dropout rate or the employment rate are used;

– Linked to the quality, the performance evaluation of the employees have progressively been implemented, despite the fact that the majority of the organizations do not have any formal evaluation system and use a casuistic approach to it (Evaristo, 2000). However, many SSO employ several professional categories, such as psychologists, professors, therapeutics, technicians, sociologists, infant teachers, auxiliary and administrative personnel, and their performance and competencies are crucial for the quality of the service provided. In some cases where evaluations are developed, indicators of punctuality and assiduity as well as productivity ratios and the 360° performance evaluation method are good examples.

All these evaluation initiatives may include mixed tools including documentary study, participant observation, interviews, questionnaire and focus group; as well as mixed indicators, i.e., both quantitative and qualitative indicators.

In order to help the search for better quality, the Social Security Institute developed the so-called "Evaluation Models of the Quality of Social Answers". This guide has a pedagogical intent, showing how an organization can develop a Quality Management System and is based on ISO norm 9001:2000 and the excellence model of the European Foundation for Quality Management (EFQM). The criteria considered are related to the means (leadership, planning and strategy; people's management; resources and partnerships; processes) and the ends (clients' satisfaction; people's satisfaction; impact on society; performance results). However, as any other evaluation methodology, it requires the commitment of the organizations. They must feel that a proactive attitude towards evaluation can help them create legitimacy, reveal transparency besides enhancing managerial practices and some of them are indeed aware of this.

2.2 Evaluation of External Initiative and its Impacts

The European Union as a funder and the Portuguese government as funder and regulator are the main responsible entities for the external initiative evaluations these organizations are submitted to.

The role of government in evaluation is twofold: one is related to the technical and financial pre-requirements to qualify SSO as an IPSS and the other is related to the control in the use of funds. The first is an *ex-ante* evaluation that includes the examination of the level of socio-communitarian activity, as well as the economic and financial capacity in order to determine if they have technical conditions to pursue its mission. Nevertheless, as noted by Hespanha *et al.* (2000) this legal procedure seems to be often dispensed, revealing some fragility in the system that reduces the impact and consequences of the legal exigencies. The second is an ongoing evaluation that consists of checking periodically if the activity has been developed according to the protocol. The control is mainly done using the number of users of each service as an indicator, which is compared with what was declared in the agreement. The control of fiscal obligations and the payment of social security taxes are also done.

This evaluation tends to have a limited impact on organizations. It is designed to follow the money, but cannot always control its use. Nevertheless, the evaluation of these organizations is not consensual. On the one hand, as some argue, who pays has the right to impose the conditions of the use of money, and control the results; on the other hand the problem of legitimacy of public intervention in the development of the activities can be raised. They are private and autonomous from the government, so they are free to make their own decisions. So, "the intervention of the State in IPSS should be limited to the cases where there are a statutory deviation or legal norms default" (Hespanha *et al.*, 2000: 226). The fact that the evaluation structure is basically imposed with pre-defined evaluation parameters may raise the debate of the autonomy of the organizations.

The European Union subsidizes and evaluates several projects in the scope of programs, but in this case, the process is more complex and rigorous. The evaluation is pursued at different moments, *ex-ante*, ongoing and *ex-post*. The *ex-ante* evaluation begins with the appraisal of applications that must include a clear definition of the objectives, the methodologies and the balance of competencies, and a mechanism to validate the organizational competences. These dimensions are pre-established by the funder. Ongoing evaluation consists of periodic and random financial auditing and monitoring the execution of the projects. The evaluation also depends on the specificity of the program. Considering the example of the Equal program, there are three evaluation methodologies to the individual projects: balances of competences, self-evaluation and independent evaluation.[10] The balance of competences is to be updated during the course of the project. However, this tool was criticized due to difficulties in the correct application which is considered a bureaucratic and rhetoric obligation. On the contrary, self-evaluations were viewed as important in changing attitudes towards evaluation and their utility were fully recognized (Capucha *et al.*, 2005). These self-evaluations can be assisted by an external evaluator that works as a facilitator during the process. There is a self-evaluation guide that includes explanations of how to develop it, by whom, as well as a set of questions that are strategic for the development of the projects in the different milestones. This guide can be adapted in accordance to each project's convenience. The purpose is to use these evaluations as a learning tool that promotes the involvement of stakeholders. Finally, the independent evaluation is developed by an external or internal entity. In any case, the Equal project managers define the evaluation content. *Ex-*

---

[10] "Key issues for the mid-term evaluation of EQUAL CIP in the Member States", Brussels 3.9.01, DG EMPL G.5, Rev. 1, available at http://ec.europa.eu/ employment_social/evaluation/docs/eval_key_en.pdf, 27/07/07.

post evaluation is concerned with the identification and analysis of final results. Besides the evaluation of projects, there are evaluations of the programs at national and European levels.

In spite of the European evaluation being oriented to programs or projects, it has contributed to the enhancing of management practices, mainly in those organizations that lacked a more professional approach. Exigencies in terms of financial reporting, project execution levels and validation of the project outputs make them develop new managerial procedures. For instance, in the Equal Program, the Portuguese product validation model is recognized as a best practice in Europe which enhances organizational practices.

Despite the main funders, SSO may be submitted to other external initiative evaluations. For instance, INSCOOP develops an annual ranking of the 100 largest cooperatives. It presents data on the participation of co-operators; professional training courses; inclusion employment policy; sportive culture and leisure activities; hygiene and security at work; consumer protection policy and ambient policy in order to evaluate their social responsibility. There is another ranking of the five largest cooperatives by branch, considering sales, cash flow, financial autonomy and productivity. Cooperatives are potentially aware of these rankings due to the significant impact they have on their reputation. This is also an incentive to innovation and good practices of cooperative values and principles.

To conclude, it is important to note that funders' evaluations focus mostly on the evaluation of direct outputs of the projects, programs or specific activities while the externalities to the community, such as the creation of employment, the increasing of local wealth or the leverage of social welfare, are in general not evaluated. Nevertheless, there are studies in some social areas devoted to the evaluation of the impact of the European funds in Portugal that may be a methodological guide to evaluate at the organizational level. For example, Capucha *et al.* (2004) studied the impacts of the European Social Fund in the rehabilitation of disabled people, considering three levels: the level of individuals (e.g. personal development, well-being, social inclusion); the level of the service providers (e.g. economic, organizational, juridical impact); and finally the level of professional rehabilitation system (e.g. policies and ideology, networking and partnerships, social and political visibility).

3. Analysis of Evaluation and its Impacts

The evaluation of the social economy organizations is a complex task. While the indicators measuring the outputs and financial performance can be identified, in a more or less consensual way, the social outcomes are much more difficult to measure and remain under-evaluated. The impact of their activities on the communities and people lives cannot be appraised using standard methods and indicators. However, it is very important to measure them in order to fully understand the social role of the social economy sector as well as to understand how they are different from the private for-profit competitors.

In Portugal, evaluation of social economy organizations is a current topic whenever the role and the relevance of this sector are discussed. Social solidarity, in particular, is one of the most relevant sub-sectors, being supported mainly by public funds. The growing number of organizations as well as their increasing social role raises questions of transparency, credibility and legitimacy in the use of public funds. Then, evaluation is becoming a social claim. In spite of this, in Portugal evaluation is still a developing area, and as Carvalho (2005: 107) states, "it is difficult for the organizations to evaluate their performance and compare it with others, because they are not concerned with it, they are small and medium sized and there are no dominant organizations with standard practices". Despite being complex and resource demanding, evaluation at the organizational level is important to see if the organization as a whole is going in the right direction and evaluate potential synergies among the different areas inside the organization.

Internal evaluation, as stated before, may help improve the efficiency, transparency that creates legitimacy, credibility and good reputation, and reinforce the principles of the social economy, or be limited to a meaningless *pro forma*. As stated by Poole *et al.* (2001), the quality of the evaluation depends on several factors, namely the organizational culture, the technology (knowledge, skills, techniques, and hardware), the management support and the involvement of people. In many SSO, there is a lack of knowledge, skills and evaluation culture what may justify the weak involvement of the boards and the workers in general. Despite the positive evolution in the last decades, much more needs to be done. In some organizations, boards are becoming younger and more educated, but still need more competences in management (Simaens, 2007).

While internal and voluntary initiative evaluation usually has a strong impact on the organization as a whole, the objective of the external evaluation asked by funders is mainly to control the use of funds. Mostly it is focused on programs or specific projects, and does not allow evaluation on all of the organization's activities. Nevertheless, the procedures to apply to European funds and ongoing evaluation have contributed to improve internal routines and some management practices. In fact, inside some organizations it can be observed the difference in routines between areas relying on European funds and the others. The internal learning process has also been beneficial to the reputation and credibility because the success on previous projects enhances the possibility of access to new funds.

Besides, the role of European funds in the development of the social economy overcomes the contribution to the individual organizations. They have changed the landscape of social economy allowing the provision of much more services, the improvement of technology and the quality of the offer. Despite of the unquestionable positive effect, some limitations may be pointed out, namely the rigidity in the use of funds. The imposed conditions leave little autonomy to the organizations to make unforeseen changes, jeopardizing the optimization of the resource allocation.

Finally, the extent to which current evaluation methods stimulate the long-term perspective of management can be discussed. The evaluation of projects is focused on their short-term results. As a consequence, organizations are stimulated to show good performance in these specific activities leaving behind the long-term concerns. However, the prosecution of their missions needs a long-term perspective in order to deal with social development and change. A balance must be found between the need of short-term accountability and long-term sustainability.

To conclude, as Guba and Lincoln (1989) refer, evaluation is an investment in people and progress. Thus, the need for more efficiency, quality of service and management procedures can be supported by the use of evaluation methods. Certainly, they not only boost SSO' efficiency but also innovation practices that will produce positive externalities in the communities where they are inserted and promote general welfare.

Conclusion

The social economy in Portugal has had an increasing role in the society, especially after the 1974's Revolution. In the present context, more than thirty years after the boom, SSO face the challenges of competition, governance and the changing role of government and evaluation could have an important role in overcoming them. Nevertheless, evaluation is still not embedded in the routines of most SSO. Despite examples of good practices in the Portuguese context, the main conclusion is that there is the need for enhanced methods of evaluation that allow the improvement of management practices and better service provision.

References

António, N., "Corporate Governance and the Stakeholder Theory – A Brief Introduction of the German-Japanese Model", *Economia e Gestão Global*, 1, 2001, pp. 29-48.

Brooks, A., "Public Subsidies and Charitable Giving: Crowding out, Crowding in, or both?", *Journal of Public Analysis and Management*, Summer 2000, 19, 3, pp. 451-464.

Bryson, J., Alston, F., *Creating and implementing your strategic plan – a workbook for public and nonprofit organizations*, Jossey Bass, 2005, 2nd edition.

Capucha, L., Cabrita, M., Salvado, A., Álvares, M., Paulino, A., Santos, S., Mendes, R., *Os Impactos do Fundo Social Europeu na Reabilitação Profissional de Pessoas com Deficiência em Portugal*, Edições Centro de Reabilitação Profissional de Gaia, 2004.

Capucha, L., Evaristo, T., Calado, A., Pereira, A., Salvado, A., Conim, C., Honório, F., Mateus, E., Santandré, J., Álvares, M., Estêvão, P., *Estudo de Actualização da Avaliação Intercalar da Intervenção Estrutural de Iniciativa Comunitária Equal*, Instituto de Estudos para o Desenvolvimento, 2005.

Carvalho, J., *Organizações Não Lucrativas – Aprendizagem Organizacional, Orientação de Mercado, Planeamento Estratégico e Desempenho*, Edições Sílabo, 2005.

Collis, D., Montgomery, C., *Corporate Strategy – A Resource-based Approach*, McGraw-Hill International Editions, 1998.

Davies, A., *Corporate Governance – Boas Práticas de Governo das Sociedades*, Monitor, 2006.

DEPP, *Carta Social – Rede de Serviços e Equipamentos 2000*, Lisboa, 2001.

Dess, G., Lumpkin, G., Taylor, M., *Strategic Management – Texts and Cases*, McGraw-Hill, 2004.

Ebrahim, A., "Accountability Myopia: Losing Sight of Organizational Learning", *Nonprofit and Voluntary Sector Quarterly*, 34, 1, March, 2005, 56-87.

Edwards, M., Hulme, D., "Too Close for Comfort? The Impact of Official Aid on Nongovernmental Organizations", *World Development*, 24, 6, 1996, pp. 961-973.

Enjolras, B., "Regimes of Governance and General Interest", CIRIEC Working Paper No. 2005/1, 2005.

Equal, *Consolidação, Visibilidade e Reconhecimento – Para uma Economia Social Organizada, Eficaz e Sustentável*, Grupo Temático Equal – Economia Social, 2004.

Evaristo, T. (coord.), *Estudo e Avaliação das Capacidades das IPSS da Região de Lisboa e Vale do Tejo*, Fundação CEBI, 2004.

Ferrão, J., "A Avaliação Comunitária de Programas Regionais: Aspectos de uma Experiência Recente", *Sociologia – Problemas e Práticas*, CIES/ISCTE, 22, 1996, pp. 29-41.

Ferreira, S., "The Places of the Third Sector in the Portuguese Welfare Regime: The Case of Social and Family Services", Presentation at the First European Conference EMES/ISTR, Paris, April 2005.

Franco, R., Sokolowski, S., Hairel E., Salamon, l., *The Portuguese Nonprofit Sector in Comparative Perspective*, Universidade Católica Portuguesa and John Hopkins University, October 2005.

Froelich, K., "Diversification of Revenue Strategies: Evolving Resource Dependence in Nonprofit Organizations", *Nonprofit and Voluntary Sector Quarterly*, 28, 3, 1999, 146-268.

GEP/MTSS, *Carta Social – Rede de Serviços e Equipamentos – Relatório 2006*, Lisboa: Centro de Investigação e Documentação, 2007.

Greening, D., Gray, B., "Testing a Model of Organizational Response to Social and Political Issues", *Academy of Management Journal*, 37, 3, 1994, pp. 467-498.

Guba, E., Lincoln, Y., *Fourth Generation Evaluation*, Sage Publications, 1989.

Hespanha, P., Monteiro, A., Ferreira, A., Nunes, M., Hespanha, M., Madeira, R., Hoven, R., Portugal, S., *Entre o Estado e o Mercado: As Fragilidades das Instituições de Protecção Social em Portugal*, Quarteto Editora, 2000.

Hodge, M. Piccolo, R., "Funding Source, Board Involvement Techniques, and Financial Vulnerability in Nonprofit Organisations: A Test of Resource Dependence", *Nonprofit Management & Leadership*, 16, 2, 2005, pp. 171-190.

Idañez, M., Ander-Egg, E., *Avaliação de Serviços e Programas Sociais*, Lisboa, Projecto Atlântica, 2002.

Keasey, K., Steve, T., Wright, M., "Introduction: The Corporate Governance Problem – Competing Diagnoses and Solutions", in K. Keasey, T. Steve and M. Wright (eds.), *Corporate Governance Economic Management and Financial Issues*, New York, Oxford University Press, 1997.

La Piana, D., Hayes, M., *Play to Win: The Nonprofit Guide to Competitive Strategy*, Jossey Bass, 2005.

Namorado, R., "Cooperativismo – um horizonte possível", *Oficina do CES*, 229, Faculdade de Economia da Universidade de Coimbra, Maio 2005.

Nielsen, R., "SMR Forum: Strategic Piggybacking – A Self-subsidization Strategy for Nonprofit Institutions", *Sloan Management Review*, Summer, 23, 4, 1982, pp. 65-69.

Nunes, F., Reto, l., Carneiro, M., *O Terceiro Sector em Portugal: Delimitação, Caracterização e Potencialidades*, Instituto António Sérgio do Sector Cooperativo, 2001.

Pereira, G., "The Portuguese Misericórdias: General Characterization and Some Insights into Non-profit Governance", Presentation at the Fifth International Conference of International Society for Third Sector Research (ISTR), Cape Town, South Africa, July, 2002.

Pereira, G., "Economia Social Solidária: O que nos Pode Dizer a Economia", Presentation at the First Portuguese-speaking Congress of the Third Sector, Porto, Portugal, November 2005.

Pfeffer, J., *Organizations and Organization Theory*, Marshfield, MA, Pitman, 1982.

Pfeffer, J., Salancik, G., *The External Control of Organizations: A Resource Dependence Perspective*, New York, NY, Harper and Row, 1978.

Poole, D., Davis, J., Reisman, J., Nelson, J., "Improving the Quality of Outcome Evaluation Plans", *Nonprofit Management & Leadership*, 11, 4, 2001, pp. 405-421.

Post, J., Preston, l., Sachs, S., *Redefining the Corporation: Stakeholder Management and Organizational Wealth*, Stanford University Press, 2002.

Rock, C., "Evaluation in the United States Welfare State Regime", Working-group CIRIEC, 2007.

Simaens, A., *Strategic Management in Third Sector Organizations: An Overview of the Social Solidarity Cooperatives*, Master Dissertation, ISCTE, 2007.

Spear, R., "Social Accounting and Social Audit in the UK", Working-group CIRIEC, 2008.

The Cadbury Committee Report, *Financial Aspects of Corporate Governance*, Burgess Science Press, 1992.

Veiga, C., *Cooperativas de Educação e Reabilitação de Crianças Inadaptadas: uma Visão Global*, Secretariado Nacional para a Reabilitação e Integração das Pessoas com Deficiência, Lisboa, 1999.

Wheelen, T., Hunger, J., *Strategic Management and Business Policy*, International Edition, Ninth edition, Pearson Education Inc., 2004.

Evaluation of Co-operative Performances and Specificities in Japan

Akira KURIMOTO

Director, Consumer Co-operative Institute of Japan

1. Introduction

The corporate scandals involving Enron, WorldCom and others have generated a wide spread distrust among people to the behaviours of large-scale corporations and triggered a series of regulations for stricter control. Private sector companies have to demonstrate that they are run in compliance with legal/moral norms and in a transparent way. The public and social economies are no exception. In Japan, the government largely lost its credibility, failing to secure safety in food, drugs and housing, while the public sector utility and transportation companies caused serious accidents. Zennoh, a giant agricultural co-operative federation, was given a number of ministerial orders for the reform of its business operations while the charismatic CEO of Co-op Sapporo, the 2nd largest consumer co-op, was dismissed for improper management associated with manipulating accounts. It is of urgent necessity to improve corporate governance and enhance social accountability toward a wide range of stakeholders.

To this end the evaluation of Social Economy (SE) sector and organizations is indispensable prerequisite. It may have common elements with that of for-profit sector but should have the specific features deriving from the different goals and unique ways of organizing. This paper will describe the context of evaluation, examining the notions of SE, recent evolution of and major issues facing SE in Japan, and increasing importance of evaluation. Then it will characterize the main trends in evaluation methods and indicators pertaining to co-operatives in the national context. Some cases are to be illustrated to show the different models of evaluation. Finally it will analyze the major implications of evaluation practices to co-operatives.

2. Context of Evaluation of Social Economy

The Social Economy (SE) is not a term widely recognized by neither administration nor media in Japan. There is neither institutional framework nor representative body of SE while conceptualising and mapping of SE is yet to be undertaken. To be worse, the term 'Third Sector' is neither appropriate to describe the SE sector since it means a group of enterprises which are jointly owned by the public and for-profit sectors and often badly criticized for their lack of proper governance. However, it is not to say there is no phenomenon in Japan pertaining to SE; there exist strong elements of SE described hereafter but they lack both recognition and cohesion as a sector so far.

A. Changing Governance Regime

Japan has been based on the market economy strongly regulated by the state that had played a predominant role in promoting national economy by elaborate industrial development policies and regulations (accelerating and braking). The 'iron triangle among politicians, bureaucrats and industries' was formed to seek rents in the regulations while industries protected themselves from overseas competition by cross-shareholding and indirect control of main banks. The government' interventionist and protectionist role had been supplemented by the collectivism crystallized in corporations and families which had protected their members from a variety of risks while sacrificing individual's choice. In this regard, Japan had taken a State control governance model, which was often commended as attributes for the most successful 'socialist' regime. Although Japan's social security system was built on the conservative or corporatist model of social insurance following the continental Europe, its expenditure in the national income remained relatively small in the OECD countries thanks to the 'hidden assets' of corporations and families in providing social safety net based on single bread-winner model.

However, the globalization and ICT revolution gave strong and far-reaching impacts to the Japanese governance regime. It forced the government to deregulate and liberalize socio-economic policies to cope with the mega competition in the enlarged borderless market. The economic policy was shifted from protectionist to pro-competition enabling industries to have free hand. Following the liberalization of products markets facing strong resistance since 1960, the financial, property and labour markets were liberalized to a large extent in 1990s. Since this process coincided with the lingering recession in 'the lost decade', the transformation was exceptionally painful as shown in a number of bankruptcies of major financial institutions and large retailers, unprecedented high rate of unemployment and suicide, increased dropouts and social exclusion. The companies and families could not provide the traditional social safety nets any more while the local communities were devastated in both inner cities and under populated villages. The recent administrations sought to shift to neo-liberal model of governance with expansion of market opportunities and minimal public interventions. Under such circumstances, SE is expected to play important roles. How is SE understood? How has it evolved and what are the major issues it faces? What is the implication of increasing importance of evaluation to SE? This section addresses these questions.

B. Understanding of Social Economy in Japan

Some researchers introduced the concept of Social Economy (SE) into Japan in the early 1990s. Prof. K. Tomizawa and Prof. K. Kawaguchi edited and translated some books with other researchers on this subject. The Consumer Co-operative Institute of Japan (CCIJ) hosted a research project on SE under their auspices during 1995-1998 and organized an international research conference in 1998 in Tokyo inviting seven researchers from EMES network. The result of these studies and conference proceedings were published in two volumes (Tomizawa and Kawaguchi, 1996; 1999). The Policy Research Institute for the Civil Sector founded by Seikatsu Club Co-op organized the SE Promotion Project aiming at popularising the concept among MPs and published a book entitled "Toward Promotion of Social Economy" in 2003.

There were some attempts to conceptualize SE by some academicians. Based on the extensive survey on the discourse in Europe, Tomizawa presented a tentative definition of SE (Tomizawa, 1999).

Social Economy Organizations are the open, autonomous and democratic entities undertaking economic activities to accomplish not profit but social purposes. Social Economy is economic activities undertaken by those organizations. Social Economy Sector is a sphere of national economy undertaken by those organizations.

Kawaguchi and Tomizawa proposed a new label 'Non-profit and Co-operative Economy' as an equivalent to SE, combining both negative and positive purposes, i.e. operating not for profit and meeting common needs through co-operation. But it was generally neglected in either co-operatives or nonprofits and still remains to be a minor subject in the academic circles. In this regard we are still halfway in conceptualising SE.

The terminology of SE or the third sector used to label it varies largely and shifts over time. It may provide information on the composition of the population addressed or an indication of what it wishes/is wished to become (Pestoff and Stryjan). 'Non-profit Sector' is widely used by researchers associated with the Johns Hopkins Project but it tends to limit the scope to the NPOs with distribution constraints and often ignores co-operatives and mutuals. 'Voluntary Sector' is used as a synonym of non-profit sector but may cover a wider spectrum of volunteer activities. 'Community Business'' is defined as a business aiming to solve community problems by citizen's initiatives and entrepreneurial techniques. It covers a variety of legal forms including companies. It is a brand often promoted by the small business unit of the Ministry of Economy, Trade and Industry (METI). Those who seek to create a fair civil society use 'Civic Sector' but it is too wide to define as a concept. As such, there is no consensus in the terminology on the label of SE. On the part of the organizations concerned, there exists very weak identification with SE. The established organizations are becoming more concerned about problems facing many communities where they operate beyond their immediate preoccupation of survival in the competitive market, their concerns for community have not yet been crystallized to address problems and allocate resources. At the same time we can observe changes at the grass roots where they started spinning off and collaborating with the emerging small organizations.

C. Recent Evolution of Social Economy Organizations in Japan

There are both established organizations and emerging ones, which are counted as components of SE. Agricultural co-ops have been established as a main distributor of the agricultural products, operating one of the largest banks, insurers and trading houses in the country.[1] They organized almost all farmers as full-fledged members but also involved a large number of non-farming residents in suburban areas as associate members. They have played highly institutionalized roles as agents for implementing public agricultural policy and therefore organized themselves as the biggest pressure group. Fishery co-ops and forest-owners co-ops are much smaller but have the same features. On the contrary, consumer co-ops have evolved from grass roots and become the largest mass organization covering one third of households. Their presence in the market is still marginal (ca. 5% of food retailing) but they exercised a strong influence as a social movement (consumer, environment and peace campaigns etc.). In the financial sector, agricultural co-ops, Shinkin banks, SME credit co-ops and labour banks are operating to cater to the specific needs of farmers, SMEs and workers while the size of credit unions remains very small in comparison with these existing

---

[1]   Zennoh (National federation of Agricultural Co-ops) and Zenkyoren (National Federation of Agricultural Insurance Co-ops) occupied No. 1 and No. 2 in the ICA Global 300 Ranking released in 2006.

organizations and counterparts in other countries. In addition, agricultural, consumer and SME co-ops run the extensive insurance business (Kyosai) that occupies 20% of total insurance policies. Agricultural and consumer co-ops are also active in providing health and social care, running hospitals/clinics, nursing homes and in-home care support centres.

Workers co-ops and non-profit organizations (NPOs) are emerging since 1990s reflecting the economic downturn and weakened social safety nets. The globalization made it difficult to maintain the expensive social welfare services to be financed by higher taxation and the generous corporate welfare schemes for employees linked with lifelong employment. The traditional community ties have been largely depleted both in cities and villages while downsizing families faced problems in caring weak members (infant, aged and handicapped). To fill the enlarged gap those new organizations emerged by local initiatives. Workers co-ops were created by under-employed workers, mostly the elderly, who were threatened to the drastic cut of public allotment schemes for them while 'workers collectives' were set up by female co-operators as spin-offs of consumer co-ops to cater to the growing needs in communities. These co-ops offered a variety of care services for infants, the elderly and the handicapped, the cleaning and maintenance of offices, public catering and community café, and so on. Today it is estimated more than 700 workers co-ops/collectives are operating involving ca. 26,000 workers (Fujiki, 2006). They are still suffered from the lack of suitable legislation despite of their campaigns for 2 decades. Although some academicians proposed a uniform co-operative law, it drew little attention among leaders of the established co-ops.

The nonprofits were set up recently, *inter alia*, after the Great Earthquake in Kobe area in 1995 when an explosion of volunteerism was witnessed. They campaigned for the legal recognition and succeeded to enact the NPO Law in 1998. More than 30,000 NPOs are registered under this law as of Jan. 2007. They are active in a wide range of areas including social welfare, health, education, environment, and community building etc. attracting a wide concern among people, in particular the younger generation. The local governments encouraged the creation of nonprofits by subsidizing local NPO Support Centres. But they are very small, lacking effective manpower and financial resources; 52% of them have staffing of less than 10 (including volunteers) while 57% have annual budget of less than 5 million yen (Cabinet Office, 2005).

According to the Johns Hopkins International Comparison Project, the Japanese nonprofits have 4.2% of economically active population, the bulk of them are semi-governmental organizations including Public Interest Corporations (PIC), Social Welfare Corporations and so on. The history of PIC can be dated back to 1896 when the Civil Code was enacted. Article 34 on Establishment of Public Interest Corporation reads 'Any association or foundation relating to any academic activities, art, charity, worship, religion, or other public interest which is not for profit may be established as a juridical person with the permission of the competent government agency.' The underlying philosophy was that the public interests should be realized by the public authorities as a rule and could be undertaken by only specially permitted entities as an exception. PICs could enjoy some tax concessions although the preferable treatment on donations was not allowed. After WW2, the new legal entities such as Social Welfare Corporations, Medical Corporations and School Corporations were created by special acts to serve to the public policy purposes under the ministries' initiatives. As such these organizations have not been associated with the SE sector either from internal perception or external recognition, but closely linked with the public sector.

The institutional framework has hampered these old and new organizations to create a visible SE sector having common identity and effective collaboration among them. The co-operatives are splintered by more than 10 separated co-operative laws under the supervision of different ministries, which lacked coordinated policies and crosscutting statistics. Except for Kyosai sector (Japan Co-operative Insurance Association) and the international relations, co-ops have no coordinating body for representation and collaboration. In the non-profit sector the existing semi-governmental bodies have played vital roles in providing health/social care and education services but they are now subject to the drastic reform aiming at increasing autonomy and transparency while the newly created nonprofits are still struggling to survive and largely seek to get subsidies and/or contracts from public sectors. The gap between established organizations and emerging ones is even bigger. The former, preoccupied with its own problems, is generally indifferent to the latter and lacking a vision of creating the SE sector.

D. Major Issues Facing Social Economy Sector and Organizations

Both agricultural and consumer co-ops are facing the stiffer competition accelerated by trade liberalization and deregulation. To cope with such situation, they undertake major restructuring of business operations. Agricultural co-ops have offset the growing deficit of marketing and supply business with the surplus earned in financial businesses over decades that are now encountering the tougher competition in the global market. To enhance the profitability they have reduced the number of primary societies through mergers and eliminated secondary federations to link primaries directly with national centrals (Norinchukin, Zenkyoren and Zennoh) while transforming unprofitable operations (agricultural input stores, supermarkets, service stations etc.) into the subsidiary companies covering wider areas. Consumer co-ops are also consolidating their buying power by forming regional consortiums and integrating them with national organization (JCCU). They are still struggling to turn the loss making store operations while maintaining higher return in the unique non-store operations. In both cases they need to enhance profitability in all business areas and improve governance and management. They are also obliged to demonstrate responsiveness to reduce impact of their operations to the environment and society at large to foster understanding and solicit support among people including political and opinion leaders.

The 'big bang' policy aiming at accelerated competition in the financial sector posed unprecedented challenges to the co-operative financial institutions. They were requested to streamline operations by merger/consolidation and install the early warning system against insolvency. Thus the integrated agricultural banking system (JA Bank) was established by integrating Norinchukin, prefectural federation and primary co-ops in 2000. The insurance co-ops were also under pressure from domestic and international insurance companies that insisted on the equal footing in regulations. In 2005, the Insurance Business Law was amended to institutionalise the Kyosai, including those not regulated by any laws. Accordingly the co-operative laws were amended.

The nonprofits have lacked the institutional support in financing and taxation. The tax deduction scheme for the donation was introduced in 2001 but the requirements were too severe that only 56 nonprofits were approved to enjoy this privilege as of February 2007. In contrast, PICs have enjoyed some favourable tax treatments in return for strict control by the supervising government agencies, which have often created them to distribute public money and secure the executive posts for the ex-bureaucrats. Such government sponsored PICs were badly criticized in 1990s and the reform was introduced in 2006 separating juridical persons and tax treatment; any association or foundation will be established only by certification of the public notaries and registration while public interest status will be given to qualified organizations that can demonstrate their contribution to the public goods. The Public Interests Accreditation Commission was formed in April 2007. The same kind of reforms is anticipated for Social Welfare Corporations, Medical Corporations and so on.

E. Increasing Importance of Evaluation

Before moving to the next section, it is necessary to see the overall implication of increasing importance of evaluation. First of all, a special attention has been given to the corporate social responsibility (CSR) after a number of corporate scandals has been unveiled, which involved not only the private sector but also the public sector. The top brands such as Snow Brand or Mitsubishi Motors had lost public confidence while the mismanagement in some electric power or railway companies caused serious radioactivity leakage or traffic accidents. Some architecture and construction companies had bankrupted due to frauds seeking unlawful rents in the deregulated market. Under such circumstances major corporations rushed into the CSR, which became a boom where a large number of consultancy and audit firms came in looking for new business opportunities. They competed in demonstrating their legitimacy by publishing sustainability, environmental or social reports. The Japan Business Federation (Keidanren) urged its members to adhere to its Charter of Corporate Behaviour and Global Environment Charter while the Japan Association of Corporate Executives published Corporate White Paper entitled 'Market Evolution and CSR Management: Toward Building Integrity and Creating Stakeholder Value'. These activities are voluntary in nature and therefore there is no criteria except for the statutory obligations in social and environmental matters.

Secondly, the emphasis has been given to the conformity assessment to the ISO standards, which became hallmarks in the industrial, technical and business sectors. Thus, ISO 9000 (Quality Management System) and ISO 14000 (Environmental Management System) became most known standards in Japan that led obtaining certificates for ISO 14001; 19,477 certificates were registered out of total 103,583 as of January 2006. It was taken as a prerequisite for the Japanese manufacturers to sell consumer products in other countries but it was also widely accepted by domestic industries (constructors, retailers, schools, hospitals etc.) and public bodies (municipal governments, refuse incineration factories, water supplies etc) as a tool for having environmental consideration built in the management practice. China is swiftly catching up with 12,683 certificates reflecting the rapid export-led industrialization, to be followed by Spain (7,872), Italy (7,080), the UK (6,223) and the USA (5,100).

Thirdly, the providers of quasi-public goods are increasingly subject to the third party evaluation. The privatization of public services spurred this tendency, but the evaluation of quality of services is not limited to the private sector; the public and social economy sectors are also subject to it. In the social service sector, the introduction of Long-term Care

Insurance Law in 2000 opened door to all types of legal entities, resulting in a drastic increase in providers and competition. The hitherto local government's administrative placement was replaced by user's voluntary contracts. To help users to make the right choice based on the information on the quality of care services and encourage providers to improve their services, the evaluation is being introduced. The Tokyo Metropolitan Government initiated the Third Party Evaluation Scheme of Welfare Services since 2003 in which the accredited evaluation agents would conclude contracts with the assessed organizations, make investigation through questionnaires to users and business assessment, and feedback their findings, which would be publicized upon approval of the latter. During 2005, 1,352 evaluations were made including one in two nursing homes for the elderly, one in 6 licensed day-care centres for children. In the health care sector that is characterized by a sheer asymmetry of information, the evaluation of medical service providers is of great significance. The Japan Council of Quality Health Care (JCQHC) was set up in 1995 to provide the third party evaluation of hospitals. It gave certificates to 2,268 hospitals out of total 9,014 as of December 2006 and publicized its evaluation results. In the school education sector, the Ministry's survey in 2005 found that 98% of public schools carried out self-evaluation while only 52% of them undertook the external evaluation as well. The 'school advisory council' system was introduced in 2000 to facilitate understanding and co-operation through listening to parents and communities and 92% of public schools set up such councils in 2006. The National Institute for Academic Degrees and University Evaluation conducts evaluation for the higher education institutions.

The criteria of evaluation mentioned above are applied to any kind of entities irrespective of their organizational forms. Given the blurred boundaries and hybridizations among the organizations, it is advisable to apply them universally. However they may overlook specificities of SE organizations, particularly social dimensions. Therefore the proper attention should be paid to the evaluation of SE.

3. Major Trends in Evaluation of Co-operatives

The evaluation of the SE organizations is a field of enquiry that has to be elaborated by them and supervisory organs. As far as the financial aspects are concerned, the regulating authorities and accounting firms have promoted the standardization of accounting and auditing procedures. They are developing the international accounting and reporting standards under the auspice of IASB and FASB. At the same time, more attention is now being paid to non-financial aspects such as impact to environment, social justice and human rights. A number of new initiatives for evaluating and reporting these aspects came into existence in each country and international bodies such as GRI, AA1000 and SA8000. The ISO is also working to formulate the guidelines for Social Responsibly in the years to come. How will the SE organizations be affected by these standards/guidelines? Are they to develop their own standards? To answer these questions, I will present major trends in evaluation of the Japanese co-operatives.

A. Who is Asking for and Conducting Evaluation

A number of stakeholders are asking for evaluation of co-ops. The member-owners are concerned about their voice being heard and their participation to the governance. The users or customers wish to know what kinds of benefit co-ops are offering in terms of quality and price of goods/services. The employees are concerned with the working conditions and their treatment in terms of equal opportunity for promotion and training. They are also interested in being involved in the decision-making process. The suppliers and banks are concerned with the long-term transaction and co-ops' financial situation. The local authorities watch if co-ops are doing business in compliance with legal requirement and environmental/social standards. The wider communities and future generations can be counted as stakeholders who may ask for evaluation since they will be affected by the conducts of these organizations. In any case, the stakeholder engagement is very important to take their inputs and give impact to them.

The mode of evaluation can be either internal or external. In most cases, the board or management, non-executive directors or evaluation committees of co-ops conduct evaluation of their own organizations. On the other hand, the authorities, banks, public accountants, accreditation agencies, universities or think tanks may conduct the external evaluation. Unlike nonprofits that are dependant to the public money or private donations, co-operatives are to be evaluated/controlled by their members as principals and not necessarily subject to the external evaluation.

There exist self-evaluation, mutual evaluation and the third party evaluation. The self-evaluation is being done by the organization itself and tends to be complacent or end with just advertisement without the objective grounding. To avoid such tendency, the mutual evaluation is undertaken by Pal System Co-op Federation where both producers and consumers undertaking direct transaction (Sanchoku) jointly evaluate the mode/process of production where produce is grown. They check how produce is grown in compliance with contracts, use of chemicals are adequately controlled, records are properly kept and so on, which in turn help nurturing mutual understanding and trust. The third party evaluation is conducted to verify the practice against predetermined criteria/standards for quality or environmental management and so on; the actors have to obtain certificates from the specified accreditation bodies.

These modes of evaluation are closely linked with objectives of evaluation. If it is to demonstrate the organization's legitimacy by disclosing the relevant information on its performances to key stakeholders and wider communities, the external or third party evaluation is likely to serve that objective. If it is to provide the management with tools to improve the organization's performance by assessing its strength, weakness, opportunity and threat (SWOT), internal or self evaluation may suffice.

B. Dimensions of Evaluation

The evaluation should have triple dimensions; economic, environmental and social. The GRI Guideline enlists the performance indicators for CSR reporting in line with these three dimensions. The evaluation of economic dimension had long history of accounting and auditing, but it goes beyond the traditional financial indicators; it relates to the impacts the organization will give to the economic situation of stakeholders and the economic system at local, national and global levels. For example, it includes evaluating the indirect impact coming from external effects to local communities.

The evaluation of environmental dimension had relatively short history but there is a wider consensus on which indicators are included in relation to the organization's impacts to the ecological system (water, soil, air and so on) although the impact of CO_2 emission to the global warming is still one of the hottest issues in the international politics.

The evaluation of social dimension relates to the impacts the organization gives to the society but what kinds of indicators are to be included is still a subject of discussion. The GRI Guidelines clustered indicators into Labour practices and decent work, Human rights, Society and Product responsibly while the UN's Global Compact classified Human rights, Labour and Anti-corruption. The Co-operatives UK's Key Social Performance Indicators are the good example of this field. The JCCU compiled a Report on Food Safety in June 2006 documenting co-op's initiatives in this field and published its Social Report consolidating food safety, environmental care and social contribution in September 2006.

C. Objects of Evaluation

The objects of evaluation vary from one organization to another reflecting on the priorities that the organization gives. It is often observed the organization chooses strong points while ignoring weak points. Even if some organizations would claim that their evaluation is comprehensive, they might miss important objects from outsider's points of view.

Co-op Kobe's Comprehensive Evaluation encompassed a wide range of objects from customers' shopping convenience and economic benefits to members'/employees' participation in decision making; from co-ops' involvement in community welfare and environmental protection to solidarity among co-ops, from co-op's profitability and productivity to financial and human resources. It covered almost all aspects concerning to co-op's activities and its stakeholders. However it did not involve the gender equality in its first report in 1998; the proportion of female managers was added in its second report in 2001 but the achievement (ca. 1.2%) was not so commendable.

Pal System Co-op Federation concentrated on the evaluation of Products and Services. It involved major attributes of products and services (quality, price, taste, information etc.), product development and branding policy, design of catalogue, concerns for environment, compliance to rules and manuals, communication with producers/suppliers, information and openness to members, social contribution and recognition etc.

Statistical data are collected and transformed into variables while questionnaires or interviews involving stakeholders are conducted to supplement those formal data. Such quantitative and qualitative information is used to evaluate the performances and analyze the changing trends.

D. Indicators and Criteria being used

Generally, co-ops apply the widely accepted indicators and criteria of evaluation to secure the comparability as one of the GRI principles. So, many co-ops applied the ISO standards for Environment Management System (ISO14000) and Quality Management System (ISO9000) as the criteria of evaluation while Fukui Co-op applied the assessment criteria of the Japan Quality Award (JQA).

Some co-ops have developed different sets of indicators and criteria to reflect specific nature of co-operative organization as the Association and the Enterprise. Co-op Kobe's Comprehensive Evaluation used 6 indicators clustered to 2 main categories (Basic Co-operative Values and Management Base) while Pal System Co-op Federation's Products

224

and Services Evaluation used 4 indicators. These indicators were broken down into 20 evaluation items. There are some common items such as provision of safe and reliable products and feedback of member's voice, but the scope of evaluation differs largely reflecting on fields of evaluation. These indicators were elaborated not necessarily in compliance with GRI's performance indicators. In doing so they could outline the specific features reflecting upon the co-operative values but might compromise comparability with other organizations.

4. Some Models of Evaluation of Co-operatives in Japan

There exist a number of best practices in European Co-ops. As early as in 1990s the Migros co-ops publicized their Social/Environmental Reports while the Italian co-ops elaborated Bilancio Sociale. The consumer co-ops in Nordic countries evaluated their performance in line with GRI's triple bottom-lines. The Key Commercial and Social Performance Indicators were introduced by the Co-operatives UK to evaluate the performance of the affiliated co-op societies in 2000. The Sustainability Report 2003 published by the UK Co-operative Financial Services won the international recognition as the best one by the UNEP. Herewith I'd like to illustrate some models of evaluation of co-operatives in Japan.

A. Evaluation of Performance and Process for Improved Management

The evaluation of performance and process by the ISO standards is increasingly undertaken in the private sector enterprises aiming at improving management practices and giving positive effects to enhance corporate reputation in the market. In the co-operative sector, the JCCU has encouraged affiliated co-op societies to obtain the certification of the ISO standards based on the internal and third party evaluation to incorporate quality and environment considerations in the management process since late 1990s. As a result, 61 co-ops obtained certificates of ISO 14001 while 14 co-ops obtained certificates of ISO 9001 until October 2006. 59 co-ops published Environment and/or Social Reports in which a special attention was paid to the ISO certificates.

Saitama Co-op, the 5th largest society, with 636,000 members, has conducted 'Reform in People and Organization' since 1994 when its turnover dropped by 1.2% for the first time since its inception. It decided to focus on members/employees as key stakeholders while it recognized the importance to look outside the organization and meet the higher social requirements for its operations. It obtained the certificate of ISO14001 for its food-processing plant in 1998, then for the entire organization in 2000. It also got the certificate of ISO 9001 for its food-processing plant and distribution centre in 2001, then for the entire organization in 2003. Based on its efforts to enhance safety in work places after serious accidents causing injuries to employees, it was accredited OHSAS18001 (Occupational Health and Safety) for its food-processing plant in 2003. When it faced the fraud in its transaction of chicken supplied by a subsidiary of Zennoh, it overhauled its merchandise policy in the product labelling and supply-chains while compensating members. It set up the Compliance Office to oversee the business process with special emphasis on Personal Information Protection and established the voluntary Code of Conduct in 2003. Adding the different requirements from one standard to another, however, inevitably overloaded the operational levels with increased burdens. Saitama Co-op has sought to establish an integrated CSR management system consolidating different performance/process indicators placed by these standards in each field while publishing the CSR Report incorporating some elements of the GRI guidelines (Iwaoka, 2006). This effort was followed up by the JCCU, which produced a guideline for the Integrated Management System for CSR in Consumer Co-ops.

The other approach taken by *Fukui Co-op* was Management Quality Award. Fukui Co-op is a medium sized co-op with 115,000 members (43% of households) in a small prefecture facing the Sea of Japan. It has made efforts to improve management quality at all levels and make active engagement in social and environmental matters in partnership with local communities. In 2001 Fukui Co-op started taking part to the Fukui Prefecture Quality Award (FPQA) a local version of the Japan Quality Award (JQA).[2] JQA has set out the assessment criteria ranging from business results to processes including leadership, understanding customers/markets, capacity building, value creation and so on (see Table 1). Co-op sought to have the third party evaluation on its business performance and processes. It applied for FPQA in 2003 and undertook both documentary examination and on-site investigation. As a result it won the Excellence Award in 2004 (CCIJ, 2004) and 2005, and finally a Grand Prix in 2006.

---

[2] The JQA was created by the Japan Productivity Center for Socio-economic Development in 1995 to enhance the management quality of firms and local governments by evaluating performance and process through 8 assessment criteria. It modeled the Malcolm Baldrige National Quality Award in 1987, which sought to revitalize the competitiveness of the American products and was named after the US Secretary of Commerce. The JQA was extended to nonprofits and supplemented by the local Quality Awards.

226

B. Evaluation According to Specific Missions

The health care is conceived to be quasi-public goods, but how to finance it differs from one country to another; tax (national health services), compulsory insurances, private insurances and/or patient's co-payment. In Japan it is accessible by all the population under universal coverage of public health insurance schemes. The Medical Care Law stipulates the providers of medical care have specific mission to respond to patients. Patients have free access to any medical institutions but they have very limited information for choosing hospitals/clinics and their voice has been rarely heard. The revelation of a series of medical mal-practices and unlawful billings has spurred the consumer's distrust to the medical industry. These are the reasons why evaluation according to specific missions of medical institutions is needed in addition of finan-cial evaluation. The Japan Council of Quality Health Care (JCQHC) conducted the third party evaluation on the structure and process of hospitals since 1997 but the evaluation of medical care is still underde-veloped.

The co-operatives in the health and social care sector are not excep-tion. Being user-driven organizations, they have specific mission of enhancing well being of the recipients in the industry where a sheer asymmetry of information exists between professionals and users. Some medical co-ops undertook the third party evaluation such as JCQHC and ISO 9001 (Quality Management). The *Health Co-operative Association* (HCA) as a national coordinating body of 126 medical co-ops con-ducted periodical surveys on the evaluation of health care services since 1983 aiming to enhance user's satisfaction by listening to their voice and improving quality of care. There are two types of surveys: evalua-tion of nursing services and that of medical/dental care services. The former focuses on nursing practices while the latter covers overall services provided in medical/social care institutions.

In 2002 the HCA conducted the 7th evaluation of nursing services composed of surveys on patient's satisfaction, nurse's consciousness and managerial nurse's self-assessment (HCA, 2003). These surveys were made independently through different sets of questionnaires that were designed to facilitate cross evaluation. Ca. 27,000 outpatients, 4,600 inpatients and 5,800 nurses in 61 co-ops were involved in the patient's satisfaction survey. Some problems were revealed where satisfaction level of patients and nurses were less than 50%. The notable example was 'instruction on evacuation in case of emergency', which necessitated co-ops to take the immediate action in view of risk man-agement. It was also found that there existed some significant percep-tion gaps among patients, nurses and managers in some questions. For example, patients scored even higher appreciation than nurses in many items while the former's satisfaction level were lower than the latter's self-assessment in such items as aid to voiding, countermeasures to contagion and safe injection (See Graph 1). Likewise, the gap was also apparent between nurses and managers. Such results showing perception gaps were used to identify the problems and take necessary corrective actions to improve the quality of services.

In 2004 the HCA carried out the 7th evaluation of medical/dental care services, which was composed of surveys on patient's satisfaction, employee's consciousness and medical functions (HCA, 2005). In the patient's satisfaction survey ca. 26,300 outpatients, 5,100 inpatients released from hospitals and 5,400 dental patients responded to the questionnaires. The satisfaction levels were expressed in scores ranging from minus 10 (fully disagree) to plus 10 (fully agree). The outpatient's survey unveiled that human factors (easy to understand, good behaviour etc) won higher scores while hardware factors (physical amenity, medical facilities etc.) earned lower scores. The inpatients expressed higher satisfaction to the core services but lowest satisfaction to the hospital meals (See Table 2). Such results are compared with the previous surveys and relevant data compiled by the ministry. The employee's consciousness survey involved 12,300 personnel including doctors (4%), nurses (45%), paramedical (16%) and administration staff (17%). Its enquiries covered the quality of medical care, work environment and education/training. It is interesting to see the different perception of medical co-op staff on the quality of medical care that prioritised mental care to patients rather than assured medical techniques, prevention centred rather than treatment centred, patients self determination rather than doctor's decision while subtle balance was observed between better amenity for patients and lesser economic burden for them. The evaluation of medical functions was designed to gauge medical institution's performance based on JCQHC's evaluation criteria. Managers of 252 hospitals/clinics replied to questionnaires. It was found they needed to address those areas where poor performance was revealed, i.e. information management system, arrangement for second opinions, analysis of treatment practices and nurse's capacity development programs.

C. Evaluation According to Specific Organizational Nature

Co-operatives have the distinct values as mutual organizations and accordingly different organizational and institutional nature. So they require to be evaluated according to their specificities. The problem is how co-operative values or difference are incorporated in the evaluation. In case of the listed companies (PLCs), their performance is measured by such financial indicators as total share values, ROE, PER and so on, while that of co-operatives must be measured by the different criteria since the latter aims at meeting members' economic and social needs rather than earning the highest return on investment. In particular, Co-operative values such as participation, democracy and equity must be incorporated in designing indicators. The Co-operatives UK added 'co-operative' elements such as member economic involvement or democratic participation to its Key Social Performance Indicators. The Italian consumer co-ops added 'Co-operative Movement' to the key stakeholders, i.e. Consumers, Members, Employees and Communities in their Bilancio Sociale.

Co-op Kobe is the largest consumer co-op in Japan with nearly 1.3 million members. It started designing its own evaluation system and set up a study team composed of executives and academics in 1993. After several years of studies, Prof. N. Tsuda of St. Andrew's University and Prof. K. Nakakubo of Himeji Dokkyo University developed the method of Co-operative Comprehensive Evaluation (CCE) in 1996. Although data correction was disrupted by the serious damages caused by the earthquake in 1995, Co-op could publish the first CCE Report for 1995-1997 in 1998. Then it published the CCE Reports every three years, i.e. in 2001 and 2004 (Co-op Kobe, 1998, 2001, 2004; Tsuda, 2003; Kurimoto, 2003). The CCE is defined as the multifaceted evaluation of overall operations and activities of a Co-op in the past, present and future, on the basis of two evaluation axes, namely Co-operative Basic Values and Management Base, The former derives from the ICA Statement on Co-operative Identity while the latter is the precondition to support the fulfilment of the former. The evaluation methods include the indicators for the relative analysis through the numerical data and the absolute evaluation through a questionnaire to stakeholders. The time span of the evaluation extends from achievements till now to the formulation of action plans for the future. These are the reasons why this concept claimed to be 'comprehensive'. The objectives of the CCE were stated in twofold way; self-examination of the organization's performance and reporting to the diverse stakeholders.

Co-op Kobe intended to develop the criteria in order to conduct an objective evaluation that takes into account the co-op's characteristics, ensuring that the evaluation method stands up to any scrutiny from the general public. It also intended to establish the comprehensive evaluation so that one can evaluate both association and enterprise sides. Therefore, the Co-operative Basic Values and the Management Base were set out as the major evaluation axes. These two axes clustered six evaluation indicators; 'Honest and Caring Services', 'Participation and Democracy', 'Social Responsibility and Fairness', 'Autonomy and Solidarity' belong to the former while 'Management Efficiency' and 'Future Potential' belong to the latter. The former includes both associational and entrepreneurial elements while the latter concerns only entrepreneurial elements. Each indicator was broken down to 5 evaluation items, which were in turn linked with the numerical data (See Table 3). During the evaluation ca. 140 kinds of data were collected from a wide range of sources from operational figures to attendance to the AGM, from consumer adviser's rating to employee's wage compared with competitors. In order to enhance the reliability of the evaluation and involve members, employees and managers in the evaluation process, questionnaires were distributed to ca. 2,800 persons and their responses were collated in a way that ensured that the survey results would closely reflect actual circumstances. The results were used to analyze the evaluation, set the weights among evaluation indicators/items and as data themselves.

Since it was difficult to set the fixed criteria or target figures for all items, the relative evaluation was adopted.[3] Indices from relative evaluations of each year (points gained) were tabulated on radar charts to display satisfaction levels and identify problem areas or they were plotted in line charts to display evolution from the base year (See Graph 2 and 3). The first CCE Report revealed the contrasting picture; management base axis took the downward trend while the basic value axis demonstrated the steady improvement during 1995-1997. These diverging trends clearly showed the trade-off between economy and democracy. Although Co-op Kobe could recover its operations from damages caused by the earthquake earlier than originally expected but in this process it faced tougher competition, which opened new outlets with selling space largely exceeding that of the co-op stores. The lingering recession triggered the price war, which resulted in shrinking margins and necessitated to curtail the labour costs. Based on these findings, Co-op Kobe had to undertake a drastic restructuring of facilities and employees. Nearly 10% of work force was laid off, sacrificing mainly middle-aged workers. This process had not been implemented without serious conflicts between the board and employees. As a result, the evaluation in the items such as 'employee's participation' and 'fair treatment of employees' dropped to a large extent. The second CCE Report in 2001 could show the improvement in management basis in contrast with declining basic values during 1998-2000. Again the trade-off between economy and democracy was apparently revealed. The third CCE Report in 2004 could record improvements in both axes during 2001-2003, showing win-win relation between economy and democracy that has been longed for by all concerned (See Graph 4).

---

[3]   To obtain indices from a large number of heterogeneous data, Standardized Index Method was used. It was developed by the government's Economic Planning Agency.

The CCE had undergone some modifications in weights between axes, contents of questionnaires, collected data, starting year and tallying method although the core methodology remained intact. At the same time, the CCE model is organization-specific but it was meant to facilitate comparative analysis with other co-operatives or nonprofits. However only Fukui Co-op introduced CCE with minor modifications while other co-ops are not likely to use it because it was custom-made to meet specific needs and it would involve a large amount of costs and work.

The other example is the evaluation of co-operative products and services. *The Pal System Co-op Federation* (PSCF) is composed of 10 consumer co-ops operating in the greater Tokyo area with total membership of 940,000. It pioneered home delivery system to individual households instead of Han groups in mid 1990s and succeeded to accomplish rapid expansion in both membership and turnover. It has been active in promoting Sanchoku (direct transaction between producers and consumers) and accredited ISO14001 for environmental management in 2000. As the next step it developed the Products/Services Evaluation (PSE) system in 2004. The objective of the PSE is to improve management quality and enhance social commitments for all aspects of products, services and their delivery. It was built on the processes of self-evaluation of products and services provided by the PSCF, members' opinion poll through questionnaires, assessment and reporting by the Evaluation Committee mainly composed of external experts, and publication of the PSE report by the PSCF board for the AGM and the public. There are four indicators concerning to product development, management base, member's satisfaction and brand values. These indicators have 20 evaluation items (See Table 4). The first PSE report was published in 2005. There were 9 items out of 20 showing discrepancy between internal self-evaluation and external evaluation. The Evaluation Committee gave more stringent assessment in the fields of product development as well as brand values after examining the management report and interviews, and made concrete suggestions item by item to improve management in these fields. The PSCF board made commitment to carry out reforms in responding to the given suggestions. It seeks to establish the Comprehensive Evaluation system in the years to come after improving the current PSE (Tohgasa, 2006).

5. Analysis of the Effects of Evaluation

It is not possible to give any kind of evaluation of Social Economy sector at macro level in Japan since there are neither representative bodies nor reliable statistics although there exist its components at micro level. Even co-operatives had evolved quite differently due to institutional and organizational reasons, diverging into either those who implemented public policy or those who maintained social dimensions, and achieved very weak cohesion among them to advance the idea of co-operative sector. So I will confine myself to making a short analysis on the evaluation of consumer co-ops.

A. *Outputs versus Outcomes*

It is necessary to distinguish the evaluation of outputs from that of outcomes. Outputs are defined as the amount of something that a person or an organization produces and shown in the quantity such as population, production, turnover, costs and surplus, amounts of saved materials and so on. Outcomes are the results or effects of an action or event and may involve the immeasurable ones. For example, outputs of the sheltered workshops for the handicapped will be measured by the amount of production, paid salaries or the hours spent by volunteers while outcomes may be gauged by the improved living/working conditions and satisfaction of those involved.

It is more difficult to evaluate the indirect or long-term effects to the market or the society at large (externality). Consumer co-ops have pioneered to eliminate the hazardous products or ingredients by campaigning against them and developing the alternative products. They won consumer's trust through such initiatives and helped to eliminate those hazardous products in the market as a whole because competitors had followed co-op's practices to gain consumer's patronage. Today we can hardly see fancy colour milk or pickles, which were once prevailing in the market. Co-ops have contributed to the institutional change toward the safer foods by pushing the government to modify the Food Sanitation Law and enact the Food Safety Basic Law in 2003. Another example was a 'My Bag' campaign to reduce total amount of shopping bags delivered at checkouts. Many co-ops asked members to bring their own bags or boxes to replace the plastic shopping bags so as to reduce the use of un-renewable resources and impact to the environment. They charged a small sum (mostly 5 yen) to those who wished to buy plastic bags or gave FSP points to those who did not claim plastic bags.[4] Members were well informed on this campaign and made positive response by bringing their own bags. It is estimated ca. 290 million shopping bags or 49% were saved in co-ops in 2005, which correspond to saving of 5,200 kilolitres of oil for producing bags and JPY 110 million of tax to be spent for garbage disposal. As such economic incentive combined with consumer education worked in consumer co-ops (JCCU, 2004). Such practices might give impact to the enactment of local government's ordnances and the modification of Containers and Packaging

---

[4] Members can exchange points with products or services.

Materials Recycling Law in 2006, which requested retailers to reduce one-way containers such as shopping bags by charging customers for them. These initiatives have been acknowledged by the government and widely recognized by the media, as documented in the JCCU's Food Safety Report 2006 or Environment Reports. It can be said co-ops had played a 'pacemaker role' or provided a 'competitive yardstick' even though such advantage would be copied and co-ops would be caught up by competitors sooner or later. But it is difficult to quantify and evaluate these contributions without risk of complacency.

The surveys on consumer's perception would provide a substitute to the evaluation. According to the online opinion poll conducted by the Hakuhodo Institute in 2003 co-ops won much higher score as reliable supplier of safe food while private supermarkets won higher score in assortments and stock level (see Table 5) (JCCU, 2004: 128).[5] Since co-ops have taken initiatives to enhance food safety and reliability, such a result showed their goal was accomplished.

B. Standardization and Isomorphism

In Japan the third party evaluation based on the ISO standards are widely accepted by industries and government bodies as mentioned earlier. It is used as effective management tools, which enable organizations to make continuous improvement of management through regular surveillance and renewal processes. The standardized procedures may ensure integrity and comparability. But the ISO standards are not in any way binding on either governments or industries; it is voluntary will of organizations whether to undergo the evaluation/auditing by the accredited agents or just make self-declaration based on the ISO standards without certification.

In addition organizations are measured against contents and targets of actions which they set by themselves and which do not necessarily ensure to generate real effects or impacts. Simply what are not set as targets won't be measured. For instance, the certificate of the ISO14001 means the organization has a system of management dealing with environmental problems in accordance with requirements stipulated by standards but does not ensure its superior performance on environment in terms of reduced CO_2 emission or refuses.

The third party evaluation schemes on health and social care services are being applied to all entities irrespective of their legal forms. They are voluntary in nature and cover a smaller part of providers in various categories at this moment but may become compulsory to those who are

---

[5] 2,000 consumers including 1,132 non-members were randomly selected for the survey on websites in April-may 2003.

entrusted service delivery by public authorities or who receive government subsidies. The objects and process of such evaluation are highly standardized to facilitate users to make comparison among providers. Some co-ops undertook both internal and external evaluation to improve the quality of services while involving key stakeholders and emphasizing the organization's profile in the process of evaluation. So far the risk of isomorphism through the third party evaluation seems negligible.

6. Conclusion: Consumer Co-operative's Role in Building the Social Economy Sector

Historically consumer co-ops have been expected to play an active role to enhance food safety and reliability through introducing comprehensive quality control system as well as promoting alternative products and Sanchoku (direct transaction with producers) that were accepted by consumers and gave impact to the industry. In this regard they played a corrective role to cope with the problems associated with market failure as shown in the hazardous food additives, controlled price, misleading labelling, excessive packaging etc. At the same time they have been making campaigns as consumer movement pressing government to enact/enforce stricter regulations. In this regard they have played an advocacy role to cope with the government failure. They are definitely expected to play a leading role in this field.

At the same time, they are expected to play more active role to build the social capital at mezzo level to cope with the community's failure, i.e. deteriorated local economy and social exclusion by mobilizing resources accumulated in them. They have the active members who have got knowledge and experiences through serving on the boards or committees. They have the experienced managers and employees who have been trained in running business and organizations. They can offer their premises to be used as meeting places by local community groups. They are financially stable in comparison with the majority of nonprofits and often offer small funds to encourage local groups that undertake the community activities for social welfare, education, and environment etc.

It does mean consumer co-ops will not only enter the social welfare business but also encourage their members to undertake various kinds of community-related businesses and activities and help to create community networks to cope with social exclusion. There are some examples of worker co-ops and non-profits created by co-operators as spin-offs from consumer co-ops. The local networks for building sustainable communities are also emerging involving consumer, agricultural, worker co-ops and nonprofits. By promoting such local initiatives, co-operative will be able to renovate their organization and business, contribute to development of local economies and democratization of local society, thus contributing to create the visible SE sector.

References

Bromqvist, K., *Social Reporting of ICMIF Members*, ICMIF Collaborative research Series, 4, 1997.

Cabinet Office, *Report of Civic Organizations Basic Survey for FY*, 2004.

CCIJ, *Proceeding of the 14th National Research Conference*, 2004.

Consumer Co-operative Institute of Japan, *Proceedings of the 14th National Research Conference*, 2004.

– *Report on Consumer Co-op's CSR Evaluation and reporting part 1*, CCIJ Report, 45, 2004.

– *Report on Consumer Co-op's CSR Evaluation and reporting Part 2*, CCIJ Report, 49, 2006.

Co-operative Financial Services, *Sustainability Report*, 2003.

Co-op Kobe, *The Report on the Comprehensive Evaluation of Co-op Kobe*, 1998, 2001, 2004.

Fujiki, C., "Practices of Social Enterprises and Tasks for developing Social Economy in Japan", *Emerging Social Enterprises and social Economy*, Doji-daisha, pp. 46-50, 2006.

HCA, *Medical Co-op Report*, 47, 2003.

HCA, *Medical Co-op Report*, 57, 2005.

Iwaoka, H., "Saitama Co-op's CSR Report", *CCIJ Report*, 49, 2006.

JCCU, *Social Report*, 2006.

JCCU, *Report on the 6th National Survey on Co-ops Sanchoku*, 2004.

Kawaguchi, K., Tomizawa, K. (eds.), *Welfare Society and Nonprofit/Co-operative Sector*, Nihon Keizai Hyoronsha, 1999.

Kurimoto, A., "Evaluation and Reporting of Social Responsibility in Consumer Co-ops", *CCIJ Report*, 49, 2006.

Kurimoto, A., "Evaluating performance by Co-operative Values and Efficiency", *Review of International Co-operation*, 93, 1, 2000.

Pestoff, V. A., *Beyond the Market and State*, Ashgate, 1998.

Quarter, J. et al., *What Counts: Social Accounting for Nonprofits and Cooperatives*, Pearson Education Inc., 2003.

Spear, R., *Social Audit and the Social Economy; Approaches and Issues*, CCIJ Special Seminar, Tokyo, March 1998.

Tohgasa, K., "Pal System Group's PSE System", CCIJ Report, 49, 2006.

Tomizawa, K., *An Analysis of Social Economy Sector: Theory and Practice of Nonprofit Organizations*, Iwanami Shoten, 1999.

Tomizawa, K., Kawaguchi, K. (eds.), *Theory and Practice of Nonprofit Co-operative Sector*, Nihon Keizai Hyoronsha, 1996.

Tsuda, N., *The Methods and Practice of the Co-operative Comprehensive Evaluation*, 1999.

Tsuda, N., "Basic Values and efficiency in Co-op Kobe", *Measurement, Evaluation*, and Policy Making, Japan, 2003.

Viviani, M., *Social Responsibility, Transparency and Efficiency; The Social Account of the Italian Consumer Co-operative*, 1996.

Table 1. Assessment Criteria of the Japan Quality Award

Categories	Sub-categories	Pts
A. Leadership and decision-making	Management leadership	120
B. Social responsibility in business	Response to social requirement Social contribution	50
C. Understanding/ responding customers and markets	Understanding customers and markets Trust relationship with customers Clarified customer satisfaction	110
D. Formation and development of strategies	Formation of strategies Development of strategies	60
E. Capacity building of individuals and organizations	Organizational capacity Employees capacity development Employees satisfaction	100
F. Value creation process	Core business process Support process Collaboration with business partners	100
G. Information management	Collecting/analysing management information Information system management	60
H. Business results	Results in leadership and CSR Results in capacity building Results in process Financial results Results in customer satisfaction	400
Grand total		1,000

Japan Quality Award Council.

Graph 1. Comparison of Satisfaction Levels: Items Showing Gaps of more than 10% in Patient's and Nurse's Perception (Inpatients)

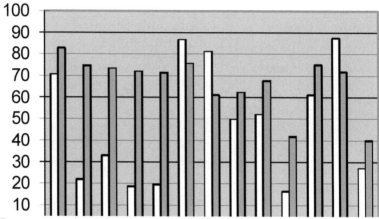

1. Respect to patient's human right
2. Proper explanation of cure plan
3. Cure plan responding to patient's voice
4. Cure plan understandable to patient
5. Cure plan enhancing patient's eagerness
6. Safe injection for identified patients
7. Sufficient aid in case of patient's voiding
8. Instruction suitable to patient's life
9. Aid to discharge from hospitals
10. Instruction on Han meeting and prevention
11. Amenity of hospital facilities
12. Countermeasures to contagion
13. Instruction on emergent evacuation

Table 2. Patient's Satisfaction to Medical Care
and Related Matters

Outpatients	Points
Receptionists/cashiers were amicable.	7.4
It was easy to question doctors.	7.3
Staff's language/attitude was good.	7.4
I understood staff's words on medication.	7.0
Doctor's prognosis/treatment was acceptable.	7.1
Waiting room and lavatory were clean.	6.8
Medical facilities/equipments were adequate.	5.2
Waiting time in hospital was acceptable.	4.4
It was easy to utilize as a whole.	7.0
I wish to introduce this hospital to friends.	6.0
Inpatients released from hospitals	
I received proper explanations from doctors.	7.9
Doctor's prognosis/treatment was acceptable.	7.8
Medical facilities/equipments were adequate.	7.5
Nursing in sickroom was satisfying.	7.9
Explanations on hospitalizing was adequate.	7.1
Hospital facilities were adequate.	6.6
Meals in hospital were satisfying.	4.9
Staff's language/attitude was good.	8.0
Protecting patient's privacy was adequate.	6.9
Overall impression was satisfying.	7.2
I learned how to lead life after leaving.	5.9
I wish to introduce this hospital to friends.	6.9

HCA, Medical Co-op Report No. 57, 2004.

Table 3. The Axes, Indicators, Items and Data
Selected for Comprehensive Evaluation

Axes	Co-operative Basic Values			
Indicators	Honest and caring services	Participation and democracy	Social responsibility and fairness	Autonomy and solidarity
Item 1	Shopping convenience	Participation to decision making	Involvement in social welfare	Solidarity among co-ops
Item 2	Economic benefits	Participation to implemen-tation	Involvement in environ-mental issues	Solidarity among members
Item 3	Product availability	Participation in everyday activities	Liaison with community	Members' education
Item 4	Product safety and reliability	Reflecting members' views	Fair governance	Employees' education
Item 5	Employees' reception of customers	Employees' participation perception	Fair treatment of employees	Co-op's autonomy
No. of data	25	19	33	25

Axes	Management Base	
Indicators	Management efficiency	Future potential
Item 1	Profitability	Financial resource base
Item 2	Productivity of capital	Organizational base
Item 3	Productivity of labor	Growth potential
Item 4	Financial stability	Investment in assets
Item 5	Efficiency of operations	Human resource base
No. of data	18	20

240

Graph 2. Rader Chart to Display Satisfaction Levels
for *Honest and Caring Services*

Graph 3. Line Chart to Display Evolution from the
Base Year for *Social Responsibility and Fairness*

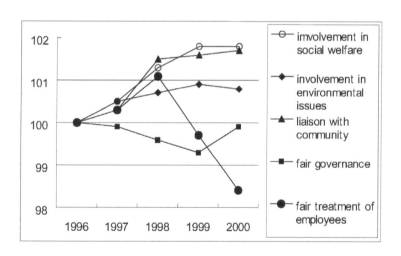

Graph 4. Trade off between Basic Values & Management Base

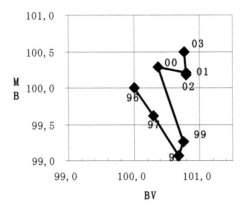

Table 4. PSCF's Evaluation Indicators and Items

Evaluation indicators	Evaluation items
A. Attractive products being patronized by members	A1: Product development based on product policy A2: Provision of safe and reliable products A3: Offering of reasonable price A4: Improved product's taste A5: Product development capacity A7: Creative design of catalogue A8: Concerns for environment in product development
B. Management base which ensures high quality	B1: Proper labelling on products B2: Compliance to rules and manuals B3: Product development process control (trace ability) B4: Enhanced checking functions B5: Communication with producers/suppliers
C. Enhanced member satisfaction	C1: Information and openness to members C2: Reflection of member's voice C3: Improved operation system C4: Response to member's inquiries
D. Brand values supporting growth	D1: Promotion of brand strategy D2: Direct transaction with producers D3: Initiatives in support of living D4: Social contribution and recognition

Table 5. Consumer's Image to Food Retailers

	Consumer co-op	Private supermarket	Independent retailer
Likely safe	1.2	-0.2	0.6
Reliable	1.15	0.1	0.55
Clean interior	1.1	0.8	0.1
Good quality	1.1	0.2	0.6
Can see producers	1	-0.7	0.15
High price	0.95	0	0.6
High freshness	0.9	0.1	0.8
Tasty food	0.85	0.2	1
Good labeling	0.85	-0.1	-0.4
Handmade products	0.75	-0.8	1.1
Rarely out of stock	0.6	0.8	-0.5
Good assortment	0.2	0.9	-0.7

Conclusions

Marie J. BOUCHARD & Nadine RICHEZ-BATTESTI

*Professor and Director of the Canada Research Chair on
the Social Economy, Université du Québec à Montréal (Canada)
Professor, LEST-CNRS
and Université de la Méditerranée (France)*

Introduction[1]

The social economy brings forth in the institutional arena initiatives
that aim at involving citizens, producers, workers or consumers in the
orientation of the economic and social activities that are of concern to
them. In the recent decades, the social economy has proven to be an
important actor in the developed world as well as in developing or
transitional economies. It plays multiple roles going from providing
answers to unmet or badly met needs, to creating public spaces to
debate about development and participate in policy planning. The social
economy has the potential of acting as a genuine institutional pole of a
plural economy, alongside with the State and the market agents.

In the present context, where signals coming from the market can be
more than doubtful and where the States' capacities to regulate are
constantly being challenged, all forms of organizations – whether
public, for-profit or of the social economy – are exposed to more complex forms of evaluation in order to improve their accountability and
reinforce their legitimacy. More and more, evaluation frameworks tend
to involve the stakeholders, i.e. those parties that can influence or be
influenced by the organization's activities (Freeman, 1984). Those can
be internal (members, owners, managers, workers) or external (customers, providers, funders, public authorities, economic partners, etc.). This
leads to complexifying the evaluation exercise, as performance criteria
and signals may be varied and, sometimes even, contradictory.

---

[1] We thank Benoît Lévesque, president of the International Scientific Council of Ciriec
for his comments on a preliminary version of this text.

Up to now, little was known about how the social economy is actually being evaluated, and how these procedures may affect or reinforce the specificity of this particular form or economy. In order to tackle this issue, the CIRIEC Working Group on Methods and Indicators of Evaluation of the Social Economy chose to adopt an inductive – rather than deductive – approach, by which former studies, recent evaluative research results and empirical observations were first discussed among members of the group in the context of seminars. Further on, the analysis of those cases called for a variety of concepts coming from different theoretical backgrounds. Each author was invited to inspire his or her analysis from that of others. The result of such a process may not lead to a strong theorization but, in return, it offers the grounds for interpreting the complexity of the phenomena. The objectives of this work was to identify the methods and indicators for evaluating the social economy, appreciate their advantages and limits, and situate them in relation to the organizational, institutional and societal aspects of the social economy. We also wanted to pinpoint the conceptual frameworks underlying the evaluation approaches and see how they were related to different views of the social economy.

This book is therefore composed of two sets of contributions. A first is made of four theoretical papers inspired by various disciplinary fields: management, economy, sociology, philosophy. A second set of contributions is composed of seven national analysis of how the social economy is evaluated in different institutional contexts: France, Québec (Canada), United Kingdom, United-States, Brazil, Portugal and Japan. Without summarizing the contributions of the chapters in this book, each having its own particularities, we can draw from them three transversal dimensions. The first relates to some contextual factors that influence the evaluation practices in the present context. A second concerns majors trends identified in this work in terms of methods and indicators for evaluating the social economy. The third is about how evaluation practices convey a vision of the place and role of the social economy, showing different modalities of evaluation acting in various modes of governance. These remarks lead to identifying some of the tensions to which the social economy is submitted in the present period and to formulating comments that we wish to address primarily to social economy actors and to those – politicians, funders, evaluation specialists and researchers – that are involved with the evaluation of the social economy. In the end, some key questions for future research are also formulated.

Evaluating the Social Economy in the Present Context

The notion of social economy is polysemic, covering a wide range of practices. With variations from one national environment to another, the present context is marked by the existence of various views on the social economy (see: Bouchard, chap. 1; Enjolras, chap. 3), which offer as many angles from which to appreciate performance. We also assist at transformations of the institutional setting (legal framework, renewal of public action, etc.) and to the accentuation of market regulation (competition for niches but also for subsidies and public contracts). Societal aspects also have their influence such as the rise of new social movements (civil society, environmental issues, alternative globalization, etc.), as well as the proliferation of technical and scientific debates (the place and role of evaluation in the administration of public policies, in the management of organizations, etc.). This context impacts the evaluation practices of the social economy.

At the *organizational and sectoral level*, the fact that the social economy combines social missions and economic activities, that it aims at producing not-for-profit benefits to members and to communities, that it internalizes social costs and produces long term intangible collective impacts, complicates the evaluation procedures. The criteria for evaluating its socioeconomic and productive function will be quite different from those that will appraise its sociopolitical aptitude to foster democracy or solidarity (Enjolras, chap. 3). While indicators for evaluating economic dimensions might be quite consensual, those relating to the social aspects are anchored in a variety of theoretical settings which are still matter of debate (Perret, chap. 2). The social economy being a diversified field, it is not surprisingly animated by an array of logics for action. It also bears strong common traits such as a governance system that involves the participation of consumers, workers or producers in the decision making process. Other that conveying a plurality of expectations, the evaluation activity can also lead to reducing sociological distances between what otherwise would be conflicting private interests.

Many *institutional factors* have influenced the evaluation practices of the social economy in the recent two or three decades. A first factor has to do with the responsiveness of the social economy to its environment. New social economy organizations are increasingly present in services of general interest (health, social services, etc.), in employment creation and training (workers collectives, workplace insertion, etc.) and community needs (childcare, elderly homecare, youth activities, etc.). On their part, the traditional sectors of the social economy (agriculture, financial and insurance services, consumption, etc.) are facing a stiffer competition accelerated by trade liberalization and deregulation. The differentiation can come by showing how the social economy as a whole

– new emerging *and* long lasting sectors, market *and* non-market activities, mutual interest *and* general interest orientations – performs in times of difficulties or crisis (Draperi, 2009). A second factor is the general trend for *marketization*, which enhances the competition for resources of all kinds, human, financial, reputational, etc. What we think of as "market" is not solely related to commercial monetary exchanges but also concerns competing for public resources, donations, even volunteer workers. Contracts, tendering, vouchers systems introduce market incentives in services formally provided by public authorities or by family and various forms of charity (Enjolras, ch. 3; Nicolau and Simaens, ch. 10; Spear, ch.7).

At the *societal level*, we assist at the increasing participation of civil society, both in former authoritarian regimes (e.g. Brazil, Portugal) and in older democracies (e.g. France, Québec, United Kingdom, United-States). The demands for a greater say on the part of citizens has been accompanied by the decentralization of public services and increased responsibilities and powers of local organizations. The issue of a sustainable development, the preoccupation for the preservation of the environment, the problem of food security and the subject of ethical governance (e.g. Japan) have increased the general public's concern about the economy. The professionalization of evaluation activities also reveals the important issue of legitimacy: who is entitled to ask for an evaluation, for what purpose, with what consequences for the stakeholders? The evaluative authorities play a dual role of control and legitimizing. The proliferation of specialized consultancy and audit firms, the emergence of accreditation agencies and the rising of methodologies pretending to offer universalistic indicators show that the game is played at a different level than it was ten or twenty years ago.

Modalities for Evaluating the Social Economy

While our study has revealed many variations on the theme of evaluating the social economy, we can point three major trends: corporate social responsibility (CRS), third party evaluation, and participatory evaluation.

Corporate Social Responsibility

The traditional market social economy and the large social economy organizations face the growing concern for ethical, environmental and social responsibility. We summarize them here in the expression "corporate social responsibility" (CSR). The scandals and corruption disclosures have affected the image of capitalist firms but also of some large nonprofit and cooperative organizations (Kurimoto, chap. 11). This challenges the boundaries of the social economy and brings the organizations, namely the cooperatives and mutual societies, to demonstrate their own performance in social, ethical and environmental terms (Bouchard, chap. 6; Richez-Battesti, *et al.*, chap. 5; Kurimoto, chap. 11). There is a boom in consultancy and audit firms that compete with various grids of sustainability, environmental or social reporting, and conformity assessment to ISO standards. Though some of these practices rely on universalistic methods of measures (e.g. Global Reporting Initiative, ISO 9000), most of the reporting is done on a voluntary and discretionary basis (Kurimoto, chap. 11). One of the reasons for this is the high costs of producing and publishing such reports that keep many organizations from going about it. And one can even question if the evaluation leads – or not – to actual changes in the organizations (Alberola and Richez-Battesti, 2005).

However, more and more social economy institutions, such as those of the financial services, are adopting forms of social and environmental reporting. A common sectorial or "industrial" set of norms is emerging, where the content of the CSR reporting is strongly correlated with social economy values and principles but also mixed to norms that are typical of the CSR fashion, such as in the British Key Performance Indicators, or the French Societal Balance Sheet (*bilan sociétal*).

Hence, the social economy distinction can be seen as an indigenous source of normativity that influences CSR practices, which can therefore be seen as a hybrid between strategic positioning and the affirmation of a specific identity (Ramboarisata, 2009).

Third Party Evaluation

In the area of public and quasi-public goods, third party evaluation has become a common demand. Evaluation has grown to be a tool for the governance of public policies (Perret, 2001). It is conducted to verify the practice against predetermined criteria and standards. This type of evaluation has taken more importance, whether as a result of privatization and deregulation of State services (e.g. Japan), or new regulation of activities formally in the areas of traditional philanthropy or households (e.g. Brazil, Portugal), or because of the reengineering of the public services (e.g. France, Québec) and of New Public Management's influence over public administration practices (e.g. United Kingdom, United-States). This has led the development of evaluation practices both externally commanded – by government or donators – and internally initiated. The role of experts and independent agencies has become important, organizations often having to obtain certificates from specified accreditation bodies.

As many authors have noticed, third party evaluation often aims at evaluating results with regards to policy or programme's objectives, utilizing tools that contribute to standardize the actions. The focus can be put on what organizations do (outputs, or direct effects) or on the changes that result from their actions (outcomes, or indirect effects) (Rock, chap. 8). Measuring outputs offers a simple and rather cheap option for evaluating the resources involved in producing an intervention or an action.[2] But in many cases with the social economy, much of the results are intangible and even collective. Hence, a better angle may be to look at the outcomes or the effects produced over the client or the community, which sometimes only occur in the long run (e.g. workplace insertion, reduction of social costs, social cohesion). However, a downside of evaluation modes that are centered on individual change is that they neglect the institutional features that may be generating or contributing to the problems (Rock, chap. 8). Another drawback comes from the technical difficulties and costs of evaluating outcomes, which imply being able to isolate the effects proper to the intervention of the changes that would have occurred independent of the action of the latter (Perret, 2001).

One of the key issues is whether the methodology conveys the recognition of the social economy and its specific way of doing things. Some of these "evaluation failures" can be overcome by negotiating or debating the evaluation framework with those who are concerned.

Participatory Evaluation

A third modality is identified in participatory evaluation. The normative finality of the evaluation, often implicit when it comes to resorting to standard indicators may, conversely, be part of an explicit strategy to establish specific norms to the social economy regarding its effectiveness and performance, even to develop new standards. There can be strategic value in promoting evaluative systems that measure the social economy difference, since such systems may lead to changes in behaviour both of social economy organizations and their competitors in the public and private sectors.

This purpose is often best served by participatory evaluation procedures. The decisions dealing with the objects evaluated are made with the stakeholders concerned, in an approach where the sense of the action is debated to reflect the plurality of the different points of view (Perret, chap. 2). This involves bringing the tensions and controversies into the limelight, and talking them through in spaces of public deliberation (Eme, chap. 4; Richez-Battesti, *et al.*, chap 5). Those interactions give way to the production of ideas, representations and common values

---

[2] The co-production with members and voluntary resources still needs to be assessed, for example with social accounting methods.

that enable collective actions (Bouchard, chap. 6). Here, evaluation has a cognitive function and serves to reinforce the organization or the sector's autonomy.

In order to play such a role, evaluation needs to be institutionalized (Perret, chap. 2). But such a perspective requires a transformation of the normative modes of regulation of the public sphere and of politics that are not particularly prone to entering deliberative arenas, through granting all actors an equal and legitimate right and opportunity to express themselves (Eme, chap. 4).

Evaluation as Modes of Governance

Many chapters in this book show that the mode of evaluation is constitutive of the mode of governance of the social economy. Broadly defined, governance encompasses the institutional and organizational mechanisms which define the power zone and influence the decision making of management in order to allow organizations to pursue their mission. Governance bears two main dimensions, power distribution and motivations of actors (Hollingworth and Boyer, 1997). Typically, power distribution varies between market (which distributes power horizontally) and hierarchy (which organizes power in a vertical top-down manner). The motivation of actors varies from self-interest and social obligations.

The notion of "new governance" stems from a reconsideration of the role of the State as the central agent, creating openings for demands for participation and democracy from social actors, for critiques of the State, and for the introduction of private sector methods into the public sphere (Bernier, Bouchard and Lévesque, 2002). The new partnership governance resists hierarchy and centralization and builds on networks of differentiated actors. Negotiation, persuasion and evaluation replace command and control (Enjolras, 2008). This type of governance involves an effort to capture synergies and raise the level of social learning within and between organizations (Paquet, 2000). Governance plays a role in the way organizations interpret and internalize the constraining rules from their institutional context and, conversely, in the process by which organizations build their own shared meanings and influence institutions in return.

The evaluation practices that we observed of the social economy vary accordingly to the modes of governance to which they participate. Different typologies have been mentioned throughout this book but, to summarize, three main types of governance can be distinguished: public, competitive and partnership governance. In each of these, the evaluation criteria and the instance to which the organization is accountable vary.

Public Governance

In the public governance mode, evaluation seeks to show if and how the policy and its results fit the expectations of the elected government.[3] The evaluation procedure aims to control the conformity of the results to the prescriptions. According to the proportion of public or donation sources of resources, the social economy organizations can be more or less submitted to this form of evaluation. They can eventually fall into a "subsidiary trap", where autonomy is traded off for compliance to the public policies or donator's interests (Nicolau and Simaens, chap. 10). Where their input is most important such as in the United-States non-profit sector, we see the evaluation procedures reflect the public and the donators' interests to "follow the money" and insuring the good governance and the accountability of those in charge (Rock, chap. 8). The emergence of accreditation agencies controlled by a plurality of stakeholders (Bouchard, chap. 6), appears as a new modality that could allow the cross-fertilization of views and enrich the interpretation grids (Perret, chap. 2). Nevertheless, standard norms and rigid criteria will always seem hard to apply in small and young organizations, or in fields of activities where the social economy proposes innovative forms of action.

Competitive Governance

In many of the observed cases, evaluation has become a tool for competing for resources (Portugal, United-States, United Kingdom) or for public recognition (Brazil, France), or for both as they are correlated. As a previous CIRIEC Transversal Working Group has demonstrated (Enjolras, 2008), a competitive regime of governance gives new challenges to the social economy as more for-profit enterprises are penetrating the field of social and health services. In the case of competitive governance, evaluation is turned towards consumers and clients, their exit being the very first type of judgement. In this perspective, evaluation helps governments identify those organizations which can introduce competitiveness in providing social services, as shows the case of Portuguese Social Solidarity Organizations.

Markets (or quasi-market in the case of public contracts, voucher payment, tendering, etc.) require mechanisms for comparative assess-

---

[3]   A variant would be the corporative mode, in which the evaluation is bounded to the centralized interests of large organizations that act in mutual support with government (Streek and Schmitter, 1991; Enjolras, 2008).

ment of performance (Spear, chap. 7). Large scale organizations as well as those involved in market dominant type of activities are submitted, even if implicitly, to competitive modes of evaluation. The criteria tend to have a standardizing effect on practices. However, the evaluation systems often do not reflect the specific conditions of work and functioning of the social economy, namely hybridizing public resources with market and non-monetary resources (voluntary work and donations). In addition, the causal relationships between the objectives pursued by the organizations and the evaluation indicators have yet to be clearly demonstrated, especially when trying to measure impacts of the mission organizations have set for themselves (reducing poverty, increasing the economic or social power of persons or organizations that are their members, etc.). It also needs to be said that there is not only one objective concept of performance, independent of the judgement of the parties involved.

Partnership Governance

Evaluation can be a strong instrument for generating institutionalized and long term partnerships between public administrations and the social economy sectors. Such partnerships can call for *ex ante* and ongoing types of evaluation, showing that the organization is embedded into a community and that it is able to pursue its mission (Bouchard, chap. 6; Nicolau and Simaens, chap. 10). In the partnership mode of governance, the accountability is focused on citizens and the evaluation is negotiated through direct participation procedures. The criteria for evaluating may be the object of controversies and compromises.

Still, the lack of sufficient financial resources allocated by public authorities to these evaluation procedures often renders those more symbolic than effective. The presence of social intermediaries dedicated to support the social economy may be part of the solution to this (Bouchard, chap. 6). The will to provide labels to those organizations that prove to be of social utility (*utilité sociale*) however seems to hit the wall of the very complexity and variety of what consists of "social utility" (Battesti, *et al.*, chap. 5). Most of our investigation shows that members and users remain the major source of information that organizations rely upon to monitor satisfaction and to adjust quality and quantities according to the demand. Again, the scarcity resources, namely time, makes it difficult for organizations or sectors to formalize the evaluation procedures which, in spite of their effectiveness to adjust to social demands, remain insufficient to legitimize special treatment from the public authorities.

Typology of Evaluation Methods and Governance Modes

Many authors in this book have underlined the plurality of the social economy. Acting at the interface of civil society, State and market, the social economy borrows its characteristics from all three and yet at the same time distinguishes itself from each. Its place varies accordingly to its recognition by the institutional environment and depends as well on the place occupied by the public and the capitalist sectors in the various sectors in which it may emerge. This leads to an analysis in the terms of complexity, i.e. looking at the variety of logics at work and at the tensions that generate innovative dynamics inside the social economy. The evaluation methods and indicators for the social economy should reflect this complexity, to the risk of oversimplifying its assessment or forcing it into a mold that doesn't fit its characteristics. Hence, different methodologies will serve better some of the social economy's dimensions. The debate on evaluation is thus directly linked to the definition of the field of the social economy as well as to its modes of governance. Consequently, it is closely tied to the legitimacy of the social economy.

We have typified three generic modalities for evaluating the social economy: ethical, social and environmental responsibility (summarized as corporate social responsibility or CRS); third party evaluation; and participative evaluation. We also typified three governance modes in which evaluation takes a different role: public, competitive and partnership. The modalities can be typically associated with the size and age of an organization (small and emerging, or large and institutionalized), the kind of activity (market and private, or public and collective goods and services),[4] and the ways the indicators are defined and utilized (mandatory and compulsory, discretionary and voluntary, or debated and negotiated). These typologies must be seen as ideal-types, i.e. models to which empirical cases may be compared in terms of their similarities and differences.

In this modelization (see Figure 1), third party evaluation is typically utilized in the case of public and collective goods and services, and takes place within a public mode of governance, the methods and indicators being deduced from a policy or a programme and generally imposed by the instance in charge of the evaluation. Corporate social responsibility (CSR) – in a restrictive sense (respect of regulations) or a larger meaning (proactive regarding social, ethical and environmental issues) – is generally a voluntary and discretionary practice of large social economy enterprises that produce private goods or services submitted to market competition, sometimes at the world-wide level.

---

[4] These two dimensions are inspired by R. Paton, 1992.

Participatory evaluation, which involves stakeholders in defining the methodology, is mostly seen in the case of the new social economy, where the collective social mission is supported by economic market activities, and where public authorities are open to co-constructing policies with socioeconomic actors.

Figure 1. Evaluating the social economy

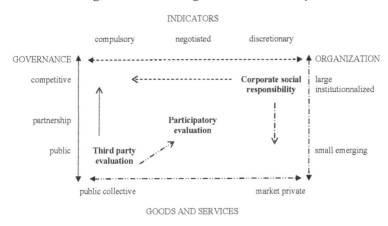

Of course, as organizations evolve from one stage to another or as they move from one type of activity to another (or to a mix of them), the evaluation modalities may also change. Also, evaluation modes have a life of their own. For example, CSR is such an important trend that the question is not so much "if" organizations will follow the movement but "when" (Zadek, Pruzan and Evans, 1997). Although it is most evidently practiced by large and institutionalized organizations, CSR is rapidly spreading to younger smaller social economy enterprises, especially in terms of environment and sustainable development. It is also becoming such an important marketing advantage, with consumers everyday more conscious and aware, that CSR is growing to be more compulsory than not. Another example is with third party evaluation. As social economy organizations resort more to market oriented activities in support of their social mission (such as the case with "social enterprises"), their lesser dependence to a single financing source may favour the debate – or at least some negotiation – between parties about the evaluation criteria. On the other hand, as public services are more subject to contracting and tendering, the governance mode shifts from a centralized authority that speaks in the name of the general interest to a competitive mode where entities are compared on the basis of cost-benefit analysis.

Therefore, this representation of evaluation modes and governance regimes needs to be interpreted in a dynamic rather than a static fashion.

Concluding Remarks

The above discussion has exposed the current trends of the social economy and situated them in the present context, identifying three principal modalities that evaluation practices take and associating them to different modes of governance. This typification also shows how the methods and indicators for evaluating the social economy may be linked to the size and age of the organization as well as to the anchorage of its activities in the market or in public policies. In addition, such a modelization helps understanding the shifts that may occur in the evaluation trends as changes happen in the regulation, the structuration of organizations and sectors, the opening to stakeholders' participation, etc. More important, in spite of noting variations in each national context, the results of this Working Group's research demonstrate clearly that evaluation has become a major stake for the social economy and that it is closely linked to the view of the social economy itself and of its role in the global picture.

Evaluation is a critical moment in the life of any organization. What it focuses on and the way it is conducted may have dramatic impacts over the strategic orientations of the organization as well as over the staff and members' motivation to follow them. In many cases, the evaluation of social economy organizations leads – or not – to the organization's access to crucial resources, may those be financial or reputational (Spear, ch. 7). Evaluation is therefore an important tool for orienting and controlling the actions.

Evaluation can serve the purposes of optimizing the usage of public resources and of insuring the accountability of entities benefiting from those. As a tool for organizational learning and social marketing, evaluation may also have an important effect over the awareness that staff, users, members and the general public have of the organization's mission, and it can influence its performance as well as its legitimacy to operate (Perret, ch. 2). As we have already discussed, this reveals at least three important roles that evaluation comes to play, as it:

– acts in the organizations and sectors' strategic positioning;
– produces norms for the field of the social economy;
– eventually develops alternative indicators of wealth and social wellbeing for societies.

In each case, some issues can be brought to the concern of those who are involved with evaluating the social economy, being policy makers, social economy actors, or researchers.

Evaluation and Strategic Positioning

In a strategic perspective, evaluation is closely linked to management. In some cases, it can induce forms of managerialism, with the adoption of models coming from the capitalist enterprises and a narrow conception of performance (Hoareau and Laville, 2008). But it can also rely upon the construction of a specific and dedicated referential tool. The trade off is between specificity and comparability.

Evaluation can also be destined to the outside, for reasons going from accountability to public relations. There again, the risk is that of a too narrow vision of performance, not very compatible with the social economy model. There is also the possibility to mimic commercial corporations or follow the donators' interests, and fail to highlight the social economy's uniqueness. Here, the trade off is with transparency, which constitutes an advantage towards stakeholders and in front of society as a whole.

Nevertheless, the strategic positioning of the social economy will always be twofold, as it straddles two types of goals. On the one hand, it aims at solving individuals' problems with collective solutions. On the other, it mobilizes individuals into participating to solve collective problems. While this duality is a strong force of the social economy in terms of producing citizenship and society, it is rarely taken into account in the logic models underlying its evaluation, which are caught between individualistic and holistic approaches. These approaches respectively stress more on the individual capabilities (Sen, 1985) or on the production of the social (Herrmann, 2009); on the substantive types of indicators (results) or on the process indicators (Leviten-Reid and Torjman, 2006); on the short term direct effects on individuals or on the long term indirect impacts on communities (Gadrey, 2002); etc. Referring to more than one methodology is probably a lesser evil but finding methodologies that better reflect the particular capacities of the social economy is certainly something to look for.

Specific Norms for the Social Economy

Evaluation helps to characterize the activities and theirs results ("lamp post" effect), to justify the financing of activities (counterpart effect) and to compare (competition effect). Expectations regarding each of these functions may be quite different and sometimes even contradictory, to the risk of provoking certain schizophrenia or a tendency towards isomorphism. This is enhanced by the permeability of the social economy's institutional field with those of the capitalist and the public sectors. The well recognized innovative function of the social economy (Bouchard, 2006; Lévesque, 2006a, 2006b; Salamon, *et al.*, 1999) is

257

consequently put to challenge by the standardization function of evaluation procedures which can, depending on what their focus is, contribute
to the institutionalization of the social economy by the State or to its
bastardization by the market.

In terms of having its specific evaluation norms, the social economy
holds a dual posture regarding the criteria from which to appreciate its
performance. The social economy produces collective goods and services and at the same time participates to the very construction of the
public good, through the revelation of demands and social innovation as
well as through its participation in the co-construction of public policies
(Bouchard, chap. 6; Eme, chap. 4; Richez-Battesti, *et al.*, chap 5). This
explains the presence – if not the opposition – of two models of evaluation. One that is centralized and hierarchic, characterized by normative
prescriptions imposed in a top-down relationship between the evaluator
and the evaluated instances. Another that is decentralized and participative, characterized by plural and adaptative indicators, and which contributes, through deliberation between parties, to level out the differences. In this sense, debates over evaluation cannot be dissociated from
those over the governance models.

As mentioned above, the social economy has the ability to bridge
over divides between individuals and society, by way of communities
but also by creating public spaces for debate. Another of its strengths is
to re-embed economic activities in the social fabric. As an alternative
form of accumulation and distribution, it also favors local empowerment
over the development modes. A logical model for evaluating the social
economy should reflect at least one of these distinctive competences.

Scaling Up Towards the General Interest

The objectives pursued by social economy organizations aim at having systemic impacts on large problems such as the reduction of poverty
and exclusion, the democratic access to resources, the promotion of
sustainable development, etc. Hence, the exploration of genuine and
innovative methods for evaluating the social economy cannot remain at
the micro level and should enable correspondence with the macro level
(Leviten-Reid and Torjman, 2006). However, a tension is present when
looking at scaling up the evaluation scope from the organizational level
to the societal level. One of the complications come from the various
anchorages of the social economy into market or into public policies, by
the fragmentation of those (welfare policies, economic policies, employment policies, etc.), and by the diversity of organizational forms
(size, age, incorporation status, etc.). Moreover, as Perret mentions it
(chap. 2), the heterogeneousness of the concepts that underpin the
diversity of global social indicators contrasts highly with the univocal

and coherent economic indicators, as social indicators have no sure conceptual basis on which to rely.

Nevertheless, developing adequate indicators for valuing social products and processes of the social economy is more important than ever, as new international accounting standards (IAS) tend to iron out the diversity of economic forms (Capron, 2005). Such findings would also contribute to the recognition of non-standard forms of analysis and help improve the clarity of social issues themselves.

The Need for Further Research

This book has showed that to study evaluation practices provides access to the diversity of action logics that cross the social economy. It is also a window from which to perceive the role the social economy is expected to play in various national contexts. Evaluation methods and indicators reflect the dynamics that animate the social economy both from the inside and with its environments. They point to the tensions at work. At the same time, they are part of a strategy to weight on them.

In spite of their diversity, the case studies showed some common aspects that allowed us to see coherence between types of evaluation practices, modes of governance, sizes of organizations and categories of mission or activity. However, the scope of this work does not permit to judge of national models, as a wide spectrum of methodologies is likely to be found in each society (see Bouchard, chap. 6). Yet, this diversity may be one of the very characteristics of the "evaluation system" of the social economy.

Further research would be necessary to document how the various evaluation methodologies of the social economy relate to each other in different national configurations. The interest of such research has a wide breadth, as it concerns a growing preoccupation within contemporary societies, the re-embedding of social preoccupations within the economy, something the social economy aims at doing. It also has to do with the demands rising from various social groups for more information and better knowledge diffusion about the ways in which the economy is being oriented and managed.

To evaluate consists in determining the value of things. Technically, it entails having a reference point, a benchmark, from which to appraise the gap between what is observed and what is expected (Enjolras, chap. 3). Hence, evaluation indicators always carry an implicit message which can be related to the ideal or normative view on the phenomenon being evaluated. But no value system or normative orientations can be seen as generally valid on a global perspective (Herrmann, 2009: 11). A plurality of legitimate forms of evaluation exist (Boltanski and

Thévenot, 1991) and should be referred to in order to capture the multiple worths (*grandeurs*) of the social economy (Eme, chap. 4).

In this sense, evaluation may be seen as a social construction or an interactive organizing process, where "organization is not in the activities as such, but in their interpretation".[5] Therefore, evaluation is one of the gate doors to understanding the social economy itself. It can be considered as a "boundary object" (Star and Greisemer, 1989, quoted in Trompette and Vinck, 2009) that holds a dual function, both separating and connecting the social economy (or any object for that matter) to its environment.[6] The links it conveys with the external environments create spaces for co-construction of reality by actors with different expertise and experience, with different situated knowledge. Evaluation – the process of its construction – can therefore be seen as a knowledge infrastructure, intersection and articulation mechanisms between the different social worlds (*mondes sociaux*). Studying evaluation as a boundary object means looking at how it coordinates actors. Namely, its role in the translation between the different worlds of worth that are involved. But evaluation also holds a strategic role, even a political charge. Research must therefore also evaluate the evaluation practices and their impact on the social economy.

This stream of research goes beyond the interest for the social economy in itself. Evaluation plays today a different role in society than it did before. The industrial period was characterized by the prevalence of universal laws, solid institutions, and independent public service. This supported a vision of evaluation practices oriented by an instrumental rationality and a "one best way" of doing things. Social integration and stability was the ultimate goal to attain. In post-industrial societies, civil society is active in producing and implementing public policies as well as in judging about ethics and responsibility of economic actors. Elected representatives, citizens and associations are conveyed to participate in defining the problems as well as in evaluating the solutions. The continuous production of societies by themselves calls for continuous evaluation and benchmarking (Dubet, 2009). This "second modernity"

---

[5]   "And the working through of an interpretation is a social process (in fact, the social process we call 'communication') by means of which members both come to an understanding (however tentative) of what the events mean, organizationally, while they simultaneously reconfirm their own position in the network through the role they play in the interpretive process" (Taylor, *et al.*, 1996: 4, quoted in Mandelli and Snehota, 2008).

[6]   Boundary objects hold four dimensions: abstraction (it facilitates dialogue between worlds); polyvalency (many activities or practices are possible); modularity (different parts of the object may serve as a basis for dialogue between actors); standardization of the information incorporated in the object (it renders information interpretable) (Wenger, 2000, quoted in Trompette and Vinck, 2009).

(or second "Great Transformation") reintroduces value-based rationality and reconnects the economy to the environment (nature is not anymore exterior – or opposite – to society), leading to take into account the intrinsic plurality of social values (Billaudot, 2008).

In this sense, studying the evaluation of the social economy in the present time is not a minor subject. It should, consequently, lead to important findings about contemporary societies.

References

Aaltonen, M., "Futures Research Methods as Boundary Objects", *Futura*, 2-3, 2005, pp. 29-38.

Alberola, E. and N. Richez-Battesti, "De la responsabilité sociale des entreprises: Evaluation du degré d'engagement et d'intégration stratégique", *La Revue des Sciences de Gestion*, No. 211-212, 2005, p. 55-71.

Bernier, L., M.J. Bouchard and B. Lévesque, "La prise en compte de l'intérêt général au Québec. Nouvelle articulation entre l'intérêt individuel, collectif et général", pp. 47-71 *in* M. L. Von Bergman, B. Enjolras and O. Saint-Martin (eds.), *Économie plurielle et régulation socio-économique*, Bruxelles, CIRIEC-International, 2002.

Billaudot, B., "Une théorie de l'État social", *Revue de la régulation*, No. 2, janvier 2008. http://regulation.revues.org/index2523.html#tocto3n10.

Boltanski, L. and L. Thévenot, *De la justification*, Paris, Gallimard, 1991.

Bouchard, M.J., "Les défis de l'innovation sociale en économie sociale", p. 121-138, in J.-L. Klein and D. Harrisson (eds.), *Innovations sociales et transformations sociales*, Québec, Presses de l'Université du Québec, 2006.

Capron, M., *Les normes comptables internationales, instrument du capitalisme financier*, Paris, La Découverte, 2005.

Draperi, J.-F., "Au bénéfice de la crise. Pour un projet d'économie sociale et solidaire", *RECMA Revue internationale d'économie sociale*, No. 313, p. 19-35, 2009.

Dubet, F., *Le travail des sociétés*, Paris, La Martinière/Seuil, 2009.

Enjolras, B., "Régimes de gouvernance et intérêt général", in B. Enjolras (ed.), *Gouvernance et intérêt général dans les services sociaux et de santé*, Bruxelles, P.I.E. Peter Lang, 2008.

Freeman, R.E., *Strategic Management: A Stakeholder Approach*, Boston, Pitman, 1984.

Gadrey, J., *Bénéfices collectifs, externalités collectives, et économie solidaire: commentaires sur le rapport européen du CRIDA*, Lille, Université de Lille 1, Laboratoire CLERSE, 2002.

Herrmann, P., *Indicators – From Where, What Goal, Which Way?*, Cork, Ireland, European Social Organisational and Science Consultancy for University of Cork, William Thompson Working paper No. 15, 2009.

Hollingworth, R. and R. Boyer (eds.), *Contemporary Capitalism. The Embeddedness of Institutions*, Cambridge, Cambridge University Press, 1997.

Hoareau, C. and J.-L. Laville, *La gouvernance des associations*, Paris, Érès, Sociologie économique, 2008.

Lévesque. B., "Le potentiel d'innovation sociale de l'économie sociale: quelques éléments de problématique", *Économie et solidarités*, Vol. 37, No. 1, pp. 13-48, 2006a.

Lévesque, B., "L'innovation dans le développement économique et dans le développement social", p. 43-70 in J.-L. Klein and D. Harrisson (eds.), *Innovations sociales et transformations sociales*, Québec, Presses de l'Université du Québec, 2006b.

Leviten-Reid, E. and S. Torjman, *Evaluation Framework for Federal Investment in the Social Economy: A Discussion Paper*, Ottawa, The Caledon Institute of Social Policy, 2006.

Mandelli, A. And I. Snehota, I., "Markets as mediated conversations", p. 99-103 in *What's an organization?, Materiality, agency and discourse*, Montréal, Université de Montréal, Language, Organization and Governance Research Group, 2008.

Paquet, G., "Vers des méso-systèmes d'innovation et de gouvernance en Europe et en Amérique du Nord", pp. 811-825, in M. Côté and T. Hafsi, *Le management aujourd'hui. Une perspective nord-américaine*, Québec, Presses de l'Université Laval/ Économica, 2000.

Paton, R., "Value-based organizations in the wider society", in Batsleer, J., C. Cornforth and R. Paton (eds.), *Issues in Voluntary and Nonprofit Management*, Wokingham, Addison Wesley, 1992.

Perret, B., 2001, *L'évaluation des politiques publiques*, Paris, La Découverte.

Ramboarisata, L., *Analyse institutionnelle de la stratégie de responsabilité sociale d'entreprise (RSE) des institutions financières coopératives*, Thèse pour le doctorat en administration, Université du Québec à Montréal, 2009.

Salamon, L.M., H.K. Anheier, R. List, S. Toepler, S.W. Sokolowski, and ass., *Global Civil Society: Dimensions of the Nonprofit Sector*, Baltimore, The Johns Hopkins University, Centre for Civil Society Studies, 1999.

Sen A., *Commodities and Capabilities*, Amsterdam, North Holland, 1985.

Star, S.L. and J. Griesemer, J., "Institutionnal ecology, 'Translations', and Boundary objects: amateurs and professionals on Berkeley's museum of vertebrate zoologie", *Social Studies of Science*, 19(3): 387-420, 1989.

Streeck, W., and P.C. Schmitter, 1991, "Community, Market, State and Associations? The Prospective Contribution of Interest Governance to Social Order", in Thompson. G.J. *et al.* (eds.), *Markets, Hierarchies and Networks: the Coordination of Social Life*, London, Sage, 1991.

Taylor, J.R., F. Cooren, F., N. Giroux and D. Robichaud, "The communicational basis of organization: Between the conversation and the text", *Communication Theory*, 6, 1-39, 1996.

Trompette, P. and D. Vinck, "Retour sur la notion d'objet-frontière", *Revue d'anthropologie des connaissances*, Vol. 3, No. 1, p. 5-27, 2009.

Wenger, E., "Communities of Practice and Social Learning Systems", *Organization*, Vol. 7, No. 2, pp. 225-246, 2000.

Zadek, S., P. Pruzan and R. Evans, *Building Corporate Accountability*, London, Earthscan Publications Limited, 1997.

Presentation of the Authors

Carolina Andion holds a Ph.D. in human sciences from the Federal University of Santa Catarina (UFSC). She is a professor at the Postgraduate Program of Administration in the Administration and Socioeconomics Sciences Center (ESAG) at the State University of Santa Catarina (UDESC). She is also a researcher at the CIRIEC-Brazil.

Marie J. Bouchard is professor at Université du Québec à Montréal (Canada). She holds a Doctorate in Sociology from the École des Hautes Études en Sciences Sociales (France). She is head of the Canada Research Chair on the Social Economy, a regular member of the Research Center on Social Innovations (CRISES), and the codirector of the Community Housing Research Group within the Community-University Research Alliance (CURA) on the Social Economy. She presently acts as Vice-President for International Affairs of CIRIEC-Canada. Member of CIRIEC's International Scientific Commission Social and Cooperative Economy, she is the coordinator of the Working Group on Methods and Indicators for Evaluating the Social Economy.

Lucila Campos holds a Ph.D. in production engineering from the Federal University of Santa Catarina (UFSC). She is a professor of the Post-graduate Program of Administration at Universidade do Vale do Itajaí (UNIVALI), and she is member of the CIRIEC International Scientific Commission "Social and Cooperative Economy". Her research interest has been on social economy, social management and sustainability.

Bernard Eme holds a Doctorate in Philosophy and the rank of full Professor in Sociology at Université de Lille 1. He is a researcher at Centre Lillois d'Études et de Recherche Sociologiques et Économiques (CLERSÉ). He previously was a researcher at CRIDA and LISE, and Maître de conférences associé at Institut d'Études Politiques de Paris. His research mainly focuses on the solidarity-based economy, of which he is one of the major contributors, namely the relations between associations and public action in the area of work insertion and proximity services.

Bernard Enjolras is director of research at the Institute for Social Research in Oslo, Norway. He received his Ph.D. from the Institut d'Études Politiques de Paris (France), he holds Ph.D. in Sociology

(Université de Québec à Montréal, Canada) and is Doctor in Economics (Université Paris I. Panthéon-Sorbonne, France). His main fields of research are civil society, social economy organizations, public policies and governance. He is author or editor of several books and scientific articles, notably: *Conventions et institutions. Essais de théorie sociale* (Paris, L'Harmattan, 2006), *L'économie solidaire face au marché. Modernité, société civile et démocratie* (Paris, L'Harmattan, 2002) and *Gouvernance et intérêt général dans les services sociaux et de santé* (Brussels, PIE Peter Lang, 2008).

Laurent Fraisse is a socio-economist, member of the Laboratoire Interdisciplinaire pour la Sociologie Economique (LISE-CNAM CNRS) since 2004. He is also member of the European EMES research network on social enterprise. He took part in several European research programmes on social economy, solidarity-based economy and social enterprises, on the governance of welfare services (child and elderly care services) and social policies.

Akira Kurimoto is Director and chief researcher of Consumer Cooperative Institute of Japan and Executive Director of Robert Owen Association. He is also Vice Chair of CIRIEC-Japan. He served as Chair of the ICA Asian Co-operative Research Forum (1998-2001) and Chair of the ICA Research Committee (2001-2005). His research interest has been on comparative analysis of co-operatives, the social economy and social enterprises.

Isabel Nicolau is a researcher at Management Research Center at ISCTE – IUL (Lisbon University Institute) where she is an Associate Professor teaching Strategic Management. She is Board member of CEEPS/CIRIEC-Portugal and member of the CIRIEC International Scientific Council and Scientific Commission "Social and Cooperative Economy". Her research interests are corporate social responsibility and social economy organizations.

Erika Onozato is a researcher for the ABIPTI (Brazilian Association of Technology Research Institute) and SENAI (Industrial Education National Service) as well as for CIRIEC-Brazil. She is also a MSc. in Business Administration from the Federal University of Paraná (UFPR) and she holds teaching at several colleges in Brazil.

Bernard Perret, born in 1951, is a graduate from *École polytechnique* (1974) and ENSAE – *École nationale de la statistique et des études économiques (1976)*, and a member of the Conseil général de l'environnement et du développement durable at the ministry of Sustainable Development. He is a member of the Laboratoire de sociologie du changement des institutions (LSCI-CNRS). He teaches at the Institut

Catholique (Paris), and is a member of the editorial board of the journals *Evaluation* (London) and *Esprit* (Paris).

Nadine Richez-Battesti is a member of the CIRIEC International Scientific Commission "Social and Cooperative Economy". Professor at the Université de la Méditerranée (France), she is director of Master in Social economy: human resources, management and project, and researcher in LEST (Center of labor economy and sociology). Her research interests are in cooperative banks and governance model in a comparative perspective.

Charles Patrick Rock is currently professor of economics at Rollins College, Winter Park, Florida and received his Ph.D. in Economics from Cornell University, his M.A. in International Studies from Ohio University and a B.A. in Psychology from Williams College. He has worked with alternative financial institutions serving low-income families for many. His current research includes the social economy, the reconstruction of the content and teaching methods in economics, comparative economic ideologies, labor history, and social welfare policy reform in the USA. He has also taught economics and several other subjects in several other countries including Denmark, Ireland, Bulgaria, Portugal, France, Russia and Botswana.

François Rousseau is associate researcher Ph.D. of the École Polytechnique Management Research Center (CRG) and Engineer Adviser. He is a member of the École de Paris du management, CIRIEC-France, Chair of the Scientific Committee of Social economy observatory and teaches management of Social Economic Organizations in HEC Group and IAE Paris-Sorbonne University. Since 1997, his research improves the elaboration and the description of the "Militant Organization" or the "Manufacture of sense". His research topics are NPOs, crisis, tools of management, project management, social utility, social entrepreneurship, evaluation.

Maurício Serva holds a Ph.D. in administration from the Getúlio Vargas Foundation (FGV), São Paulo. He is a professor and director of the Post-graduate Program of Administration at Federal University of Santa Catarina (UFSC), and he coordinates there the Center of Studies in Organizations, Rationality and Development. He also presides over CIRIEC-Brazil.

Ana Simaens is a senior teaching assistant at ISCTE – IUL (Lisbon University Institute), Board member of CEEPS/CIRIEC-Portugal and member of the CIRIEC International Scientific Commission "Social and Cooperative Economy". Her main research interest is strategic management in social sconomy organizations.

Roger Spear is a member of the CIRIEC International Scientific Commission "Social and Cooperative Economy", Chair of the Co-operatives Research Unit, founder member and Vice-President of the EMES research network on social enterprise, and teaches organizational systems and research methods (in ESRC recognized Mres degree), in the Centre for Complexity and Change at the Open University. His research interest for many years has been on co-operatives, the social economy, and more recently social enterprises.

Hélène Trouvé is doctor in economics. She is research engineer in National foundation of gerontology. She is also associated researcher in Center of economy of the Sorbonne – University of Paris Pantheon Sorbonne. Her research interest is in the domains of the non-profit organizations and the social utility of non-profit organizations, of the public policies and of the integrated networks.

Social Economy & Public Economy

The series "Social Economy & Public Economy" gathers books proposing international analytical comparisons of organizations and economic activities oriented towards the service of the general and collective interest: social services, public services, regulation, public enterprises, economic action of territorial entities (regions, local authorities), cooperatives, mutuals, non-profit organizations, etc. In a context of "large transformation", the scientific activity in this field has significantly developed, and the series aims at being a new dissemination and valorization means of this activity using a pluri-disciplinary approach (economics, social sciences, law, political sciences, etc.).

The series is placed under the editorial responsibility of CIRIEC. As an international organization with a scientific aim, CIRIEC undertakes and disseminates research on the public, social and cooperative economy. One of its main activities is the coordination of a large international network of researchers active in these fields. Members and non-members of this network are allowed to publish books in the series.

Series titles